Street Scenes:Brecht, Benjamin, and Berlin

Nicolas Whybrow

intellect™
Bristol, UK
Portland, OR, USA

First Published in the UK in 2005 by
Intellect Books, PO Box 862, Bristol BS99 1DE, UK
First Published in the USA in 2005 by
Intellect Books, ISBS, 920 NE 58th Ave. Suite 300, Portland, Oregon 97213-3786, USA
Copyright ©2005 Intellect Ltd

A catalogue record for this book is available from the British Library

ISBN 1-84150-114-X
Cover Design: Gabriel Solomons
Copy Editor: Julie Stradwick

Printed by 4edge, UK.

Contents

Acknowledgements

Formally I wish to thank the UK Arts and Humanities Research Board for two funding awards, one a small grant (in 2000) that enabled me to spend two months living in Berlin, the other a research leave grant (2001–2) that permitted the completion of this book. I am also grateful to the British Academy for enabling me to deliver two PSi conference papers based on the research material for the book, one at the Universität Mainz, Germany in 2001 ('*Schauspielplatz* Berlin: the performing city'), the other in Singapore in 2004 ('*Der Bevölkerung*'/'For the People': performative interrogations of nationhood in the new Germany'). Further relevant conference papers were given at the UK universities of Lancaster, Bristol and De Montfort in 2000, 2003 and 2004 respectively ('Locating Brecht in Berlin: performativity and the city', 'Wracked Reichstag: performative interventions in the Berlin Republic's seat of power' and 'Encountering the City: on "not taking yourself with you"').

Some of the book's content has also appeared in journals in one form or another, and I would like to thank the editors concerned for permission to include it here. *Performance Research* published two pieces, parts of which are distributed throughout chapters two, five and six: 'Leaving Berlin: on the performance of monumental change' (6i, 2001: 37–45) and 'Foot-notes' (7iv, 2002: 27–37). Chapter eight meanwhile has appeared more or less as it stands in *New Theatre Quarterly* as 'Street Scene: Berlin's Strasse des 17 Juni and the performance of (dis)unity' (76, 2003: 299–317).

Most of the quotations in the book come within 'fair use'; permission to use copyright material has been sought from all relevant parties concerned and I am grateful for their consent (though replies have not been received in all instances). I mention here those that have specifically requested to be given separate credit. Thus Suhrkamp Verlag, Frankfurt am Main holds the original rights to both Brecht and Benjamin. Excerpts from *Illuminations* by Walter Benjamin, copyright © 1955 by Suhrkamp Verlag. English translation by Harry Zohn, copyright © 1968 and renewed 1996 by Harcourt, Inc., reprinted by permission of Harcourt Inc. Extract from *Illuminations* by Walter Benjamin published by Pimlico. Used by permission of the Random House Group Limited. Methuen Publishing Ltd holds the UK rights to all Brecht's writings in translation and has granted permission for excerpts cited. In the US the plays are published by Arcade Publishing, New York. Copyright © 1995 and 1997 respectively from *Journals 1934-1955* and *Poems 1913-1956* by Bertolt Brecht. Reproduced by permission of Routledge/Taylor and Francis Books Inc, New York. Excerpts from *Brecht on Theatre* translated and edited by John Willett. Translation copyright © 1964, renewed 1992 by John Willett. Reprinted by permission of Hill and Wang, a division of Farrar, Straus and Giroux.

The copyright for Norman Ohler's *Mitte* © 2001 is by Rowohlt. Berlin Verlag GmbH, Berlin. I am, moreover, pleased to thank both the Brecht-Archiv and the Brecht-Weigel-Gedenkstätte for their respective supplying of research material. All photographs appearing in the book are by me.

On a more informal but no less important note I would like to acknowledge the invaluable contributions of certain colleagues and friends. I am particularly indebted in both capacities to Ulrike Zitzlsperger of not only Exeter University but also Berlin, past and present. Without her comprehensive support – which has included making available successive Berlin apartments for extended sojourns, maintaining an ongoing dialogue on the city, directing me towards likely places, events and publications of interest, as well as commenting critically on aspects of the material – this book would simply not have been possible. In many respects it is Ulrike's tireless enthusiasm for Berlin life in general, based on an intimate association reaching back to late Cold War times (when I first met her there), that has sustained my own interest in the city from a more detached standpoint.

I also wish to credit Baz Kershaw of the University of Bristol, Gerry Harris of Lancaster University and Richard Boon of the University of Leeds for their welcome assistance with various funding applications. May Yao and Lucinda Sanders of Intellect deserve recognition for their responsiveness and diligence. And thanks, finally, to a range of occasional and informal interlocutors, among them Kate, Jo, Jutta, Andreas, Donald and Susanna, Bernhard and Ulrike, John and Felicitas; to Marlinde for the kind bequethal of Brecht's entire *Stücke* and, not least, to the old Leeds crowd for commissioning, on the occasion of my fortieth birthday, Ronald Arthur Dewhirst's droll Warholian portrait of Bertolt Brecht (who told Bert).

Photographs

1. Passport with GDR stamps (bottom left: Brandenburg Gate, 17 June 1990).

2. Chaussee Strasse street sign.

3. Brecht House, Chaussee Strasse 125.

4. Brecht/Weigel gravestones, Dorotheenstädtischer Friedhof, Chaussee Strasse 126.

5. Chaussee Strasse street sign.

6. Brecht Bookshop, Chaussee Strasse 124.

7. Neue Synagoge, Oranienburger Strasse 30.

8. *Ampelmännchen* (red), Potsdamer Platz.

9. *Ampelmännchen* (green), Potsdamer Platz.

10. Plaque ('Never forget'), Neue Synagoge, Oranienburger Strasse 30.

11. Anti-Neo-Nazi demonstration, Neue Synagoge, Oranienburger Strasse, 2001.

12. Damaged police vehicles, anti-Neo-Nazi demonstration, Oranienburger Strasse.

13. Tacheles (rear), Oranienburger Strasse 54–56a.

14. Tacheles (frontage), Oranienburger Strasse 54–56a.

15. Grosse Hamburger Strasse/Oranienburger Strasse street signs.

16. Boltanski's *The Missing House*, Grosse Hamburger Strasse 15–16.

17. Ernst Thälmann monument, Greifswalder Strasse.

18. Libeskind's Jewish Museum, Linden Strasse 13.

19. Graffiti, Markgrafen Strasse.

20. ETA Hoffmann Garden, Jewish Museum, Linden Strasse 13.

21. Holocaust Tower, Jewish Museum, Linden Strasse 13.

22. Brecht bronze, Theater am Schiffbauerdamm, Bertolt Brecht Platz.

23. *Der Verlassene Raum*, Koppen Platz (Grosse Hamburger Strasse).

24. Will Lammert's maquette for Ravensbrück, Grosse Hamburger Strasse 26.

25. Niederkirchner Strasse street sign.

26. Anhalter Bahnhof portal, Askanischer Platz 6–7.

27. Anhalter Bahnhof terrain, Askanischer Platz 6–7.

28. Anhalter Bahnhof portal (detail), Askanischer Platz 6–7.

29. Berlin Wall (remnant), Topographie des Terrors, Niederkirchner Strasse 8.

30. Berlin Wall (detail), Topographie des Terrors, Niederkirchner Strasse 8.

31. Copper strip Wall memorial, Niederkirchner Strasse (tarmac).

32. East Side Gallery, Mühlen Strasse 47–80.

33. Graffiti, Savigny Platz S-Bahn Station.

34. Graffiti, Friedrich Strasse Station.

35. KPM advertisement, Ebert Strasse.

36. Info Box, Leipziger Strasse 21 (Potsdamer Platz).

37. Europa Centre, Tauentzien Strasse 9/Kaiser Wilhelm Gedächtniskirche, Breitscheid Platz.

38. Potsdamer Platz building site, 1998.

39. Sony Centre (northern side), Potsdamer Platz.

40. Hotel Esplanade (interior fragment), Sony Centre, Potsdamer Platz.

41. Headquarters of German Railways (DB), Sony Centre, Potsdamer Platz.

42. Sony Centre (interior), Potsdamer Platz.

43. Strasse des 17 Juni street sign, Brandenburger Tor.

44. Soviet T-34 tank, German-Russian Museum, Berlin-Karlshorst.

45. Reichstag/Bundestag building portal (with Behrens's 1916 inscription).

46. Poster for exhibition of Christo's *Wrapped Reichstag* project, Martin Gropius Bau, Stresemann Strasse 110.

47. Foster dome, Reichstag/Bundestag (interior).

48. Foster dome, Reichstag/Bundestag (interior).

49. Foster dome, Reichstag/Bundestag (terrace).

50. Haacke's *Der Bevölkerung*, northern courtyard installation, Reichstag/Bundestag.

51. Love Parade 2000, Strasse des 17 Juni.

52. Karl Liebknecht Strasse/Alexander Platz street signs.

53. Palast der Republik western facade (detail), Schloss Platz.

54. Group of visitors gathered round *The Empty Library*, Bebel Platz.

55. *The Empty Library*, Bebel Platz.

56. Marx-Engels monument, Marx Engels Forum, Karl Liebknecht Strasse.

57. *Weltzeituhr*, Alexander Platz.

58. *Fernsehturm* (exterior), Panorama Strasse.

59. *Fernsehturm* (interior), Panorama Strasse.

Introduction

Preamble

THIS SPACE FOR RENT

Fools lament the decay of criticism. For its day is long past. Criticism is a matter of correct distancing. It was at home in a world where perspectives and prospects counted and where it was still possible to take a standpoint. Now things press too closely on human society.

(Walter Benjamin, One-Way Street)

Measurement is thus displacement. One not only displaces oneself, in order to take the measure, but one also displaces the territory in its representation, in its geometric or cartographic reproduction.

(Paul Virilio, Lost Dimension)

Taking Brecht

This book began life as a research project into Bertolt Brecht. It was 1998, his centenary year, and as the spotlight swung on to him, I was fascinated in general terms by the way the life and work of a key twentieth century writer and theatre practitioner, as well as radical thinker about art and politics, was being portrayed. Two factors in particular struck me. First, the desire of critical commentators to *pin down* Brecht: to interpret and assess and categorise; ultimately, whether positively or negatively, to fetishise him. There seemed, in this, to be a form of 'taking' in operation, implying an objectification that would inevitably culminate in a dead end (each 'take' the successful taking of a life). At the same time it put me in mind of Brecht's own alleged 'taking' tendency, the collagist's 'thieving' of ideas and practices, and the way *that* implied a renewed life-giving: taking 'this' and 'that' and allowing dialectical horns to be locked within a certain framework. Residing within the 'this and that' is the notion of the re-charged fragment, which is what brings me to the second factor. Here, I was intrigued by the way Brecht continued to have paths trodden for him roughly around two nodes: on the one hand, an alignment with radical Marxist commitment and a form of rationalist, agitational didacticism, both of which had had their day; on the other, serving as a frequent and productive point of reference in the most contemporary of discourses concerning interdisciplinary cultural practice generally, and art-making in particular. The dichotomy seemed to be exemplified by the position of Richard Foreman, the long-time director of the groundbreaking New York Company, the Ontological-Hysteric Theatre. In an interview for a centenary collection of articles entitled *drive B,* he concluded that things were 'as simple as that: Brecht no longer pushes the envelope'. *Mother Courage*, for instance, was 'supposed to be one of the great plays of the world but [...] to me is one of the most boring things I've ever had to sit through …[laughing] I get it, I get it'. In the same breath, he readily acknowledged that '[w]ithout Brecht's example and influence I doubt that I'd be able to do what I'm doing today. I don't question that for a moment' (Silberman 1998: 91–2).

It may be 'someone else's house' (92) in which Foreman now wishes to live, but what I mean to suggest is that there seem to be certain residual aspects of Brecht's praxis that hang significantly in the air. They're less to do with the writer's individual works then, as Fredric Jameson proposes in another centennial publication – one which tries to 'release' Brechtian technique – the 'more general lesson or spirit disengaged by [them]' (1998: 29). Central in this respect is the decisive contribution Brecht has made in a conceptual sense to the way art's functioning relates to both 'real' and 'everyday' life. In essence his points of influence would include, first, the situating of the spectator in an active role as the conscious maker of decisions rather than just as passive recipient. Second, the concept of 'making strange' as a means by which to create a 'pensive space' which would suggest the possibility of 'things in the world being otherwise'. Third, the application of a collage/montage technique which would emphasise the fragmentary, changing and *constructed* nature of what is thought of as 'reality'. And, fourth, the notion of the 'usability' of art; that is, its performative insertion into practices of everyday life. All of these ideas begin with a car crash, the event of Brecht's 'Street Scene' model, which encapsulated his theory of an epic theatre (Willett 1978: 121–9).

The notion of 'usability' or 'usefulness' captures best perhaps my own preoccupation with Brecht (if not the practice of art and the flow of ideas generally). For what is of interest to me is the extent to which his praxis not only seeks a direct application to the 'everyday-real' but also thereby sets up the criteria by which its value may be determined. In other words, the work will only figure *if* the circumstances in which it looks to operate deem it to be significant or at least 'of interest'. Art is judged by its impact in context – what it can *do* (or how it does what it does where it does it) – rather than merely for the 'intrinsic' qualities it may have that would, in the last instance, confine and make it the desired object of 'civilised' private experience and ownership. As Klaus Völker puts it: 'Brecht's epic theatre was an attempt to wrench this "artistic experience" away from metaphysics and "bring it down to earth"' (1979: 245). So it is that I am concerned with writing 'in and around' Brecht but also 'away' from him, picking up on traces which seem 'usable' and can perhaps be 'sent off' in certain productive directions. In a way the approach builds on a paraphrasing in which the architect Daniel Libeskind – who figures significantly in this book – once indulged in public debate with Jacques Derrida:

> Kafka somewhere says that authors really begin their work when they are dead. While they are alive, they are not really at work – they are just preparing themselves. But when they die, then they begin to write, and that is how they are great writers – the good ones begin only when they die.

> *(Libeskind 1997: 113)*

Whilst obviously anathema in one respect precisely to a Brechtian notion of 'immanent usefulness', embedded in this thought is the possibility of a writing which occurs *in absentia*, which circles around the post-mortal Brechtian *imago* and becomes, in a sense how he writes in me (or us), rather than what I write about him. There is in this something of the symbiotic ecology of the saprophyte, as Greg Ulmer delineates it, organic matter 'living off the decay of dead organisms in a way that makes life possible for living plants'. In other words, it facilitates a 'living *on*' or *sur*vival (Foster 1983: 105–6).

The notion of the 'afterlife' is, of course, also central to the work of Walter Benjamin, as we shall see. It permeates his thinking on phenomena ranging from the revelatory nature of ruins, to criticism of artistic production and translation as writings of 'renewal' or 'continued life' (Gilloch 1997: 196). The practice in question proposes a certain performativity inasmuch as I, as writer, am accorded an active role which essentially stages – that is, brings to life rather than represses – the drama of my activity. In other words, the book becomes to some degree about the writing of it. The best example of this is perhaps Geoff Dyer's book about D.H. Lawrence, *Out of Sheer Rage* (1997). Effectively adopting a position of 'enacting the now of writing in the present time' (that is, 'enacting the enacting of the now'), as Peggy Phelan says of the performative (1993: 149), Dyer tells one long tale of prevarication as it takes place: his *avoidance* of reading Lawrence's books, let alone writing about them despite meaning to. In narrating this frustrating process of deferral, which occurs simultaneously against the backdrop of his own highly-pleasurable 'ethnographic' retracing of Lawrence's travels (in Italy, in New Mexico), Dyer seems to evoke far more about the writer's 'essence' in practice – that which remains as a decisive trace – than any methodical critical analysis he may have attempted. The tension that Lawrence's impatient moodiness or 'rage' holds as the prerequisite of a life-enhancing creativity and sensitivity is played out through Dyer's – or his writer-protagonist's – own actions and experiences. Allotting himself this role sets up an important opportunity – as Dyer states elsewhere (citing George Steiner's *Real Presences*) – in which 'the performer "invests his own being in the process of interpretation". Such interpretation is automatically *responsible* because the performer is answerable to the work in a way that even the most scrupulous reviewer is not' (Dyer 1992: 165–6). So if the supposed paradigm of Lawrentian inspiration is premised on a practice of avoidance, there is in that a synchronous critique of conventional criticism implied. It is one which recalls Susan Sontag's words on Roland Barthes, for whom the radical decision that 'the point of criticism is to alter and to relocate meaning – adding, subtracting, multiplying it – is in effect to base the critic's exertions on an enterprise of avoidance'. Like Foreman's condemnation of the obvious in Brecht ('I get it. I get it'), 'the message is already understood, or is obsolete'. It is then a matter of moving on: 'the work with its received valuations already exists. Now, what *else* can be said?' (Sontag 1983: 428).

Performing Berlin

When I visited friends in Berlin in Brecht's centennial year of 1998, I looked in at the writer's archive in Chaussee Strasse one morning. It was an initial gesture towards the research I had in mind, a putting out of feelers, and it led to the beginnings of a decisive shift of emphasis. I had witnessed Berlin on three separate occasions in the first half-decade after the fall of the Wall in 1989. That was a very special, intoxicating time for the city, when the implications of such radical change were replete with anxiety as well as a sense of potential, and I always felt sorry only to be able to dip into this atmosphere for short bursts at a time. Now, nearly a full decade later, the times were clearly less heady but nevertheless heavily loaded with the imminent effects of those transformations set in train in the first five years. Things were happening to Berlin in a way – and at a speed – that was simply tremendously exciting. They were changes, moreover, which were becoming properly comprehensible and articulable in a manner that the severely limited eloquence of *Wahnsinn* ('unbelievable', 'madness') – the word for the inexpressible on everyone's lips in the early days – had not been able to capture. The blank space of uncertainty was beginning to acquire colour and definition. And it should be remembered that the shock of 1989 had applied as much to the western half of the city as its eastern counterpart.

The day before my visit to the archive I had witnessed, in a public park in the Neukölln district of the city, the world premier of *Run Lola Run*, Tom Tykwer's hugely enjoyable and – subsequently – internationally successful film. Three times the flame-haired Lola dashes through the streets of Berlin – in a superimposed montage effectively of the same story 'differently told' (and 'ended') – to bale out her naïve boyfriend, who has become embroiled in a dodgy gangster heist.

Entrusted with a massive lump sum of 100,000 Deutschmarks, he has panicked and left it in a carrier bag on the Underground and now has to face his mean bosses empty-handed. Lola's route is the same each of the three times, but variations of incident along the way – including encounters which spark conjectural flights down narrative 'side streets' – as she attempts to scrape together the money within an improbable time-span of twenty minutes, produce distinct outcomes. It amounts to a witty, inventive comment on temptation, risk, corruption and, above all, chance: the suddenness with which your fortunes can shift in a fast-moving, bewildering world where money is the currency and love too seems to come at a price. A huge, beer-swilling audience, packed into open-air, raked seating on a hot, humid August evening, laughed and cheered and quipped throughout, as if it were at a football match (Brecht would have been pleased). Without explicitly *trying* the film had tapped into something recognisable: the everyday familiar Berlin streetscape in a direct sense, but, far more importantly, a wry sense of the bizarre narratives of renewal that the unsettled 'temper of the times' was producing.

To me, then, the contrast between the stuffy 'inside' of the archive that morning and the vibrant 'outside' that was the city could not have been more marked. In that spatial dialectic, though, there seemed to exist an opportunity. Brecht, declared by Florian Vaßen to be one of the most important poets of the city in the twentieth century (1998: 74), was, after all, someone whose art sought an immediate connection with the 'theatre of everyday life', a move which recognised the 'real' as performed. And Berlin was fully engaged in just such a 'theatre', as it attempted to negotiate the relationship between old and new identities. Thus, between the 'archive' that represented the Brechtian body of work, and the quotidian city, there existed, as Ben Highmore suggests of Michel de Certeau's practice:

> the possibility that existing archives might be attended to by focusing on the every-
> day as a tenacious irruption and interruption within them, or as a potentiality to be
> extracted by a range of speculative approaches. On the one hand an archive of the
> everyday; on the other the everyday-ing of archives.
>
> *(2002: 162)*

What is more, Berlin was a city that exuded a powerful sense of itself performing, a kind of intense self-awareness that permeated all aspects of the everyday and that had, moreover, a historical typicality. As Alexandra Richie reports, the verdict on Wilhelmine Berlin of the famous cultural guide Baedeker was that it was 'theatrical' and 'showy' (1999: 232). And, a quarter of a century later, Franz Hessel is referring to the construction workers on Frankfurter Allee as engaging in a 'theatre spectacle of work' for young and old alike, for 'spectating is something Berliners still do as in times of old when they weren't in such a hurry as these days' (1984: 204). If, as John and Katya Berger intimate, cities possess governing behavioural characteristics – Vienna the nostalgic city, Lisbon the 'city in waiting'

(2000: 13) – then Berlin is the performing city, not only in its tendency toward self-conscious display but also in the sense that it is, more obviously than other places, in constant process, an unfinished city trying out identities. And like the reflexive Brechtian actor, it does not seem merely to perform but to *show itself* performing.

But Brecht also had a very particular connection with the city, spending approximately a third of his life there and founding probably its most famous ever theatre institution, the Berliner Ensemble. It was, moreover, a life that embodied precisely those preceding, radically shifting Berlin histories of Weimar, the Nazi era (experienced in exile, of course) and the beginnings of the Cold War. Thus, *locating* Brecht in contemporary Berlin – in the threefold sense of 'seeking', 'finding' and 'situating' – as well as reading the ever-evolving city through a writer who emphasised the ceaselessness of change, seemed a viable as well as exciting proposition. In many respects *locating* Brecht can be said to amount to a process corresponding to Jameson's championing of Brechtian method, which is:

> defined and constituted by the search and discovery of contradictions. Perhaps one might even say: by the construction of contradictions – since it is as a reordering process that it is necessary to grasp the dialectical method in Brecht: as the restructuring of juxtapositions, dissonances, *Trennungen*, distances of all kinds, in terms of contradictions as such.

> *(1998: 79–80)*

Hence, what we take to be the city, a naturalized, totalising space of 'normality' and 'immutability', can be shown to be (historically) constructed – contradictorily so – and, as such, subject potentially to a 'dismantling'.

And if Berlin does indeed present a performing paradigm or 'theatre of the streets', it simultaneously 'gives license' to the visitor or 'stranger' to take part in some way. It is surely no coincidence that the city boasts a long line of distinguished twentieth century socio-cultural commentators preoccupied with direct immersion in and observation of street life as a means by which to arrive at an index of modernity, from Simmel and his student Kracauer to Hessel and Benjamin. All concerned in their respective ways with the performative encounter between the phenomenon of the everyday and the metropolitan dweller (within the space of the city), it was Walter Benjamin who articulated as well as enacted most comprehensively a praxis relating to the figure of the *flâneur*: the idle stroller, mingling with the urban masses on the streets, yet remaining a detached observer. Benjamin expounded his thinking chiefly in relation to Baudelaire and nineteenth century Paris. But his Berlin writings – and he was of course a resident of the city from birth – including (or perhaps particularly) *One-Way Street* (1928), are clear examples of the interactive conjunction of walking and reflecting embodied by the *flâneur*, a drifting figure, prone to distracted digression, to whom, supposedly, the detritus of modern life – from architectural ruins to banal 'things', 'the neglected and the chance […] the marginal and the forgotten' (Vidler 2000: 116) – reveals the macroscopic. Hessel, of course, also produced a whole collection of Berlin sketches based on his excursions as *flâneur* (see *Ein Flaneur in Berlin*, 1984). Reviewing his friend's work, Benjamin welcomes the return of the 'endless spectacle of *flânerie*' (1999b: 263).

Benjamin/Brecht

Apart from both being bound up intimately with Berlin, Benjamin and Brecht were also friends, and the former remains one of the key readers of the latter's work (within a triad incorporating Barthes and Jameson, according to Darko Suvin [1999: 140]). In his commentaries on Brecht's early city-dwellers poetry, Benjamin suggests his colleague 'is probably the first important poet who has something to say about urban man' (1977: 61). For Benjamin himself it was more the locales and contours of the cityscape itself to which he was attracted. As Carol Jacobs suggests in her discussion of 'A Berlin Chronicle': 'People are displaced: they become outskirts to the city's privileging of "*Schauplätze*". The images of *Schauplätze*, literally translated as those "places to view", are the endless theatres that, one could claim, are the critical scene of *Berlin Chronicle*' (1999: 23).

Whilst very different in both method and manner of expression, there are evident points of contact in the two men's respective praxes, not only in terms of subject matter – their mutual preoccupation with the mythology of the city for a start – but conceptually speaking. Frequently lines can be drawn between similar processes of thought 'differently articulated' or, indeed, distinct ones that can be 'usefully linked'. In his comprehensive study of Benjamin's relationship to the metropolitan, Graeme Gilloch describes his approach as one in which the city:

> is rendered strange not so much through a simple effect of distance, but rather
> through the continual movement or fluctuation of vantage-points. There is flux
> between the minutely detailed close-up and the distant observation. Benjamin's
> images of the city are not static but dialectical in character.

> *(1997: 62)*

The locating of 'correct distance' (Benjamin 1997: 89) implied by this view is, as Gilloch points out in a note, 'clearly related to the "estrangement effect" (*Verfremdungseffekt*) pioneered – or at least refined – by Brecht's "epic theatre". The quiet contemplation of the drama by the spectator is disturbed as the dramatic action itself is subject to interruption' (Gilloch 1997: 194). Indeed, Benjamin's sketches of cities conform to the practice he developed of *Denkbilder* or 'pensive portraits', which similarly recall Brecht's concern with creating a space of 'conceptual intervention' for the spectator. For Gilloch the *Denkbilder* 'fundamentally prefigure the dialectical image' (23) – played out by both writers via the critical practice of 'montage' – 'in which the historical object comes into being in the momentary intersection of past and present' (35). The Benjaminian notion of 'dialectics at a standstill', as we shall see, is one which has a direct relationship to Brecht's *Gestus* in which the contradictory nature of the social and/or historical is crystallised by what is at stake in the detail of a single action or moment. In their respective studies both Jameson and Gilloch refer to the significance of the 'monadic' in which 'traces of the general (the social totality) are discernible within the particular (the mundane and trivial)' (Gilloch 1997: 186). A concrete wall is everyday, but what if it divides a city? And what happens when the people on one side knock it down one day? Thus the implications of the general contradict the ordinary; the *construction* of the Wall already contained the seeds of its own destruction since its impulse was dehumanising. (It is interesting, possibly, that the German term for the event of the 'Fall' tends to be *Wende* [rather than *Fall,* which has implications of finality as opposed to a sense of continuity], a turning point or turn around, [a half-turn, perhaps, but not the radical full-turn of a revolution]. It is as if it were an end that had in any case been expected and, as such, one that is superceded in fact by the notion of *transition*. At some point the change will have come; '*[W]ende*' already contains the German for 'end'.)

Benjamin's central concept of 'porosity', moreover, developed specifically as a designation for the 'characteristic form of social, spatial and temporal organisation in Naples', refers to the 'clear lack of boundaries between phenomena, a permeation of one thing by another, a merger, for example, of old and new, public and private, sacred and profane' in that city (Gilloch 1997: 25). Extrapolated so as to serve as a general motif within the narrative of cities, it is a term which points eventually 'to the relationship between architecture and action, and in particular the indeterminate, improvised character of everyday life as dramatic performance' (25).

Wa/ondering

Between Brecht's epic street scene model and Benjamin's one-way streetscapes a speculative tension presents itself, then, one calling to be played out within the space of the city. Where one proposes a performative theory of looking, the other points to a haptic practice of experiencing firsthand the dramatic 'shock' of contemporary urban life. Both these are, of course, forms of witnessing: of seeing, feeling implicated, and responding. Out of this emerges a poetics of walking and writing, a conjunction of wandering and wondering, which seeks to find a relationship between the immediacy of the encountered (the city as 'text') and the complex elaboration of that encounter (the text as 'city'). Hence, the 'prompt language [that] shows itself actively equal to the moment', which Benjamin advocates for writing at the onset of *One-Way Street* (1997: 45), is subject at the same time to a 'delayed reaction' in the form of the considered introduction and juxtaposition of related factors. (As David Frisby reminds us in relation to the practice of the monumental and unfinished *Arcades Project*, 'when Benjamin declares, "I am in the arcades", he is in fact in the Bibliothèque Nationale in Paris' [2001: 29].) If 'wandering' is a performative act – both a doing which 'gets you somewhere' (even if you don't know at the outset where exactly that will be) and a unique, ephemeral 'enunciation', as de Certeau theorises (1988: 98), of the route you happen to take – 'wondering' recontextualises that performance within the dimensions of the page. The latter *(re)iterate*s – to invoke Derrida (1988: 53) – presupposing a change that leaves but a remainder – albeit a significant one – of the former activity. 'In this context', as Frisby also reminds us, '(and in the historical analysis of the *flâneur*) a neglected dimension of *flânerie* is revealed, namely the *flâneur* as producer (of texts, images, etc.)' (2001: 13). Again, the method implies a meeting of Brechtian and Benjaminian minds within the space of the everyday: the collagist's or ragpicker's principle in which '[d]iverse, incongruent elements are rudely dragged from their intellectual moorings to be reassembled in radical and illuminating configurations. The shock-like character of modern social life finds expression in this montage of heterogeneous fragments' (Gilloch 1997: 19).

There is also an important elusiveness in the action of the walker, which is redolent of the city's own unforeseen movement as it seeks to negotiate identities for itself: I move because the city does. The concept of characterising cities according to their 'mobilisations' was also a Benjaminian preoccupation: the improvisational 'porosity' of Naples, Moscow's interpenetration of the technological and primitive (Caygill 1998: 125–6). Thus, there was a dialectic that emerged between how cities moved and how you moved in them. In Neil Leach's words: 'the "wanderer" represents the freedom and flux of the city. As such the "wanderer" is the archetypal creature of our contemporary condition, a creature whose existence reflects the very transiency of the city' (1999: 159). Walking promises, moreover, a corporeal brushing with the 'real' and 'immediate' (as well as 'ever-shifting'), emphasising it as a *practice*, an unpredictable wa/ondering from the self-generating, circular tendency of discourse's meta-functioning (commentary on commentary), whilst simultaneously acknowledging a debt. Highmore's explication of de Certeau's creative subversion of the power of 'authorised knowledge' via a tactics of the everyday – 'a research practice that would embrace "artistic" forms' – is relevant here. De Certeau's practice is:

> based in heterological sources that doesn't reduce these sources to illustrations of
> theoretical arguments, but uses the sources to provide and provoke theory. Faced
> with an archive of unmanageable proportions (novels, ethnographies, sociologies,

police reports, interviews, conversations, diaries, newspapers and so on), the researcher of everyday life is faced with the demand to find ways of 'listening' that are capable of hearing the tactical where it can. The two ambitions (to produce an archive of the everyday and to 'everyday' existing archives) become one: a practice of listening to the murmurs of everyday life.

(Highmore 2002: 169)

Like Wim Wenders' angel-protagonist in *Wings of Desire* (1987) – played by Bruno Ganz – I have tuned in, then, to current Berlin conversations, detached snatches picked up in passing. But like the angel I have craved finally to partake of the mortal's implication in this life, to become, as he says, 'worded'. I spent two periods of extended time in Berlin, a long summer in 2000 and a shorter winter in 2001, 'walking the streets' but also – in between as well as subsequently – reading, talking and writing about the city. There is no doubt that the practice corresponded to a form of situated nomadism – if that isn't too much of a contradiction in terms – an ethnographic impulse which seems to me turned around two contiguous points delineated by James Meyer as follows:

The first nomadism is lyrical – a mobility thematised as a random and poetic inter-action with the objects and spaces of everyday life. Reconciling the Dada/Surrealist strategy of an arbitrary encounter with the real with a contemporary 'Slacker' feeling of aimlessness, this nomadism transfigures the most ephemeral and incidental contacts for aesthetic contemplation. The second nomadism is critical: it does not enact or record an action or movement for the spectator's delectation, so much as to locate travel itself within historical and institutional frameworks. Whilst one nomadism is personalised, presenting the body's circulations as a series of phenomenological encounters occurring in real time, and tends to veil the material conditions in which this mobility occurs, the other nomadism locates the mobile self within a periodised, discursive schema.

(Coles 2000: 11–12)

Whilst Meyer would like strictly to hold apart those first and third person relationships to the environment, for me the Benjaminian 'immersed but detached' *flâneur* and the Brechtian 'performing performer', whose referent is the social, points usefully towards a potential interaction. Private experience is forced into a public realm, the lyrical enters epic space in a move which also recalls Benjamin's distinction between the immediate, lived experience that is *Erlebnis* and the experience of social discourse that is *Erfahrung*. The enframing of *Erlebnis* within *Erfahrung* marks the transitional point at which experience as 'that which is simply lived-through and experience as something that can be accumulated, reflected upon and communicated' is reached (Highmore 2002: 66–7). Perhaps Richard Shusterman's version of 'pragmatism', 'a philosophy of embodied, situated experience', comes closest to defining the desired approach:

> Experience is inevitably contextual, since it involves the interaction of an experiencing subject and the environing field, both of which are in flux and are affected by their interaction. But this contextuality of experience does not entail a hopeless subjectivism that precludes generalisations. For human subjects and environments share many contextual features. Nonetheless, a philosophy that argues from experience and recognises its contextuality should be reflective enough to declare its own experiential situatedness.

(2000: 96)

Berlin Streets

So, for me, Benjamin and Brecht are vital travelling companions – my walking stick and spectacles, if that doesn't sound too anachronistic for the beginning of the twenty-first century – whereby the former perhaps makes his presence felt more as a methodological influence, corresponding to his physiognomic way of probing and getting the measure of cities, as against the latter's integration as the producer of artistic proposals, as well as proposals about art. But, as Shusterman's comments imply, ultimately it is the immediacy of *locale* that is central in this practice, not least in this case the city of Berlin specifically.

Part one of the book, comprising chapters two and three, is directly concerned to bring these various elements – space, performers, action and technique – together in a literal and figurative mapping of Brechtian and Benjaminian territory. The first port of call in Berlin is, thus, the Brechtian 'site' at Chaussee Strasse, incorporating amongst other things his former house (a museum), the archive, his grave in the cemetery immediately next door, as well as the Brecht Bookshop. Wandering around this site affords the opportunity to identify aspects of the 'Brechtian trace'. Aware of the various, contradictory attempts to lay claim to Brecht, the chapter seeks to advocate an approach to the body of his work that corresponds instead to his own sense of 'lawlessness' and 'always being on the move'. In mapping key signposts of Brechtian terrain, the Benjaminian aphorism that 'to live is to leave traces' (1978: 155) is set against the deathly impulse to 'take' or assert narrative ownership over the absent Brechtian body.

Taking its cue from the Brechtian 'Street Scene' model, as well as personally encountered events, chapter three develops the notion of the shock situation or extraordinary circumstance, not to say *transgression*, as stimulating an incisive connection with 'otherness', or that which has not been articulated. Hence, the dislocation effected by the hypothetical occurrence of an accident on the street produces conditions in which unexpected perspectives present themselves. Brecht's model seeks not only to find the performative in everyday life, but also to emphasise the dual role of the witness as both compromised and responsible raconteur, character and performer. That function flows into Benjamin's preoccupations with the *flâneur*, a figure who is also both a spectator of and performer in 'scenes of the street', that 'dwelling place of the collective' (2002: 423). The chapter concludes by reiterating the case for the 'new *flâneur*' as the physical location, as 'moving body', of the material experience of the contemporary city.

To return briefly to the beginning: as the commencement of a topographical excursion around a 'strange city', the first chapter – strictly still part of the introduction – concerns itself with the business of getting to Berlin in the first place and the implications for the traveller of encountering the 'terror of the unfamiliar'. Drawing on psycho-geographical theories of place as propagated by Freud (the 'Uncanny') and Marc Augé (the non-places of supermodernity), the chapter argues for the necessity of 'leaving yourself behind', of temporarily 'losing yourself' as well as 'losing sight of yourself'. This emerges as the prerequisite for experiencing the unknown in a way that opens itself to the 'remarkable' rather than being foreclosed. Both Benjamin and Brecht address this issue, the former in his musings about the *flâneur*, the latter in his early 'city poetry' (on which Benjamin comments). In fact, the chapter's implicit concern is to portray the process of travel to unknown locations as equivalent to the Brechtian technique of rendering the familiar strange.

But the chapter also marks out the encounter with the strange city as one that is about the subject's identity, less in the sense of (re-)establishing it in a foreign place than in recognising its contingency and ephemerality: displacement or the failure to become permanently situated as the condition of being. Hence, as Jane Rendell proposes 'where I am makes a difference to what I can know and who I can be. (But I am not going to be [t]here for ever)' (Blamey 2002: 46). Operating between two places, moreover, potentially constitutes the subject not merely as the one 'who maps the tears and rifts, the places where things have come apart, and the overlaps and joins, the places where things come together', but also as the one who can allow him/herself to be changed by new surroundings (47).

The remaining chapters (four to nine) – making up part two – each take a specific Berlin street as their topographical space of encounter and speculation. Whilst clearly framed by the first part of the book, as I have outlined, I do wish to lay claim to a certain 'creative autonomy' for part two. In other words, the latter is certainly not conceived as a slavish, teleological exemplification of any theoretical foundation perceived to have been laid down by the former. Rather it grants itself permission

– in the true manner of the *flâneur* – to meander where it may, invoking Benjamin and Brecht directly where opportunities present themselves, all the while bearing in mind that their formal presence is in any case always already implicit. As such these chapters are effectively self-contained, though an inherent continuity of theme prevails; the final chapter, moreover, does not seek to present a conclusion to the book.

The locations in question produce the opportunity to explore both general and particular issues. On the one hand, as Libeskind implies, there is in the experiencing of the city the unavoidable physical *detail* of the street, which has an instigative function:

> the impression one gets when looking at the photographs of a bombed Berlin – and I have looked at them – is that the one thing that was not erased in all the bombings – and almost everything was – were the streets: the markings of the streets, the curb, only a few centimetres high. Here again is the logic of Kafka, which says that the most dangerous line is the line only three centimetres above your foot. That is the line you stumble on, a line low to the ground. I take this as a technique.

> *(1997: 113)*

On the other hand, the streets form a pattern, a shifting locus, in which a range of discourses meet and rub against (or scratch at) one another, ultimately *producing* – with a nod to Henri Lefebvre (1998) – the city's spatial organisation. It is in this sense that the city can be said to be performing itself into being, a practice which always remains provisional. I know of no other cityscape whose configuration has been so demonstrably inscribed, over and over, by its recent histories, a fact attributable to the sheer turbulence, the rapid rise and fall, of successive eras. Thus, as Andreas Huyssen sums up:

> the city on the Spree is a text frantically being written and rewritten. As Berlin has left behind its heroic and propagandistic role as flashpoint of the cold war and struggles to imagine itself as the new capital of a reunited nation, the city has become something like a prism through which we can focus issues of contemporary urbanism and architecture, national identity and statehood, historical memory and forgetting.

> *(1997: 57)*

Turning its attention to aspects of the new Berlin, chapter four finds itself in the Scheunenviertel area of the city, controversially known as the Jewish quarter. Concerned with the concept of historical superimposition, an account is given not only of the area's shifting status at various points in history but also how spurious, nostalgic claims on the past are made. This manifests itself in different ways. On the one hand, there is the spawning of an *ersatz*-Weimar culture that seeks to reproduce the twenties bohemia for which the city, but not necessarily the quarter, was once renowned; on the other, the area turns into a startling arena for the playing out of neo-Nazi histrionics in front of the synagogue on Oranienburger Strasse that featured significantly in the *Kristallnacht* fire attacks in 1938. The neo-Nazi antics, which I witnessed firsthand in the winter of 2001 in the largest fascist demonstration in Germany since the war, are related to Benjamin's comment on one of Brecht's 'city poems', suggesting Nazism needed anti-Semitism as a form of parody.

Contemplating several memorial sites, ranging from public installations to monuments, museums to cemeteries, chapter five tackles the highly topical question of memory and forgetting in a city attempting to reconcile two distinct post-war legitimising narratives of history. Drawing on examples of work by artists such as Boltanski, Whiteread and Calle, as well as former GDR statues of heroic figures (including Brecht's own bronze), the question of the circumstances under which memory-work can actually take place is addressed. Two factors in particular emerge as significant: first, the creation of a 'thinking space' which encourages interaction and, second, the application of Brecht's notion of *Gestus* (Benjamin's 'dialectic at a standstill'). Though not situated on Grosse Hamburger Strasse (the location for the chapter), Libeskind's Jewish Museum is integrated into this discussion as a performative building which, as the embodiment of a 'dialectical zigzag' organised around voids of disappearance, demands the visitor's participation in memory-work.

Chapter six, based on Niederkirchner Strasse, takes one of the last remaining stretches of Wall in the city as the impulse to reflect on its (and other walls') significance as signifier(s) of cultural conditions. Viewing the Wall from the perspective of physical and symbolic barrier as well as canvas of expression, its changing function from Cold War construct to reunification relic is analysed as an index of division and repression. Even its rapid disappearance, it is argued, points to a form of displacement – that of the actual chasm between East and West – into an 'invisible' psychic space of denial. The most evident sign for that is in the epidemic spread of graffiti, a performative 'writing on the wall' which warns of the unsighted presence of the dispossessed.

Expanding further on the theme of historical superimposition, chapter seven contrasts the changing status of Potsdamer Platz. Once the 'Piccadilly Circus of Berlin', a highly active intersection (captured to some degree in Brecht's early plays), it fell into Cold War inactivity as non-land positioned precisely in the death-strip zone of the Wall. After reunification it re-emerged as the focal point for the development of a 'new Berlin'. The chapter considers the direction it appears to be taking in the context of the rebuilding debate between city planners and architects over historicism and critical reconstruction. Picking up Derrida's notion of the *Riss*, the breach that defies master planning, the chapter relates this to the Brechtian shock of 'making strange' as well as to Libeskind's advocacy of a heterogeneous 'site-as-puzzle'. The centre-piece of the new square, the giant glass citadel that is the Sony Centre, is critiqued as an alienating exclusion zone, the epitome of 'loud' corporate colonising of public space.

Strasse des 17 Juni, one of Berlin's most prominent streets, named after the East German workers' uprising of 1953 (in which Brecht was controversially implicated), serves as the location for an interrogation of the politics of German nationhood in chapter eight. Particular attention is given to the new parliament building, the Reichstag, which has been out of action for the majority of its troubled history. The chapter considers its attempts to evoke democracy and unity through various 'mediations', including Norman Foster's refunctioning of the building, Christo's facilitation of its rebirth and Hans Haacke's installation, which rewrites its prominent inscription of 1916 'For the German People'. Finally, placing it in the context of a long history of mass marches and demonstrations on this particular street, the annual July Love Parade is analysed in terms of its claims to be a unifying political event.

Running through the former 'royal Berlin' as well as the centre of the Cold War East, Karl Liebknecht Strasse provides the opportunity to consider the ideological construction of the built environment in the final chapter. This is of especial pertinence to perhaps the most dogged debate in the city since 1989: whether or not to resurrect the vast Royal Palace, ruthlessly demolished by the East Germans in 1950. Doing so would imply removing the ugly People's Palace, put in its place under socialism and held in affection by many East Berliners. The polarised issue exemplifies existing anxieties of identity in the city, which manifest themselves in respective forms of nostalgia. The debate is framed by a Galilean perspective, both in terms of his introduction of an opened out 'enlightenment space of movement' and in the dilemma he faced in revealing his revolutionary research. Brecht addresses the conundrum of scientific discovery versus the ideology of reactionary authority in his play about Galileo, intending a Benjaminian telescoping of the issue into the (post-) World War II present. The epitomising figure in this move, it is suggested in the chapter, is the physicist Heisenberg, who played an ambiguous role in the Nazi era as one of the potential developers of a nuclear capability. However, his principle of 'uncertainty', arrived at through observing and measuring the play of light, is used, finally, as a figurative correlative – evoked in the realm of art by Tacita Dean's Berlin TV tower film – to both 'seeing' the city and the city 'seeing itself'.

1. *Terra* Terror: the Unlikely Event

'You know why they put oxygen masks on planes?

So you can breathe.

[Shaking head] Oxygen gets you high. In a catastrophic emergency, you're taking giant panic breaths. Suddenly you become euphoric. You accept your fate. [Indicating drawings on safety procedure card] It's all right here. Emergency water landing. 600 miles an hour. Blank faces. Calm as Hindu cows.

That's an...that's an interesting theory.'

(Fight Club)

[...] travel to forget they used to advise the neurasthenic, travelling lessens the suicidal tension in opposing a substitute for it; the little death of the departure, the gain acquired in the increase in rapidity of displacement was a disappearance into a holiday where there's no tomorrow, which amounts, for each, to a deferred rehearsal of his *last day*.

(Paul Virilio, The Aesthetics of Disappearance)

Dying to Go

I'll begin on the plane from London Heathrow to Berlin Tegel. Still on *terra firma*, just easing out of the blocks and taxiing towards take-off.

'In the event of the aircraft landing on water...'.

Wait. Slip up or customer relations policy change? 'Unlikely event', surely. That is what they have always said in the past: *unlikely*. What is going on? The tables have turned and we have to bank on the event being *likely* or at least even odds? After all, there is a quite confounding argument to say that the outcome of all risk situations is ultimately two to one. It either happens or it does not, and it could do so at any time. So perhaps the airlines are finally coming clean. Or maybe we are talking evolution. The airlines have come to the conclusion that, as a species, we humans have become so conversant with the global discourse of air travel – so sky-wise – that we do not require that little linguistic prop anymore. It is now inscribed in our cultural genes, as it were. In fact, retaining it may in the meantime produce the reverse effect, namely to draw attention to rather than disguise the very real possibility of the plane crashing. Sophisticated beings that we are, we have developed an immunising capability against such rhetorical charms, which, let's face it, did have the tricky task of deflecting our thoughts *from* death by raising the possibility of its imminence. From the airlines' point of view, then, it is best to be matter of fact. Play it straight, deliver the instructions and hope *the fearful thought* keeps its distance.

And, as the cabin crew continues the performance of its emergency ritual, it strikes me how odd it all is, that tugging of toggles and tapping of top-up pipes. Deeply familiar, but strangely abstract. And somehow archaic, the vestige of a primeval era of travel by air. Like activating propeller blades by spinning them manually. It seems to stand in no relation to the advanced degree of sophistication represented by present-day aircraft technology. Will they still be doing that fifty years from now? Or will there be an assumption by then that safety procedure is generally *known*; that we do not require to be taught or reminded anymore of how to behave in the unlikely event? Well, perhaps. But I suspect the survival of this survival ritual is safeguarded by a purpose exceeding – or even superseding – the communication of a code of safe practice. That purpose might be the perfunctory playing out of an exercise designed to insure the airlines against liability in the event of litigation following an accident. Rumour has it after all that when things actually go wrong, the notion of *procedure* in any case goes out of the window (so to speak). Hence, *being seen* to be taking precautionary measures is the most important factor from the point of view of the post-crash determination of responsibility. On a less cynical note, I would suggest the ritual is chiefly about managing terror. Not in the (unlikely) event of it arising at some future point in the flight, but in the extremely likely event of it being present *here* and *now*.

As I have pointed out, the problem for airline companies is how to deal with the very tangible association of the service they provide with the idea of death: that which is unknown and unforeseeable, which you fear – literally and figuratively, the last thing you want to happen. There cannot be many modern, everyday phenomena that confront you with the possibility of death with quite the same immediacy as travelling by plane. There are, for instance, visits to hospital. But hospitals are designated 'death sites'. They are prepared for it. They have real procedures that are implemented when it occurs. We accept that mortality, however it is handled by medical discourse, is one of the features of hospital culture. It deals in it. Air travel does not, *supposedly*. Moreover, whereas a visit to a hospital may invoke the 'smell of death', it is not necessarily *yours*, though ultimately it is probably that of which you are thinking. Airlines are faced not only with having to invoke death's possibility – without mentioning it – but also with palliating the implication that if it takes place, it will be within the next few hours and it will affect *you*. They are caught, then, in the unenviable position, on the one hand, of causing you to contemplate the potential occurrence of death – a nasty one at that – whilst reassuring you, on the other, that the risk to which you have committed yourself was really worth taking. To enable the latter thought to gain ascendancy, the former needs to be displaced or, if you want to be Freudian, sublimated. Like the plane itself our attention is elevated to a higher channel, away from the earth and thoughts of interment. So, if we are in fact talking survival tactics in the cabin crew's performance, the element of *survival* is more accurately ascribed to the strategic redirection of terror than the passing on of 'handy tips' for certain unmentionable eventualities. The whole procedure might be called *entertaining* the unbearable idea of death, a performative action that marks the collapse of the terror of contemplation into the ritual of its *diversion*. In Freudian terms that can be said to correspond to the move towards language and away from the 'lived experience of the real', a process analogous to the well-known allegory of *fort/da*, which both Freud and Lacan viewed as the linguistic distancing or mastery of the drives.[1] (For the latter that process of encodification implied, of course, the disappearance of the self.) Drawing on both Bauman (1992) and Baudrillard (1993), Adrian Heathfield's article 'Facing the Other: the Performance Encounter and Death' usefully sums up the notion of the social organization of cultural production as originating in a defensive reaction to the threat of mortality:

> Modern societies are predicated on 'survival strategies' which frequently involve the temporary resolution of death's threat through objecthood: the fixing of that which eludes understanding and explanation into identifiable and knowable objects. Objecthood draws phenomena into the field of the rationally explicable and is a condition which implies containment through place, name and identity.

(1997)

Terra Nullius

We are airborne and rising. A member of the cabin crew places before me a flat, rectangular box. My squarish meal.

'What would you like to drink, sir?'

'Oh, er, got any white wine?'

'Bordeaux or Australian Chardonnay? Be with you in a moment, madam...'

But this is precisely not a square meal. This is a mini-banquet of delicacies: smoked salmon for starters, then roast chicken and Russian salad, followed by tiramisu. And these are delectable angels, unconditionally indulging my every desire: pleasing to behold, silky in their movements, charming and obliging of manner. Burp and they would probably pretend to find it alluring. I may not be God – we'll be hearing from him later, I expect, delivering his report on the state of play 35,000 feet above Hanover or thereabouts – but I've certainly got some sort of minor fiefdom to my name. As the air gets thinner and the alcohol begins to cloud my brain, I'm not in heaven just yet, but it is giving me a pretty good foretaste.

But where am I in fact? 'In between', no-man's land (or air), nowhere? Well, it could be the occasion of my last supper. But that is a retrogressive thought. Death, or the fear of it, has long since been lulled out of my system. I am in full trance now, a state which began to work its spell at Heathrow, actually. A kind of sickly-sweet shopping and eating delirium. I realised, as I waited for the sugar to disappear into the depths of my third cappuccino, that the hive of activity all around me in the departure area, that constant stream of people parading past my observation post outside *Prêt à Manger*, was entirely without aim. It dawned on me when the same characters would reappear at intervals, still apparently on their way somewhere. And I recognised what was going on because I had been there myself, circulating endlessly, prowling the precinct, a trapped soul, thinking: there must be something interesting, something I haven't seen; there must be *more*. In some respects the activity suggests the aimless strolling of the *flanêur*. In fact, it's the antithesis because its possibilities are finite and predictable. You cannot get lost, only pointlessly ensnared.

The anthropologist Marc Augé refers to airports, or the locations of air travel generally, as instances of the non-places of supermodernity (Augé 1995). The latter is meant in the sense of a modernity that is '*over-determined*, in the language of Freud or Lacan' (Augé in Read 2000: 8), containing an excess of information which no longer allows human beings to recognise themselves:

> This overabundance of images has perverse consequences in so far as the more we get a chance to see everything, the less we can be sure we are still able to really look at them. The world becomes, one might say, abstractly familiar to us, so that, socially speaking, there are literally no more relations between the world and us, in so far as we are content with the images imparted to us, as is the case today for a lot of people.

(10–11)

Augé's notion of the 'abstractly familiar' recalls Freud's musings on *das Unheimliche*. Translated correctly, but nevertheless incompletely as (the) 'uncanny', the German *unheimlich(keit)* also has literal connotations of being 'unhomely' or even, as Paul Auster's alter ego muses in *The Invention of Solitude,* the state of 'not belonging to the home' (1988: 148). More commonly, it refers to that which arouses a sense of fear, insecurity or foreboding. Running these various senses together leads you to equate the experience of terror with the notion of not being home(ly), or of being in the realm of the unfamiliar: 'what is "uncanny" is frightening precisely because it is *not* known' (Freud 1990: 341). There is a link here too with Heathfield's summary of objecthood as that which 'draws phenomena into the field of the rationally explicable' (1997). A secure condition of *Heimlichkeit* or 'home(li)ness' is restored through a network of familiar or knowable objects. However, Freud's actual thesis is based on the curious way in which *heimlich* ('homely', 'familiar', 'native') 'is a word the meaning of which develops in the direction of ambivalence, until it finally coincides with its opposite, *unheimlich*' (1990: 347). This is premised on the fact that *heimlich* also means 'secret' – *ergo*: the home, or its objects, as the protector of secrets – which is in fact its dominant sense in common usage. A 'warm and secure' phenomenon harbours something 'ugly and threatening'. (Neil Leach gives an illuminating example of the dialectic in operation: 'within the *heimlich* of the homeland there lurks the *unheimlich* of nationalism' [1999: 159].) Hence, for Freud, 'it may be true that the uncanny is something which is secretly familiar, which has undergone repression and then returned from it, and that everything that is uncanny fulfils this condition' (1990: 308). As such, the 'uncanny is in reality nothing new or alien, but something which is familiar and old-established in the mind and which has become alienated from it' (363).

Augé concludes that 'in the world of supermodernity people are always, and never at home' (1995: 109). Non-places not only produce a form of suspended identity (or temporary non-identity), they also – or therefore – preclude significant interaction with the subject's environment. Like white noise, they effect a 'blanding out', a state of alienation in which you cannot properly *sense*. Hence, the non-places of travel can be said to promote an experience that is *forgettable*, in which no significant trace is left either in or by you although, paradoxically, it is a location to which you may return repeatedly. The 'abstractly familiar' emerges, then, as the effective antithesis to the 'secretly familiar' action of the uncanny inasmuch as the latter implies an *acute* sensing or 'coming home' of *something* previously witnessed, something that had absented itself. Augé's non-places evoke a return which produces an absenting.

Paradoxically, the traveller 'accedes to his anonymity only when he has given proof of his identity', according to Augé, a process which produces 'solitude and similitude':

Alone, but one of many, the user of a non-place is in contractual relations with it (or with the powers that govern it). He is reminded, when necessary, that the contract exists. One element in this is the way the non-place is to be used […] The contract always relates to the individual identity of the contracting party. To get into the departure lounge of an airport, a ticket – always inscribed with the passenger's name – must first be presented at the airport desk; proof that the contract has been respected comes at the immigration desk, with simultaneous presentation of the boarding pass and an identity document […] and checks are made at departure time to ensure that these will be properly fulfilled.

(1995: 101–3)

The English version of the French *non-lieu* (non-place) does not, as the translator of Augé's book points out, capture an important juridical application of the expression, namely 'no case to answer' or 'no grounds for prosecution'. In other words, it is 'a recognition that the accused is innocent [Tr.]'. As Augé himself states: 'In a way, the user of the non-place is always required to prove his innocence' (102) or, one might add to underline the paradox: to attest to his or her anonymity, to confirm their disappearance or absence. As Shusterman points out, the latter's 'etymology (*ab + esse*: 'away from being') reveals its link to the ancient philosophical puzzle of non-being, the paradoxical nature of 'things' that don't exist or simply fail to be 'here and now' (that is, present)' (2000: 99).

Terra Incognita

My mind drifts back fifteen years to the mid-1980s when I lived and worked in West Berlin for a year, frequently undertaking trips by train or car on the designated transit routes to and from West Germany. Every time it was an adventure both terrifying and exhilarating because you never knew what the East German frontier guards had in store for you. Procedures were rigorous but absurdly so, for in truth they were superfluous. You weren't permitted to turn off the motorways – not that many would have wanted to, save out of curiosity – and the trains did not stop till they got to the border at the other end. If the guards could find a way of pulling you up for some flaw in your behaviour or ID so as to fleece you of western currency, they would. It happened to me once when leaving the city. I was not in possession of my West Berlin resident's pass, something I wasn't even required to carry with me by the *western* authorities. What possible relevance could it have had to the German Democratic Republic on whose territory I was not intending, literally, to set foot?

The checks were conceived as an exercise in intimidation, providing the basis for the state to assert a sense of its ideological superiority. Ironically, then, if there was any real *proving* going on, it was in the reverse direction. But in the same way as you tended to mistrust East German Olympic success, which was supposed to be indicative of the way that this superiority produced better human beings, there was always something 'incredible' about the checks. In fact, they navigated a fine line, from the traveller's point of view, between fear, irritation and amusement. On the trains, the guards – carrying guns, of course – would flip open little portable 'bureaux' in stiff black leather, which hung round their necks. In scrutinizing your passport they would indulge in a cameo performance of studied efficiency. Ostentatiously they reassured themselves of your authenticity as they tested your photo not once but twice against your actual face, which could not help but break into a smile. The double take as a popular comic convention of high farce. Your smile disappeared fast, though, as it met with a look of steel and the stamp thudded down on your passport with the conclusive action of a guillotine. But it was a look that seemed to speak – or so you fancied – as much of entrapment as the confident assertion of authority. Who was really in control? Whilst there was no question that a guard could make life difficult for you on a whim for the three or so hours that you were occupying GDR territory, there also seemed to be a hint of acknowledgement of *something else*, as if s/he were saying: I know how this must look, but what's amusing to you, mate, is my life. In other words, it was a ritual, which somehow could not disguise the paradox produced by having to go to such lengths to prove its moral superiority.

There is no doubting the sense of *Unheimlichkeit* created by these encounters, but one of a different order. There were all those associations relating typically to the arousal of unease and fear: the sense of threat and unfamiliarity, of 'not being homely/at home'. The last of these did not, of course, take you into the 'comforting' abstracted realm of the non-place, though, but into the relative insecurity of the 'incognisant place', one which was at once terrifying and thrilling because it was secret(ive) (*geheim/heimlich*), repressive and unpredictable on the one hand, yet somehow 'pleasurably safe' on the other. Not unlike those paradigmatic situations of serious disciplinary enforcement experienced as a school child, in which the teacher makes an exposing example of some unfortunate, unruly student in front of the whole class, you feel, as witness, the very real authoritarian danger of the moment, whilst simultaneously basking in the pleasure of knowing you personally are above incrimination. At the same time, though, you could be drawn in if, in some small way, your demeanour were to encroach unfavourably upon the field of the 'riled gaze' (or at least the gaze that is burning to demonstrate its authority). In other words, the authority in question is dangerously volatile and could transfer the object of its attention at the slightest flicker of 'disobedience' elsewhere.[2]

The most common use of *unheimlich* in informal speech is as an adverbial intensifier meaning 'incredibly' (as in 'incredibly interesting'). The unknown place is just that: *incredible*, but in a dual sense; that which you would not believe – which seems unlikely – because its 'unknownness' is both sinister *and* amazing.

The type of encounter with the GDR guards was one which seemed to *play* with the serious possibility of something being or going wrong, of there being a question-mark over your authenticity in this place. There *was* a 'case to answer', but one, which in true Kafkaesque style, you yourself were not actually capacitated to effectuate. Ultimately, it was an experience that was unforgettable. Even now, Augé suggests, 'the countries of Eastern Europe retain a measure of exoticism, for the simple reason that they do not yet have all the necessary means to accede to the worldwide consumption space' (1995: 106–7). By comparison, the sickly alienation of the non-place of supermodernity implies submission to the pacifying over determination of objecthood, that saturated network (or *cul-de-sac*) of consumerist signification that serves to deny or forget the extraordinary or unlikely. As Edensor observes in his analysis of the culture of the Indian street, Western streets tend to be marked by non-sensuality. Within the touristic order there is organised and disorganised space, the former corresponding to a 'manufactured otherness' as against the latter's unregulated stimulation of both desire and fear (Fyfe 1998: 215–16).

Tegel Terror

We're going down. The plane banks and turns in a broad sweep over the eastern part of Berlin, which looks flat and grey. Row upon row of systems-built residential blocks: the *Plattenbauten* of Hellersdorf. A character in Norman Ohler's novel *Mitte* maintains: 'If you look down from a plane, the buildings form letters which spell NOT HERE' (2001: 217). A dull pain has begun to occupy the right half of my skull. Migraine. Or perhaps a touch of vertigo, now that I can see the ground below. I wince as the television tower, that beacon of advanced GDR technology, comes into view. 365 meters high, its spindly, red and white needlepoint is slowly piercing the inner corner of my right eye. All I can think of is the title of a collection of Bruce Chatwin's writings – his last – which I haven't even read: *What Am I Doing Here*. I remember reading in one of his biographies how some people believed there to have been a typographical error: a forgotten question mark. In fact, it was a cosmetic matter. The publishers didn't consider such punctuation to look good on the cover (Clapp 1998: 175). I also recall reading now that one of Chatwin's intentions before he died was to walk the boundary of east and West Berlin (220). He never did. Ten months after his death in January 1989, 28 years after partition began, the boundary was being crossed by thousands of people all at once. In retrospect the historian, Alexandra Richie, describes the experience of that transitional moment itself as 'quite banal – one simply walked a few metres past a large, ugly structure and into another district.' At the same time, though, 'it meant so much [...] everyone sensed that this was a moment they would savour for the rest of their lives' (1999: 835). And another seven months after that, on 17 June of the following year, I myself recall walking down the avenue in the western part of the city named after that very date and passing through the re-opened Brandenburg

Gate.[3] Reunification not yet in place, I received a token 'DDR' stamp in my passport, placed neatly, but to me with staggering nonchalance – the frontier guard grinned and winked, I swear – alongside some of the other ones I had chalked up in the mid-80s. Perhaps, when you find yourself caught in the middle of such momentous events all you can do is perform in them as if they were the most mundane.

We have just crossed the former border, or what no longer remains of it. There is virtually no trace of the Wall now. It's a void space. That reminds me of another book title with a question mark apparently missing: the East German novelist Christa Wolf's *Was Bleibt* (What's Left). It was published in 1990, but she had written it some eleven years earlier and not dared to release it, for which she was heavily taken to task after the fall. Its subject matter is surveillance and the dilemma of the writer living in a state whose ethos she supports, if critically, but whose praxis constrains her creative freedom, thereby turning her effectively into a prisoner or outcast. A writer without language. As Graves reports, Wolf's writer-narrator, 'suspecting that one of her close friends could be informing on her, debates with herself whether he would have had any choice but to cooperate with the *Stasi*, and she ponders on various stratagems he might have adopted to outwit them' (1994: 4). What avenues are left? Ironically, it emerged in 1993 that Wolf herself had been involved in passing on low-grade information to the *Stasi* early in her career. Before that she had already been vilified by Western commentators for her supposed quietism, for failing to voice opposition to the GDR in the time of its existence. The characteristic ambiguity of her writings was nothing less than an apology for the state, one which ensured not only her but its endurance, too.[4]

Judith Sallis suggests that '[in] the absence of punctuation, the title can be interpreted as either a question or a statement, implying the search for and the assessment of that which is permanent in a world characterized by transience' (1996: 111). Perhaps, so soon after the fall of the Wall, the disappointment directed at Wolf stemmed in subconscious part from the book's title which promised certain answers that neither the content itself nor the context in which it emerged was to deliver. Instead it presented a conundrum relating to the country's past. Given that artists and intellectuals were accorded considerable significance within GDR society for the views they held – and Wolf in particular was 'lumbered' with the status of respected 'moral authority' (Graves 1994: 5) – she would not have fulfilled the desperate need at the time for the matter of the future identity of the GDR to be resolved. Revealing her position as *problematic* rather than heroically chaste resulted in Wolf being cast as the villain. Now the Wall – that terrifying symbol of a divided identity and the most celebrated demarcation of no-man's land in recent history – has disappeared, and with it, seemingly, the GDR.

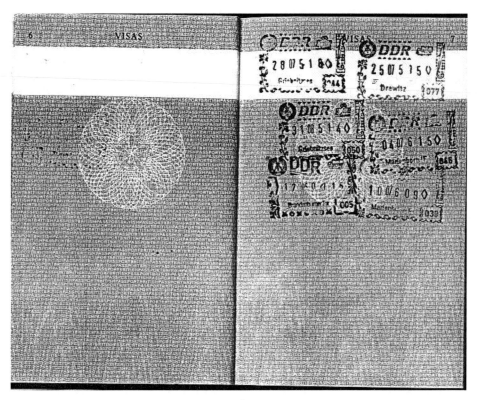

1.

But that's a view from above. As Benjamin proposes in *One-Way Street*, a landscape is only experienced properly by walking through it:

> The airplane passenger sees only how the road pushes through the landscape, how it unfolds according to the same laws as the terrain surrounding it. Only he who walks the road on foot learns of the power it commands, and of how, from the very scenery that for the flier is only the unfurled plain, it calls forth distances, belvederes, clearings, prospects at each of its turns.

(1997: 50)

And, as if to confirm the physical immediacy of Benjamin's spatial invocations, it is when the plane touches down at Tegel Airport that the real terror strikes. To be precise it is when the reverse-thrust of the brakes kicks in; that delayed counter-surge which finally propels me out of my air travel trance because I think, having already survived the bump and swerve of landing, that something has gone wrong. All I can see as I peer in alarm out of the window are the wing flaps turned up, hysterically exposing mechanical innards. It is not exactly reassuring to have the

airplane bare itself like that just at a point when I need it to demonstrate its robustness. And not an angel in sight now.

But for me it's not really crash terror. This is terror *incognita*. I have descended on a strange – though once-known – city for the next two months and my whole being feels as if it has been blasted out of me. The migraine – the migrant's curse? – that has replaced it is forcing my right eyelid shut, as my body tries valiantly to find ways of alleviating the pain. My visual field is blurred as a result. I cannot see. I seem to have lost sight of myself. Really, what am I doing here?

Later I realize that what is happening to me is a necessary prerequisite for the discovery of strange territory. Strange but familiar. I have been here before. The experience of terror is what spurs me on to seek curative *terra firma*. A little crisis has been opened and I must 'look into it'. As Barthes proposes, 'one never speaks of fear: it is foreclosed from discourse, and even from writing (could there be a writing of fear?). Posited at the origin, it has a value as method; from it leads an initiatic path' (1989: 350). I have travelled through non-place to unknown-place, but I am still 'passing through' or 'infected', both of which are meanings attributed to the Latin *transitio*, according to the Berlin poet Durs Grünbein (Stein 1999: 89). A third is 'going over to the enemy', which puts me in mind of the 'unlikely events' of the *Wende* of 9 November 1989. Victor Burgin refers to this form of transition as representing 'the economic and political equivalent of "osmosis" – the movement of a fluid through a semi-permeable membrane, from the weaker to the stronger solution' (1996: 156). And, as Franco La Cecla points out, 'the feeling of a possible and imminent danger' – the source of my terror – 'is the sense of adventure [...] Getting lost in these cases is a condition of beginning, the need and the ground on which to start or to resume getting orientated' (Read 2000: 34). The imperatives, on the one hand, of a child-like perception 'at first sight', as Gilloch puts it (1997: 63), and, on the other, of 'getting lost', are precisely the points of departure for Benjamin in his series of autobiographical vignettes 'Berlin Childhood around 1900', also contained in slightly different form in 'A Berlin Chronicle':

> Not to find one's way in a city may well be uninteresting and banal. It requires igno-
> rance – nothing more. But to lose oneself in a city – as one loses oneself in a forest
> – that calls for a quite different schooling. Then, signboards and street names,
> passers-by, roofs, kiosks, or bars must speak to the wanderer like a cracking twig
> under his feet in the forest, like the startling call of a bittern in the distance, like the
> stillness of a clearing with a lily standing erect in the centre. Paris taught me this art
> of straying; it fulfilled a dream that had shown its first traces in the labyrinths on the
> blotting pages of my school exercise book.

(1997: 298)

Importantly La Cecla also refers to the Socratean warning against 'taking yourself with you' on your travels; the danger, if we do, that we risk 'colonizing with our presence every step of the journey' for 'to know new places corresponds in this century with denying their difference' (Read 2000: 39). That is what tourists generally do, eliminate the 'real experience of otherness', in the same way colonialists did before them. In Helen Liggett's discussion of Levebvre the encounter with the city is then deemed by the latter to be 'no longer lived' and 'no longer understood practically'. What is left is but a 'virtual object', one of cultural consumption, which leads him to the question: 'If man is dead, for whom will we build?' (Liggett 2003: 91). Thus, as Silverman proposes, two modes of identification can be sketched: on the one hand '"heteropathic", where the subject aims to go outside the self, to identify with something/someone/somewhere different'. And, on the other, '"cannibalistic" where the subject brings something other into the self to make it the same' (Blamey 2002: 259).

The young Brecht wrote a cycle of poems for the 'city dweller' in the 1920s, the first of which echoes the sentiment of guarding against the known. Stern advice is offered on what to avoid on arrival in the new place. As Vaßen puts it: 'Already with the entry to the city all old ties are to be cut. The *Mitgebrachte* ("the ones brought with you"), in the shape of travelling companions are discarded' (1998: 79–80).

> Part from your friends at the station
>
> Enter the city in the morning with your coat buttoned up
>
> Look for a room, and when your friend knocks:
>
> Do not, o do not, open the door
>
> But
>
> Cover your tracks.

(Brecht 1976: 131)

Walter Benjamin identifies Brecht's state of mind in these poems as that of the political émigré in his own country, not only foreshadowing the emigrant's experience of foreign lands – Brecht's in exile – but also equating the condition with illegality: 'Cover your tracks' (Benjamin 1977: 60). Coupled with the tone of address – what can be read as a coaxing dialogue with the self – a clear duality of persona emerges, a split expressed in the second stanza as existing between a 'lost face' and the 'hat' that stands in: 'Pull the hat they gave you over your face, and/Do not, o do not, show your face' (1976: 131). Like the epic actor's portrayal of a role, then, it is as if you are standing temporarily and invisibly beside yourself, watching a character perform the part of a stranger.

But there is also the suggestion that what is happening to me here, this necessary emptying of selfhood, is replicated somehow in the very topographic turmoil of the city. I haven't even left the plane, but I sense that the 'new Berlin' with its 'identity in transition', will somehow suit my own displaced frame of mind. If my self has disappeared temporarily, the promise of its return lies in wait in the unpredictability of the strange yet familiar terrain I'm about to negotiate. In his review of Franz Hessel's 1920s book about *flânerie* in Berlin, Benjamin isolates its deepest insight as being the writer's observation that 'We see only that which looks back at us' (1999b: 198).[5] His subsequent reference to 'the lingering [after-]gaze [*nachschauende Blick*] of things and people' (198) recalls the 'deferred action' of Freudian *Nachträglichkeit*, described by Foster as 'an event [which] is registered as traumatic only through a later event that recodes it retroactively' (1996: xii). Related to the 'return of the repressed' that corresponds to the experience of the 'uncanny', Burgin points to its generalisation as 'what appears to come to us from the outside is often the return of that which we ourselves have placed there – something drawn from a repository of suppressed or repressed memories or fantasies' (1996: 95). So, as Steve Pile summarises:

> There is a dynamic exchange of looks which takes place within a spatio-scopic regime [...] Lacan's ideas begin to undo a notion that space is somehow a passive backdrop against which bodies and subjectivity can be mapped – *space looks back* [my emphasis]. Space is dynamic and active: assembling, showing, containing, blurring, hiding, defining, separating, territorialising and naming many points of capture for power, identity and meaning.

> *(1996: 129)*

Not to 'over-subjectivise' the process in operation here, though, it is the abstracted notion of a reciprocal or performative relationship between viewer and viewed that I wish to emphasise, one which echoes the transitive practice introduced by minimalist art of, as Nick Kaye formulates it, 'forcing an incursion of the time and space of viewing into the experience of the work' (2000: 3). For 'work' read locale or city. Thus, as Liggett neatly concludes of Benjamin, he:

> sees active engagement with the material of the world as generative. His relationship with the city is not subjective, of the lone witness to events, nor is it objective in the positivist sense, of the discoverer. The relationship is performative and mutually generative. A space that attracts meanings is made as he moves through the city [...] not reporting as a correspondent would or assuming correspondence with the truth [but] using [himself] as the instrument [...] The life of the city and the life of its

artists are intertwined as the fragments of modernity are reconfigured into a montage based on encounters with the city.

(2003: 103)

Notes

1. See Freud (1991: 283–7) and Lacan (1997: 103–4). Invoking the child's game of *fort/da* seems particularly apposite here given the pampered conditions of security and dependency imposed on the airplane passenger: the replication of the baby-seat with its safety straps, the high-tolerance, 'motherly' attention of the cabin crew, the easily-digestible comfort food, eaten (often) with plastic cutlery from a fold-down table reminiscent of the circumstances of the high-chair, and so on. On this particular trip the gravelly-voiced captain – radiating the heroic, man-of-action responsibility of the 'absent father with a very important job to do' – even asked his passengers over the intercom to do him the 'special favour' of keeping their safety-belts on during the flight. Anything for you, Daddy, if it means you'll take good care of me.

2. Again, the childhood analogy seems appropriate since Freud attributes the experience of the uncanny to the revival of repressed infantile complexes (Freud 1990: 372).

3. The main thoroughfare extending westwards from Brandenburg Gate was named Strasse des 17 Juni in memory of the victims of the workers' uprising against the GDR government in 1953 (see chapter eight).

4. See Frank Schirrmacher (1990) 'Dem Druck des härteren, strengeren Lebens standhalten. Auch eine Studie über den autoritären Charakter: Christa Wolfs Aufsätze, Reden und ihre jüngste Erzählung *Was bleibt', Frankfurter Allgemeine Zeitung*, 2 June 1990.

5. Benjamin makes a similar reference in 'On Some Motifs in Baudelaire': 'To perceive the aura of an object we look at means to invest it with the ability to look at us in return' (1999a: 184). In a note he adds: 'This endowment is the wellspring of poetry. Wherever a human being, an animal, or an inanimate object thus endowed by the poet lifts up its eyes, it draws him into the distance. The gaze of nature thus awakened dreams and pulls the poet after its dream' (196).

Part 1

2. Chaussee Strasse: the Last Place

In the vast 'city' of art and possibility the Brecht house was at one time an exciting house to live in.

(Richard Foreman, 'Like First-Class Advertising', drive B: brecht 100)

The interior is not only the universe but also the etui of the private person. To live means to leave traces. In the interior these are emphasized. An abundance of covers and protractors, liners and cases is devised, on which the traces of objects of everyday use are imprinted. The traces of the occupant also leave their impressions on the interior. The detective story that follows these traces comes into being.

(Walter Benjamin, 'Paris, Capital of the 19th Century')

Sometimes all that remains of the past is a name – it becomes the connective space, the passage to other experiences.

(M. Christine Boyer, The City of Collective Memory)

Staging Brecht

Feeling lonesome and bereft I go round to Brecht's, a man who knows about migration. A friend in exile. The house, which incorporates the archive, is at Chaussee Strasse number 125 in Berlin's Mitte district. That's right in the centre of the city, as the name suggests. A centre called centre. The folk there, the attendants of the Brechtian habitat, tell me he is next door at number 126. That's the funny thing about Berlin. It's not odd and even numbers on respective sides of the street. Instead you might begin at one corner, at number one, say, count your way consecutively up that side of the street to the end, and then come back down the other side. On a long boulevard like Prenzlauer Allee, for example, it means number one ends up being opposite number 249. Of course, you don't actually have to trudge laboriously up the whole length of one side and down the other till you find your number because there are indications on the street signs as to which numbers correspond to a particular block – unless they've been stolen, which is admittedly frequently the case.[1] Eventually you get the hang of it, but just to help matters along, not all of the city necessarily conforms to this pattern. The streets around the Kollwitz Platz area immediately adjoining Prenzlauer Allee, for instance, operate an odd/even dichotomy. So, whenever you're hunting for an address in Berlin – which, even as a native in a metropolis of some 3.5 million inhabitants, you frequently find yourself doing – there is always that moment of hesitation as you peer at the numbers on buildings: which system am I in here? I've attempted casually to uncover the historical reasons for the numbering discrepancy, but it seems that the highly

2.

delicate political issue of changing street names – to which I'll return – has dominated to such an extent in Berlin that no-one seems particularly alive to the matter. The one thing you can say, as the example given shows, is that neat explanations of it as the relic of a former East-West division are misplaced.

The other odd thing about Brecht being next door at number 126 is that it's a cemetery, the Dorotheenstädtischer Friedhof. I know he's dead, and the dead get buried in cemeteries, but do the latter customarily have numbers? My blind spot perhaps. (Thinking about it, though, maybe they should have several thousands.) Still, that's where he is, along with Helene (his wife), Hegel (the philosopher) and Heiner (Müller, that is, the writer and director, who hasn't been there long, of course). But let's not begin with endings. Before paying a visit to the cemetery, I had an appointment to be taken on a guided tour of Brecht's house. I was curious about this, not so much in expectation of what I might discover about the writer – I had in any case 'done' this tour twice in the past – but what the guide would be like. Some things I'd already picked up on, you see. When I'd made the appointment the previous day, the person to whom I had spoken on the phone had said, 'Yes, we can fit you in at eleven o'clock. It'll be a young 30 year old woman showing you round'. A strangely intimate volunteering of information it seemed to me. It's not as if we were meeting one-to-one at a railway station where identification might have been a problem. All it needed was for her to add, 'Her name's Candy, by the way'. As far as I could tell, though, there was no erotic spin to it, no deliberate attempt to make the prospect of the visit appear more enticing. On the contrary, it seemed utterly matter of fact: this is what you're getting.

But then maybe I was judging the situation by my two previous visits, one during the last years of the GDR, the other not long ago in 1998. Both had been characterised for me by that sense of a sober, sincere, 'truth-to-materials' consolidation of the Brechtian *imago* which the Berliner Ensemble was repeatedly taken to task for after his death in 1956, and which the British dismiss easily as humourless.[2] I distinctly remember the guide two years previously – an older one, if we're going to be particular about age – lamenting the fact that televised productions of Brecht were only ever shown on late-night TV these days, that being a pity since surely he still had so much to teach us. *Everything* for the modern generation – though she may well have meant 'Western' – seemed to be about *fun*, she complained, actually using the English word. Perhaps, then, the phone call *had* carried some sort of concession to changing times: not just a youngish person, who would barely have been out of school when the Berlin Wall collapsed, and who may therefore have a refreshing, if not cheeky, take on Brecht, but also a woman who would be bound to hold a robust view on the controversial likes of Professor Fuegi. In his biography *The Life and Lies of Bertolt Brecht* (1995), he attempts to discredit Brecht as, in Willett's words, 'a pig of variable sexuality who mastered his women collaborators by seducing them, and thereby got them to write a great part of his works' (1998: 194).[3]

As it turns out the 30 year old woman's performance is remarkable above all for its speed of delivery. Belying her interest in the situation, she rattles off her lines to our little group as if she had a train to catch. However, she is a lot freer than her predecessors with the Brechtian legacy, eager to portray the writer precisely as *fun*-loving, as well as witty, and, in what seemed like a conscious move to counter charges of manipulation and domineering egotism, as rather reserved in company – more polite and a good listener. The mischievous, charming sides, moreover, viewed mistrustfully by some as just the characteristics masking his unpleasantness, particularly in relation

3.

to women, are passed off harmlessly in an amusing anecdote about the flux and flow of people in his house. Apparently, Brecht was very keen on the two exits and entrances. It allowed certain visitors to be kept apart, one lot being seen off furtively through one door before the next was greeted at the other. (What more would you expect from the author of such models of high farce as *The Good Person of Setzuan*?)

Of course Brecht's house is also Helene Weigel's, the Berliner Ensemble's most celebrated performer, who continued living there until her own death in 1971. She had kicked him out of their villa at Weissensee in the northeastern part of the city when he called her a lousy actress once too often, according to the guide.[4] Nothing to do with 'all his women', she stresses, and I wonder how she would have come to know that. Surely not being taken seriously as a working woman would have represented some sort of final straw in the light of the validity Brecht accorded his other female 'collaborators'. Eventually he persuaded Weigel down to Chaussee Strasse, but they occupied for the most part different sections of the house.[5] This was 1953, around the time Brecht was finally given his own theatre building, the Theater am Schiffbauerdamm, about ten minutes walk down the road towards Friedrich Strasse station. Not that you would have seen Brecht dead walking down Chaussee Strasse. His love of cars is legendary.

Weigel used, in fact, to occupy the second floor of the house immediately above Brecht but moved downstairs to the ground floor after his death. The presentation of her domain is all matronly domesticity. Never mind that she was the *Intendant* (or artistic director) of the Berliner Ensemble, as well as its leading performer, which put her on a higher income from the theatre than her husband as it happens. There's a spacious bedroom with one of those prominent nineteenth century stoves typical of Berlin apartments: tiled and larger than a full-size family fridge. (The guide during my visit in 1998 felt compelled to emphasise that Helene's bed was a double one, as we could see; that separate bedrooms did not signify no sexual relations. She meant with Brecht, I presume.) A homely winter-garden functions as a living-room and looks on to a small but well-kept garden. And the kitchen is in cosy country style. Wherever you look in Weigel's rooms it's all well-worn wood, pewter, glass and earthenware; a paraphernalia of authentic antiques: hand-crafted furniture, crockery, vases, jugs and rugs. The only apparent gestures towards modernity: a Daliesque Bakelite telephone (without the lobster) and, as one witness puts it, a 'pre-Sputnik era television set' (Hooper 2000).

Nobody dares to say, it seems so corny, but Weigel's apartment really does appear like the staging of the home the nomadic Mother Courage would have had – despite a time difference of three centuries – had she not spent her life dragging a cart loaded with all manner of 'useful' nick-nacks around the European theatre of war. One of Brecht's late poems, 'Weigel's Props', refers to his wife's predilection for choosing 'the objects to accompany her characters across the stage' according to the same principles with which the poet picks 'the exact word for his verse'. As the poem goes on to observe: 'Each item [...] selected for age, function and beauty/By the eyes of the knowing/The hands of the bread-baking, net-weaving/Soup-cooking connoisseur/Of reality' (1976: 427–8). Brecht's appreciation of Weigel's talent is expressed in terms which neatly typecast her as the 'natural domestic'. The Weigel recipes – her husband's favourites – served up in the Keller Restaurant of the Brecht House represent the final endorsement of that perception. They're called *Versuche* – the name given to Brecht's collected 'experimental writings' pre-1933 – but culinary theatre might have been more accurate.

Despite my inner impulse to contradict or at least sniff at everything I'm being told, I realise I'm also enjoying this Brechtian *Heimat-Klatsch*, this 'opera'. It's like sinking into a hot, soapy bath. Wandering through these rooms, I experience a profound sense of *familiarity* and pleasure, of being in some sort of way 'at home'. That's not the consequence of having been here before but of something somehow being confirmed. It's what you would expect, the Brechtian 'always already', a *Gewohnheit* or *inhabitation*. A diary entry of Walter Benjamin's testifies to an afternoon spent debating theories of living with Brecht. The latter identifies a basic dialectic between a 'convenient' alignment to surroundings – what you might call the forming of a habitual habitat – and an attitude reminiscent of always being an invited guest in one's own home (*GS* 6: 435–6). Here, the stage-managers from the Berliner Ensemble have discreetly set the scene: all props have been checked off, cue sheets are in place, audience in, final call, the performance can begin. If this is Brechtian theatre, though, it really is more like a culinary one, the flavour of Brecht, an appetising staging of a staging that proves as dialectical as synthetic pudding.

Brecht's rooms are on the first floor and, above all, tell a story of *work*: books, manuscript cabinets, typewriters. A smaller study leads to another larger one, both overlooking different sections of the cemetery. In the former the chairs can be seen to be placed far apart from one another, because Brecht felt people thought more about what they said that way. So the guide says. Proximity encourages shooting from the lip. These rooms were, of course, one of the settings for the writer's famous collective production sessions. Here, the guide feels compelled to make a general point about the active writing role of Brecht's three main women collaborators Ruth Berlau, Elisabeth Hauptmann and Margarette Steffin (the last of which never experienced Chaussee Strasse[6]): of course they operated collectively, but Brecht was still the main mover. Without him nothing would have come about.

The emphasis in the apartment is on the authentic and simple to the point of austere, just to continue with the Brechtian myth. 'Spare, proletarian splendour', as the leftist politician Egon Bahr observed on a recent visit he made to the house

(Henrichs 2000: 9). No half-curtains, but apparently Brecht did order one of his carpenters from the theatre to distress the floorboards so as to give them more of a worn look. They're gone now, though. Dark brown as they were, they created a rather subdued atmosphere and were recently replaced by pine. ('Wood was extremely hard to come by in the GDR', the guide mutters.) With its large, south-facing windows and whitewashed interior, that gives the place a summery lightness, one epitomised by the simplicity and delicacy of the several Chinese parchment scrolls hanging on the walls. Confucius dominates in the main study, hovering majestically above a dark leather sofa as if it were his throne. Less imposing but somehow more resonant in a personal way, the scroll of *The Doubter* in Brecht's modest-size bedroom. In exile at Svendborg in 1937 he wrote a poem about the character's role as a check against complacency:

Whenever we seemed

To have found the answer to a question

One of us untied the string of the old rolled-up

Chinese scroll on the wall, so that it fell down and

Revealed to us the man on the bench who

Doubted so much.

I, he said to us

Am the doubter. I am doubtful whether

The work was well done that devoured your days.

Whether what you said would still have value for anyone

      if it were less well said.

Whether you said it well but perhaps

Were not convinced of the truth of what you said.

Whether it is not ambiguous; each possible

misunderstanding

Is your responsibility. Or it can be unambiguous

And take the contradictions out of things; is it too unambiguous?

If so, what you say is useless. Your thing has no life in it.

(1976: 270–1)

Clearly it's a poem which suggests that as a thinker and writer your work is never done because, apart from anything else, what you say has implications for those who would embrace it: 'But above all/Always above all else: how does one act/If one believes what you say?' (271). In fact, that line epitomises the performativity at the heart of Brechtian writing, the notion, reiterated by Willett (quoting Eliot), that 'the poem is something which is intended to act' (1998: 39). It does what it says, uses a question to assert an imperative of questioning, and inserts itself pragmatically in the context in which it supposedly takes place. In other words, it offers itself as instigator *or* respondent to a particular situation or moment, as a *usable* device. Brecht used poems like calling cards – as someone once said – sending out activating signals to whomsoever it might concern. There was in this an important plea for writing in the modern age of technology, one echoed, of course, in Benjamin's preoccupations with a changing notion of 'authenticity' and the rise of (urban) alienation in his famous essay 'The Work of Art in the Age of Mechanical Reproduction' (1999: 211–44). Boyer suggests that for Benjamin modernism 'attempted to describe the crisis in perception that everyday experience created [...] But these epistemological problems of perception, interpretation, and authenticity are no longer the dominant issues controlling postmodern thought in the era of electronic communication' (1998: 492). However, her explication of Perloff's argument for poetry's role as 'radical artifice' in the context of postmodern information systems has clear Brechtian overtones. Such 'writing has to be recognised as a performative practice engaged with and shaped by the material reality of the everyday world, a practice intended to transform the reader's perception of meaning and experience' (488). Whilst Brecht obviously belonged to the era of modernist experimentation, his understanding of everyday materiality as theatrically constructed, and the need for art to insert itself radically to interrupt and expose the rules of that construction – 'montage, in curves, jumps' (Willett 1978: 37) – seems as we shall see to prefigure what Boyer outlines (citing Ermarth) as a necessary response to the 'hypnosis' of postmodernity:

To see the world as a figural construct is a way of seeing double: both its structure and its affects. As the distinction between reality and fiction becomes an artifice, just one manner of constructing a series of things, 'we depart from the Euclidean universe of unity, identity, centre, and enter the non-Euclidean universe of pattern, superimposition, and differential function. Instead of continuity we have leaps in space, instead of linear time we have time warps that 'superimpose one part of the pattern on another'.

(Boyer 1998: 492)

The Doubter, then, that paradigm of agonised incredulity, of belief in unbelief, hangs next to the bed in which Brecht died on 14 August 1956. The writer had always had a heart condition, and that's what eventually killed him at the age of 58. Incessant cigar smoking didn't help. Heiner Müller maintained he need not have died, though, had he been able to take advantage of the advances in Western medicine at the time (Müller 1992: 231). For fear of being buried alive, he instructed 'that a stiletto pierce his heart before his burial', according to Stephen Barber (1995: 87).[7] Splitting it in two ensured there were no more alternatives, no more doubting to be done. Dead is dead. As he intuited in the last stanza of 'The Learner', another poem written in exile: 'The scars are painful/Now it is cold./But I often said: only the grave/Will have nothing more to teach me.' (1976: 257).

Of Dead BB

Leaving one memorial site for another, I pop next door to the Dorotheenstädtische cemetery. Brecht welcomed its proximity when he moved into Chaussee Strasse for the cheerful company its illustrious inhabitants would offer, so the guide had said.[8] The list of famous figures buried within a very compact area of inner-city terrain really is staggering. It's explained by the fact that the local district contained the academies of sciences and arts as well as the university. So, although the luminaries concerned may not have lived in the area, membership of one or other of such distinguished institutions meant they could be buried there, irrespective of religion, too (Bienert 1998: 249). A veritable celebrities graveyard. You can imagine Hollywood stars killing for that kind of post-mortal veneration, the ultimate enshrinement of their vanity. Here, though, we're talking more creative, intellectual and political achievement. As it happens, in 1960, the novelist Heinrich Mann, brother of the more-famous Thomas and, along with Brecht, one of the band of Hollywood 'anti-stars' exiled from Nazi Germany, was shipped over especially from California to be buried here with honours.[9] That was ten years after his actual death. He's the next grave but two from Brecht. Apart from the Hegels, Fichtes, Bonhoeffers and Schinkels, then, many of the notables belong at least to the Brechtian era if not his immediate 'entourage', although for the most part they post-date his own burial there: Hanns Eisler, Paul Dessau, John Heartfield, Wieland Herzfelde and so on. They're all near-neighbours but some, as Michael Bienert mischievously suggests, appear to have suffered calculated marginalisation: 'Elisabeth Hauptmann and Ruth Berlau [...] have been banished to the remotest corners – as far from Brecht and his wife as it was possible within the walls of the cemetery' (1998: 252). Whether or not Helene Weigel had anything to do with that remains unclear. It would have had to have been a pre-emptive move since she predeceased both of them. One unmistakable feature of her own grave alongside Brecht's, though, is her nominated immortalisation as Weigel-Brecht, which she wasn't known as in life. In death the speculative narratives of ownership and allegiance persist, then. In the game of strategic name-spotting the favourite is that Brecht, by his own choice, is buried diagonally opposite Hegel (Bienert 1998: 249–251; Völker 1979: 374) – or should that be 'dialectically'?

Brecht personally, it seems, was anxious to avoid drawing attention to himself, insisting on a modest, private burial. Insofar as he was in a position to dictate terms he did not, as Völker points out, wish to be the subject of praise from those official quarters he considered himself to oppose. A letter to the academy of arts testifies to his resistance to being laid in state. Nor 'do I want speeches at my graveside' (Völker 1979: 374).[10] There resides in the demands an uncanny echo of Brecht's short poem 'I Need no Gravestone' from the years immediately preceding his exile from Germany. It reads like an epitaph, which begins paradoxically by declaring itself effectively surplus to requirements: 'I need no gravestone, but/If you need one for me/I would like it to bear these words:/He made suggestions' (1976: 218). The gravestone he got bears no message other than the two words of his name:

4.

Bertolt Brecht. It seems enough. As I approach the grave – inevitably situated now on Brecht Row – a party of school children, grouped round its teacher, blocks the path. I turn and quickly quit the scene. Those words, the beginning of a sentence whose completion I fear, are responsible for my impulse. They float across, clear and precise: *'Brecht war natürlich...'*. Brecht was *naturally...* I succeeded in not hearing the rest. A misogynist? Stalinist? Closet capitalist? Plagiarist? Didact? Hypocrit? A member of the *Stasi* perhaps. Whatever suits your purpose, I suppose. Possibly even someone who made suggestions. We naturally turned them into sticks with which to beat him, even when he was already dead. In May 1990 they – anti-Semites of some order – desecrated his grave. He was a Jew-lover now (or again). Which was true literally since Helene Weigel, his partner in resting peace, was of Jewish origin. But that's obviously not what was meant. If they had known that, they would hardly, as Bienert intimates, have left *her* grave untouched (1998: 248). Brecht was a Jew-lover like Kennedy was a Berliner in 1963, by association; by identification with the predicament of (a) people. The two words on his gravestone are spare, but not sufficiently so, it seems; he should perhaps have heeded his own advice in his early city-dweller's poem:

See when you come to think of dying

That no gravestone stands and betrays where you lie

With a clear inscription to denounce you

And the year of your death to give you away.

Once again: cover your tracks.

(1976: 132)

Waiting for the coast to clear I attempt to locate Heiner Müller. Widely held to be Brecht's 'natural heir', he himself was quick to declare any potential inheritance of the Brechtian legacy as a betrayal were it not to involve a refunctioning critique of the man's practice, one appropriate to the times (Wright 1989: 122). I find myself chuckling when I find Müller's grave: a plain, meticulously-kept square of turf with a quadrate, cast-iron post, perhaps 1.5 metres high, for a gravestone. Interviewed once along with his collaborator, the director Robert Wilson, he was asked about his utilisation of the 'fragment-as-text'. Rejecting the question as 'an exercise in scholasticism', he replied: 'Fragment is a very dangerous word [...] I think the most fragmentary thing is a perfect square because you have to exclude so much to make it perfect, to make it not be fragmentary. You have to exclude curves and circles' (Holmberg 1988: 456). In other words: isn't any phenomenon a fragment, it's just that some pretend they are not? And, in asserting their wholeness, there is, moreover, a destructive act of repression in operation. As well as recalling Heidegger's corrective definition of the boundary not as 'that at which something stops but [...] that from which something *begins its presencing*' (Leach 1997: 105), it also points to Lyotard's discussion of Freudian psychoanalytic technique as it relates to the act of remembering. Here the latter emerges paradoxically as a process of forgetting, of deselection (1991: 26–30). Lyotard sets this against Freud's notion of 'working through', a 'rewriting which provides no knowledge of the past [...] One can say of what has gone that it is there, alive, lively. Not present like an object, if an object can ever be present, but present like an aura, a gentle breeze, an allusion' (31). In fact, the order of Müller's grave is broken by one of his trademark cigars, left in one corner of the perfect square. Extinguished now but keeping its shape quite well: the cigar that produced Brecht's 'natural air'. There's also a random pile of stones and pebbles heaped on top of the post by visitors. That's a well-known Jewish custom of remembrance observed in graveyards. Flowers wilt, stones endure. Müller also a Jew, then.

I circle back to Brecht's grave. *Bertolt Brecht*. White lettering, luminous but discreet, like subtitling on a foreign film. How many images could his name be a translation for?

I, Bertolt Brecht came out of the black forests.

My mother moved me into the cities as I lay

Inside her body. And the coldness of the forests

Will be inside me till my dying day.

In the asphalt city I'm at home. From the very start

Provided with every last sacrament:

With newspapers. And tobacco. And brandy

To the end mistrustful, lazy and content.

[...]

I, Bertolt Brecht, carried off to the asphalt cities

From the black forests long ago.

Standing before Brecht's grave now I am struck by the utter tranquillity that has descended on this cemetery: but for the modest ministrations of its gardeners, padding around like vergers in a church, and the occasional ripple of urban wind through the trees, its *stillness* at the heart of the big city. There's something about cemeteries that appears unchanging. I mean in their configuration. Unlike buildings, say – another form of public site – they're not really subject historically to formal innovation and, hence, indicative as well as productive of socio-cultural change. We leave them be, tending them – less so if they're Jewish ones – but essentially abandoning their form to nature, to the cycle of seasons. In part, that's to do with their practical function, of course. They're on a long haul; their inhabitants can outlive the span of several human lives combined. They're not supposed to be for moving, and so the shape of their surroundings does not change. It's also perhaps that we've found a way of more or less managing the pragmatics of a procedure – disposing of dead people – to which we'd rather not give too much thought anyway: the abject; that which we would prefer to keep 'off stage', the *obscene*. The only manner in which cemeteries seem to change, then, is if they're destroyed or desecrated, and then it is all the more shocking. In their becalming, immutable state, though, they serve as important locations for the activation of the performative mechanism of contemplation, which may well, at this memorial site, be an operation within the space of memory, though not necessarily. 'Bertolt Brecht', the gravestone inscription, is evocative because it can suggest so much by its poetic economy. The visitor is put in the classic Brechtian role of active participant, pausing for thought. As Sayre argues, art is revelatory precisely when it 'asks us to fill in the gaps [it] produces' or, quoting Roland Barthes, 'when it is *pensive*, when it thinks' (Sayre 1992: 250).

Brecht's poem 'Of Poor B.B.' also includes the observation, 'Of those cities will remain what passed through them, the wind!' (1976: 108). Ultimately it is the element that moves, the restless wind, sending puffs of the past into the present, that retains a memory of the cities. In his fragmentary notes on the poem Benjamin suggests that the experience of reading it as a whole is like passing 'through the poet [himself], as through a gate upon which, in weather-worn letters, a B.B. can be deciphered' (1977: 58). Brecht it would seem is writing, as a young man, about the need to leave himself behind, to cross a threshold and move on. At the same time, it is only he – his present self – that can make that move, so it is up to him to 'see himself in(to) that position'. Like Kafka's poor fellow before the Law – who doesn't see it, though, until it is pointed out to him on the verge of death – he must become the agent of his own agency (1992:165–6). B.B. may be Bertolt Brecht, then, or may point to a self-reflexive doubling in which the spectator's spectating itself becomes theatricalised, a 'being seen seeing' as Wright puts it (1989: 56): Brecht beside Brecht, Brecht playing Brecht, or even Brecht looking at Brecht looking at Brecht, as if to say, 'Shall we?' In a move to re-motivate Brecht in the present age – or perhaps to speculate over why he may have been important in the first place[11] – Fredric Jameson has recently come up with 'the Brechtian in Brecht', not with specific reference to the poem in question but generally speaking (1998: 85). My understanding of the suggestion is – as I shall elaborate upon later – that what remains of him, and one might include in this his aura within the city, resonates as a form of Brechtian framing of the Brechtian, a notion which may not be too far removed from Benjamin's image of passing through the poet or the gateway marked B.B. For Benjamin himself, as Carol Jacobs writes in her analysis of 'A Berlin Chronicle',

> nothing is written in stone, and certainly not the tomb inscription that might fix the relation of the city to those who once inhabited it. It is impossible to determine whether the names of the dead bear witness to the city or the other way around, whether Benjamin, say, bears witness to Berlin or the city weaves the veil of memories.

> *(1999: 26)*

Elizabeth Wright begins her book *Postmodern Brecht: a Re-presentation* with the striking question: 'What does Brecht's name mean?' (1989: 1). Using examples of postmodern performance, which include Heiner Müller, she demonstrates how the latter's call for a critical relationship to Brecht is fulfilled in this deconstructive work. Implicit in her argument is that the refunctioning taking place can be termed 'Brechtian' not because it replicates Brecht's practice as such but because Brechtian (self-)reflexivity proposes – like the figure of the Doubter – a never-ending process of looking and re-looking: '[i]ts constant disturbance of the spectator's gaze points to life as a dialectic, a continual battle of gazes to be fought out beyond the bounds of theatre' (51). Hence, Brecht's name, what it means, may be taken as indicative of this destabilising process. It is the trace that remains, a supplement that makes itself available 'beyond' the writer and his canon.

Outside the Law

As I leave the Dorotheenstädtischer Friedhof, looping back towards the Brecht House at number 125, I'm thinking about de Certeau, who maintained in *The Practice of Everyday Life* that books were a metaphor for the body (1988: 140). What the image conjured for him was the inevitable way the body is encoded: 'From birth to mourning after death, law "takes hold of" bodies in order to make them its text [...] It engraves itself on parchments made from the skin of its subjects. It articulates them in a juridical *corpus*. It makes its book out of them' (139–140). He may as well have said juridical corpse. Pausing between cemetery and house now, I'm reflecting on a previous visit to the archive with its vast collection of books and papers by and about Brecht. The body of his life and work, a tomb of a billion words. There's something rather quaint about the archive. It's not yet properly electronic, still making use of card indexes and filing systems set up in the time of the GDR. The references they contain could have been typed up on one of the old contraptions in Brecht's study rooms. In truth you have to have a pretty good idea of what you're after when you visit, because there's no scanning of shelves allowed. No rooting and burrowing. Everything has to be located by one of the attendants for your perusal in a separate study area. It's like visiting an inmate in prison.[12]

I felt lost when I visited the first time, sensing only the crushing weight of scholarship, of Brechtian law, pinning me to the floor. To escape – or at least to pretend to look the part – I requested one or two random titles off the top of my head. After twenty minutes in the reading room I'd had enough though. My throat was parched; I needed a drink. Surprisingly, when I asked if I could take the books away with me, the attendant was extraordinarily easy-going, to the point of lax. 'As long as you bring them back', she said cheerily, as if fully recognising the need for the inmates to get out on parole from time to time. Gulping down a beer in the cobbled yard below, I flicked through one of the volumes, one of several biographies. My gaze was arrested by a single word: 'lax'. It was a quotation, something Brecht himself said in defence of his alleged plagiarism of verses for *The Threepenny Opera*. Arguing that he had simply forgotten to credit the German translator of Villon's text, he added: 'This in turn I explain by the fact that I am fundamentally lax over the question of literary property' (Völker 1979: 132). Elsewhere, as the biographer points out in a footnote, he'd referred to this attitude ironically as 'my assuredly reprehensible indifference', describing the notion of intellectual property as 'an item that should be classed with allotment gardens and such like things'. In other words, a form of petit-bourgeois reification. Brecht also cited the counter example of having remembered to credit Kipling for the use of a ballad which was subsequently cut from *The Threepenny Opera* (132–3): credit where none was ultimately due. The instance is all the more ironic for the fact that it was Kipling himself who had once famously declared, 'He writeth best who cribbeth best' (Willett 1998: 47).[13]

Of course, the Brechtian image was always tainted, in life and in death, with accusations of using other people's work in various ways, whether it was stealing the text of writers or selfishly neglecting to credit adequately the contributions of his co-workers. Without becoming ensnared in the potential justification for any of these allegations here, I would like to suggest in more general terms that Brecht was an outlaw rather than a criminal. He wasn't so much thieving intellectual property, as recharging it, giving it a reconstituted material life. Laxness or 'willed forgetfulness' operated in a sense as a principle of maintaining a *necessary* freedom. What he proposed in his poetics was new, tending towards something as yet undefined, untried and untested, as true experimentation determines. Not a criminal, then, because criminals break *existing* law, but an outlaw; *outside* the law because there was no known legislation for his methods. So, as Highmore suggests of that other practitioner of an everyday poetics, de Certeau, here:

> 'poetics' needs to be understood both as an inquiry into the *forms* that the everyday takes and as an activity within language and life: de Certeau reminds us that the etymology of 'poetics' is 'from the Greek *poiein* "to create, invent, generate"' (1984: 205). It is this inventive language of 'insinuation', of 'ruses' and 'poaching', and 'multiform', 'tricky' 'stubborn' ways of operating that should determine the success or failure of de Certeau's project.

> *(2002: 154)*

There is in the figure of the outlaw a link (via de Certeau's own advocacy of 'walking the city') with the *flâneur*, whose strolling activities Hessel identifies at the beginning of his book as liable to arouse suspicion: 'in Berlin you have to have a purpose, otherwise it's against the law. You never just happen to be walking along here; you're always on your way somewhere. It's really not easy for the likes of us' (1984: 9). Benjamin's *flâneur*, as Shusterman points out, is 'characterised by being "out of place"', an "absence of proper place or purpose" which "keeps him moving through the city streets"' (2000: 107).

Brecht's methods involved precisely a process of collage (or gathering) – of ragpicking from amongst the detritus of material ideas – and montage (or reassembling): on the one hand revealing structures deliberately hidden from view, on the other allowing certain collected concepts to be re-motivated by their placing in a fresh context. As Ulmer puts it:

> 'Collage' is the transfer of materials from one context to another, and 'montage' is the 'dissemination' of these borrowings through the new setting [...] Brecht defended the mechanics of collage/montage [...] as an alternative to the organic model of growth and its classic assumptions of harmony, unity, linearity, closure. Montage does not reproduce the real, but constructs an object [...] or rather, mounts a process.

> *(Ulmer 1983: 84–6)*

If there is a 'single most important discovery' to make about Brecht, it is that he was, as outlaws tend to be, *always on the move*. In life and in his work, he was 'in process'. From his extraordinary journeys in exile, to his elusive relationships with the members of his vast entourage of acquaintances, to the continual, palimpsest-like erasures and revisions of his writings, Brecht was a shadow that could not be pinned down. Visiting him in Berlin shortly after his return there, the Swiss writer

Max Frisch described his then apartment as having something 'appealingly provisional [...] everything is as if ready for departure in 48 hours; unhomely' (Frisch 1950: 290). By choice a stranger in his own home, even, by extension, in his own country, a conflation hinted at in his post-war poem 'A New House':

Back in my country after fifteen years in exile

I have moved into a fine house.

Here I have hung

My No masks and picture scroll representing the Doubter.

Every day, as I drive through the ruins, I am reminded

Of the privileges to which I owe this house. I hope

It will not make me patient with the holes

In which so many thousands huddle. Even now

On top of the cupboard containing my manuscripts

My suitcase lies.

(1976: 416)

Even in death he strove to ensure against petrification. There would be no lying in state; his heart would be pierced. Once he was dead he would be gone but for the trace of his name. Coincidentally that name corresponds to the plural imperative of the verb to break (*brechen*). Hence, *brecht (auf)* exhorts us to break (up/open/into): the named Brechtian body issues an appeal towards rupture and shock (which ultimately it turned on itself: *Brecht mein Herz*). The continual superimposing of material produces cracks, then gaps, introducing the possibility of the new and unknown to enter discourse. It is a process fulfilling, in Ulmer's words, 'the original logic of collage/montage which "represents" not in terms of *truth* but of *change*' (Ulmer 1983: 102). And, as Walter Benjamin sums up in his essay 'The Author as Producer':

[m]ontage interrupts the context into which it is inserted [...] The interrupting of the action, the technique which entitles Brecht to describe his theatre as *epic*, always works against creating an illusion among the audience. Such illusion is of no use to a theatre which proposes to treat elements of reality as if they were elements of an

experimental set-up [...The spectator] recognises them as real, not as in the theatre of naturalism with complacency, but with astonishment. Epic theatre does not reproduce conditions; rather it discloses, it uncovers them.

(1977: 99–100)

Brechtian

Passing the Brecht House now, I'm on my way to the neighbour on the other side, the Brecht Bookshop at Chaussee Strasse number 124. I remember visiting this place back in the eighties on a day trip from West Berlin. I'd decided beforehand that I would use the 25 West German Marks, which the GDR obliged you to exchange and spend, to buy as many Brecht books as I could carry. Friends had warned me there wasn't in any case too much you could do with the money. There was little that was either worth buying or permitted to be taken back over the border at midnight. Finding ways to get rid of the currency was the more likely scenario, not least because it actually amounted to rather a lot in East Berlin, things being so cheap by comparison. Moreover, any unspent money had to be returned, a parting gift to the East German state. Entering the bookshop, I was rapidly disabused of any sense of purchasing expectation I had developed. Facing me on the bookshelves were the voids of a planned economy. The specialist Brecht Bookshop could muster approximately five of his plays, as I remember. The fact that there were quite a few copies of those few suggested one – or both – of two things: first, these plays represented his least popular – the two I ended up buying were *Days of the Commune* and *Señora Carrara's Rifles* – and, second, there had been a recent print run of those particular ones. I suppose, if I were interested enough, I could delve into the records of GDR five-year plans and find out.

Back in the present I come across the German translation of Fredric Jameson's aforementioned book on Brecht, which I've read in the original. The title literally translates *back* into English as something akin to 'Desire and Terror in the Unending Transformation of all Things: Brecht and the Future' (*Lust und Schrecken der Unaufhörlichen Verwandlung aller Dinge: Brecht und die Zukunft*). It takes me aback because that's a far cry from Jameson's original title – which doesn't even indulge in the luxury of a subtitle – the abrupt *Brecht and Method* (1998). What the tortured convolution of the translation seems to be attempting is a form of summing up of Jameson's main thesis, not unlike Brecht's practice of introducing scenes with a précis of what the audience is about to witness.[14] Picking up the English copy of the book in the shop – just to verify it really is the same book – this is stated on the jacket as being, amongst other things, that Brecht 'is not prescriptive but performative', that he merely wished to 'show people how to perform the act of thinking' – crudely, actively, dialectically[15] – and that he sought to represent 'the ceaselessness of transformation while at the same time alienating it, interrupting it, making it comprehensible by making it strange'. Thus, as Barthes agrees: 'Brecht is a permanent inventor; he reinvents quotations, accedes to the inter-text: "He thought in other heads; and in his own, others beside himself thought. This is true thinking". True thinking is more important than the (idealist) thought of truth' (1989: 213).

Apart from its sideways glance at Brecht's montage of 24 scenes of life under the Nazis, *Fear and Misery of the Third Reich* – not specifically a reference point for Jameson – the German title of *Brecht and Method* produces a form of *Verfremdungseffekt* in its own right, which corresponds, of course, to Jameson's notion of representations of ceaseless transformation being made strange themselves. In the body of the text he refers to the process as 'an estrangement which asks to be further estranged' (1998: 84).[16] Jameson's concern, as I indicated earlier, is to perform an 'actualising' reassessment of the Brechtian. In this respect the German subtitle – 'Brecht and the Future' – is a trifle forward, for Jameson's preoccupation, it seems to me, is still – or only – with the (historical) pregnancy of the present moment. In a way it's as if he had taken his cue from the invitation proffered by Brecht's gravestone (the minimalist principle of which would correlate with the brevity of his own title). It is no longer a matter of the hermeneutic deciphering of Brecht, or situating of him historically, but of seeking the 'Brechtian in Brecht' (85). *He made suggestions*. One of those related to the *usability* of writing, to making his ideas 'live' – or continue to be born inasmuch as they were relevant – in the actual world. Another was to offer up a mechanism affording the critical distance necessary to dismantle or denaturalise an ideology of false consciousness. In theatre terms, that may in the meantime be as clapped out a device as the typewriters in his apartment, but it's left a residue which plays on the constructed nature of the everyday: the basic, dynamic, destabilising action of 'making strange'. Destabilise *that* action in turn and you have the very (post)modern idea of a self-reflexive bringing of your own position into question. In other words, a recognition of the contradiction presented by being implicated in the very discourses you would wish to critique or unmask; and that those discourses effectively circle around an *absence* of truth and reality rather than one which we can eventually uncover. As Baudrillard suggests of the postmodern: '[t]he transition from signs which dissimulate something to signs which dissimulate that there is nothing, marks the decisive turning point' (1983: 12). An awareness of this would seem of particular importance in the light of the potential, inadvertent stimulation of certain 'closures' implied by distanciation. On the one hand, as Foster warns, there is the possibility of a 'refusal of engagement altogether' (1996: 203). Thus, whilst the purpose of creating critical distance is precisely to actively *enlist* the commitment of the spectator to the matter in hand, paradoxically it can produce the opposite effect: indifference. On the other hand, even new conventions easily become, as it were, *conventional*, as States argues, distance tends to close rapidly. For example, the eye quickly becomes accustomed to light or darkness; or, when I read the speech balloons in the comic strip, I am reading speech spoken by people in a world and not line drawings on a page. I hear the speech; I transfer my reception to that key of signification in roughly the way I hear subtitles of silent films.

(1987: 93–4)

Brecht's contemporary significance, if he has one, lies, then, not so much in his works as in 'the idea of Brecht', the 'more general lesson or spirit disengaged by his works' (Jameson 1998: 29), the Brechtian continually being folded back on or displacing itself. As Jameson states in conclusion:

[T]he framing of artificial arguments and reasons why Brecht would be good for us today [...] seems hypothetical in contrast to the concrete demonstration that we have in fact 'gone back to him' and that his thought is present everywhere today without bearing his name and without our being aware of it.

(171).

That would appear to be placing the Brechtian – though in reality it is a phenomenon which has 'no name' – on a formal par with the terminological derivatives attached to such as Kafka, Orwell and Dickens, all of whom lent their names to the supposed appearance in real life of the (bleak) fictional realms they had described. With Brecht it is not so much the fictive situations he evoked as the implications about art's functioning – specifically in relation to the spectator and 'real', as well as 'everyday', life – that leave their traces.

If we have gone back to Brecht, perhaps we can just as easily claim that he has come forward to us, to invoke the Benjaminian notion of telescoping the past through the present. That is, on the one hand, that the past contains within it a kernel of future events and, on the other, that it is continually transformed through its interpretation by present or newly-foregrounded circumstances and occurrences (Caygill 1998: xi). But it is important to stress the functionality of that process. It is not for the sake of it: because Brecht was viewed as 'great' once, posterity must retain a hold. What Jameson's view implies is that the Brechtian 'haunts' us because the times determine the legitimacy of (some of) the currency in which he traded, but in revalued form. Peter Berger suggested once that 'ideas do not succeed in history by virtue of their truth, but of their relationship to specific social processes' (1977: 27). In other words, ideas that assert themselves are ideas that relate powerfully to the events of an ever-changing present. Naturally they can span the spectrum of the reactionary to the progressive. As Jameson suggests elsewhere 'the political relationship of works of art to the societies they reside in can be determined according to the difference between replication (reproduction of the logic of that society) and opposition (the attempt to establish the elements of a Utopian space radically different from the one in which we reside)' (Leach 1997: 259). Even then, as he acknowledges, there is no legislating for how art is received: 'great political art (Brecht) can be taken as a pure and apolitical art; art that seems to want to be merely aesthetic and decorative can be rewritten as political with energetic interpretation' (259). One explanation for the many and varied 'takes' on Brecht – frequently seen as contentious and ambiguous – is precisely that the multiplicity, radicalism and potency of his contribution has lain him open to being claimed – or 'taken' – by those, near and far, who would have some *calculated* predilection of their own to project. For this he provides fertile ground. Hence, a figure like John Fuegi is seen in more recent times to be launching a politically correct 'male feminist' attack because of the threat felt by Brecht's status as a socialist icon (Jameson 1998: 31; Willett 1998: 194). Or, at an earlier point in history, Martin Esslin, similarly motivated, it would appear, by the perceived crassness of the politics, tries to perform a separation of the 'Communist [who] was *also* a great poet' [my emphasis] (1965: xi–xii). Marxists on the other hand, as Dickson points out, 'have on the whole endeavoured to cash in on his universal popularity by displaying him as a plaster saint of Party orthodoxy or else they have condemned him as a dangerous heretic' (1978: v). And so on.

However, if we wish to keep hold of the idea that the Brechtian might be positively useful, perhaps it is best to view the writer's legacy in a way not dissimilar to the Benjaminian angel's spatial and synchronic perspective on history, as a sprawling terrain defined not by a causal 'chain of events' but by 'wreckage upon wreckage' (1999a: 249). Whilst the Brechtian does not particularly suggest the catastrophic 'pile of debris' of the Benjaminian image[17] – though his own life experiences might come close – nor, necessarily, the 'apocalyptic blast that blows Benjamin's wide-mouthed angel out of the continuum of history', as Diamond puts it (Parker and Sedgwick 1995: 163), it is simply the practical idea of the (Brechtian) past as 'live, contemporary *site*' that carries resonance. As Kushner suggests of Marx's view of history, he did not treat it 'as a single-file line forward-moving towards an end but rather as a space, a spacious albeit bloody place, a topography, a terrain of human consciousness' (Weber 2001: xii). In fact, in her equating of the *flâneur* figure – to whom, 'aimlessly strolling through the crowds in the big cities [...], things reveal themselves' – with the angel of history, Hannah Arendt opens up the possibility of just such a Benjaminian excursion in and around a Brechtian Berlin (1999: 18–19).

Notes

1. The street sign and its corresponding house numbers slot into a frame as separate plates and can therefore easily be removed.

2. Brecht himself seems to have been aware of a certain 'problem' relating to 'ponderousness', which arguably portends the Berliner Ensemble's paradoxical stasis after his death. Shortly before the company's celebrated London visit in 1956, which Brecht did not survive long enough to make himself, he specially instructed the actors to keep their performing 'quick, light [and] strong', warning them that 'there is in England a long-standing fear that German art must be terribly heavy, slow, laborious and pedestrian' (Willett 1978: 283).

3. Alternative accounts of the controversial nature of Brecht's collaborative work are Sabine Kebir's *Ich fragte nicht nach meinem Anteil: Elisabeth Hauptman's Arbeit mit Bertolt Brecht* (Berlin: Aufbau-Verlag, 1997) and *Ein Akzeptabler Mann?: Brecht und die Frauen* (Berlin: Aufbau Verlag, 1998), subtitled in its first 1987 edition as *Streit um Brecht's Partnerbeziehungen*.

4. Fuegi maintains it was Weigel herself who moved out (1995: 551).

5. Brecht and Weigel also shared a country retreat at Buckow, some 50 kilometres east of Berlin. Here, too, Brecht had his own additional arrangements, occupying a separate house altogether some 50 metres away from the main villa.

6. Steffin died tragically in Moscow in 1941, being too ill to take up her berth on the ship with which Brecht and his family travelled to the United States (Völker 1979: 272).

7. Fuegi also refers to this event (1995: 606), implying a sinister conspiracy attaches to the story of Brecht's death. As Jameson reports in his assessment of Fuegi's book: 'Clearly its author knows how to spin a yarn; and one is not disappointed with the satisfying climax, in which it is more than suggested that at the end, among fears of Brecht's impending defection to the West (under the guise of a Munich clinic), Helene Weigel had the great man murdered, on Ulbricht's orders' (1998: 31).

8. This is confirmed in a letter to his publisher Peter Suhrkamp dated March 1954 (Brecht 1990: 528).

9. Mann is the author of *Professor Unrat*, the novel which served as the basis for the film *The Blue Angel* (1930), launching the career of Berlin's one true Hollywood star Marlene Dietrich. The film was shot in Berlin's own version of Hollywood, the UFA studios at Babelsberg.

10. The wishes were kept but, as Bienert reports, an official function held at Brecht's theatre, which it was beyond his powers to prevent, witnessed the likes of the GDR president Ulbricht and Georg Lukács – 'sworn enemies' – singing his praises (1998: 246–7).

11. In fact Jameson is resistant to any reinventing games – 'postmodern Brecht or Brecht for the future, a postsocialist or even post-Marxist Brecht, the Brecht of queer theory or of identity politics, the Deleuzian or Derridean Brecht, or perhaps the Brecht of the market and globalisation, an American mass-culture Brecht, or finance-capital Brecht' – suggesting they are in themselves 'profoundly unBrechtian […] Ignoble slogans, which may carry a repressed conception of posterity

within themselves' (1998: 5). However, ultimately Jameson cannot escape the fact that he is writing a book about Brecht, which inevitably raises the question of his contemporary significance.

12. On visiting the Goethe-Schiller archive at Weimar, Walter Benjamin referred to their works as lying there 'propped up like patients in hospital beds' (1999b: 149).

13. For all that the term 'lax' might suggest it, Brecht's attitude to the question of intellectual property was not a blasé one. For a comprehensive analysis of his commitment to addressing the issue of authorial and moral rights in copyright law see Steve Giles, *Bertolt Brecht and Critical Theory: Marxism, Modernity and the Threepenny Lawsuit* (Berne: Peter Lang AG, European Academic Publishers, 1998).

It remains deeply ironic that the Brecht estate attempted to prevent Heiner Müller's late play *Germania 3 Gespenster am toten Mann* from being published and performed on the grounds that he had lifted excerpts from Brecht's *Life of Galileo* and *Coriolanus* texts. The case was eventually thrown out in the summer of 2000, the judges declaring Müller had legitimately quoted from Brecht's work for artistic purposes. In an astonishingly progressive verdict the judges stated, amongst other things, that a work of art could no longer be considered the sole property of its creator once it had been released into the public domain (see Detlef Friedrich, 'Brecht, Müller und die Richter', *Berliner Zeitung*, 26 July 2000).

14. The purpose of this practice was, of course, so the audience would concentrate on *how* things occurred rather than be in suspense over *what* would happen next: 'eyes on the course' as opposed to 'eyes on the finish' (Willett 1978: 37).

15. These are related rather than directly interchangeable terms. Ultimately all three correspond to the practice of materialist dialectics, to the process of making the dialectical nature of the world visible and representable. However, crude thinking (*plumpes Denken*) also suggests a deliberate coarseness as well as daring (perhaps not too far from the radical notion of 'thinking the unthinkable'), which therefore produces a dynamic. That is, it attempts to get somewhere new. Active thinking (*eingreifendes Denken*) – or as Jameson proposes: conceptual intervention – implies a form of committed seeking out and thinking through of the contradictions of a situation.

16. Ironically, Dyer refers in general terms to 'the flamboyant brogue' of Jameson's own prose, 'an irritating impediment to what is being said' (*Anglo-English Attitudes: Essays, Reviews, Misadventures 1984–99*, London: Abacus, 1999, p. 263).

17. As it happens in the updated introduction to the 1998 German edition of Brecht's biography, Klaus Völker quotes the Austrian writer Ingeborg Bachmann as having suggested that his work ought to be seen as 'an ironic, catastrophic, anguished, grandiose "rescue attempt"' (*Bertolt Brecht: Eine Biographie*, München and Wien: Carl Hanser Verlag [this edition: Zweitausendeins], 1998: iii).

3. Chaussee Strasse: Brecht's Spectacles

The invitation to wander the space of the text-as-city, to inspect it, echoes a central motif of Judaic mysticism: the need to bear witness. Benjamin's cityscapes are not optical puzzles, but acts of witness, of remembering what is seen so that testimony may be given.

(Graeme Gilloch, Myth and Metropolis)

'The *flâneur*' has become an important 'location' in critical theory because he stands at the intersection not only of class, gender and race relations, and also of art, mass production and commodification, but also of the masses, the city, and the experience of modernity.

(Steve Pile, The Body and the City)

There's a version of *Baal* – the last, I think, in which Baal is a mechanic, working with machines – that came about as a result of the confrontation with Berlin, with the big city. It's a decisive moment. From that point onwards Brecht becomes interesting for me […] In the confrontation with the city he turns sharp and quick.

(Heiner Müller, Krieg ohne Schlacht)

Winds of Change

Someone has half-entered the Brecht Bookshop at Chaussee Strasse 124, casually holding open the door as they have a quick flick through the pamphlets and fliers laid out for customers to browse through at the front. A sudden gust of wind sends some of them swirling on to the street. Aware of his culpability the man concerned mumbles embarrassed apologies, promising to retrieve them as he backs hastily out of the door. I go out to help. As we do our best to rescue the various bits of paper, there's another flurry, which sends the fellow's cap reeling on to the street.

5.

'Scheisse!'

Probably suffering from an escalating sense of his whole environment descending into chaos, he scurries after it blindly. I'm reminded of Jeff Wall's breathtaking panoramic photograph in London's Tate Modern, *A Sudden Gust of Wind* (1993). It spins its actors – builders and surveyors planning some architectural intervention into the landscape – into 'baroque contortions', documents and autumn leaves mingling, and a solitary hat flying through the air against the bleak, ranging flatness somewhere on the periphery of a city.

There's a brief screech of brakes, but the sickening thud I expect doesn't materialise. The van driver's subsequent performance, a cameo of cursing and shouting from the wound-down window, provides everyone around with cathartic relief. We welcome it because it means the accident did not happen. Cap in hand now, the poor chap's second round of apologies for the day – which he must, likewise, have been pleasantly relieved to be in a position to have delivered – seem comic. The proximity of pleasure and terror, the comic and the tragic. How quickly your life can change. In this case it would, literally, have been at the drop of a hat. A sharp jangling of bells rings out as a number thirteen tram approaches, fiercely querying what on earth is going on. With a grinding of gears the van drives off and the bystanders disperse. Nothing happened, so there's no more to be said. The near-victim himself has vanished, erased into thin air by the swish of the passing tram, all intentions of gathering up leaflets abandoned. Left standing on the kerb, I find myself imagining what I might have had to confront: blood and asphalt, my trendy, new jacket cushioning the victim's head on the street, the witnesses' debrief with note-taking police. Everything perceived with that adrenaline-fuelled intensity and the faint nausea that accompanies it. I know I'm only trying to enhance my sense of inner celebration at having avoided all that.

I've often thought, above all in strange lands, how a chance occurrence or radical act, some *transgression* of circumstance, would enable you to become acquainted with the place both deeply and uniquely. Like being knocked over and taken to hospital or, even, being involved in a murder enquiry. The strange upheaval of it.

6.

The urban sociologist Richard Sennett talks, as Fyfe and Bannister observe, of the desirability of encountering disorderly, painful events in the city because of the way they force us to engage with 'otherness', to go beyond one's own defined boundaries of self (Fyfe 1998: 264). Of course, he's not talking about transgressions of law as such. On the contrary, his concern is in a sense to 'naturalise' the experience of disruption because without it our lives become alienated, intolerant of the concept of disorder to such an extent that our responses turn all the more aggressive when we do encounter situations of conflict.

To a large extent this is the subject-matter of Brecht's early play *In the Jungle of Cities* (1922). Set in Chicago it portrays the seemingly motiveless pursuit of a confrontation by the wealthy timber merchant Shlink with the mild-mannered lending library clerk Garga, whom he has never met. All the former wishes to do is *buy* the latter's opinion about a book. Garga refuses. Shlink's tactics are to offer him more and more, including eventually his whole business, whilst Garga's response is to view his 'generosity' as a compromising insult. 'Small man' that he is, he will not be bought and thereby humiliated. Locked into an escalating battle of wills, the situation results in the destruction of everything both characters have in life. Garga even goes to prison in place of Shlink, triumphantly taking the blame for a fraudulent deal, which he himself had contrived so as to implicate the other. The play's climax witnesses the two men finally facing each other in the gravel pits of Lake Michigan. Shlink sketches the scene: 'The perpetual roar of Chicago has stopped [...] Now the silence has come, that conceals nothing' (*Plays* 1: 171). In the jungle of a world based on the profit motive, human contact is forced to take contorted forms. All social interactions, however harmless or benevolent they may appear, are ultimately hardwired into a destructive psychology of gaining the upper hand. Even then, as Shlink concludes, 'so great is man's isolation that not even a fight is possible' (172).

The director David Fincher's 1998 film *Fight Club* picks up a related theme: young men finding appealing the paradox of *agreeing* to beat one another to a bare-knuckle pulp in controlled, clandestine circumstances. The pain and violence of these situations, the physical sacrifice under terms which imply *no consequence*, promise a momentary connection that is real because it is *felt*. It is an activity that exists only for its own sake. At the same time it is a form of acquiescent punishment-taking, an inverted corporeal therapy, that speaks of an aberrant self-loathing produced by an aggressive, alienating urban environment. Interestingly, in a twist that introduces a Brechtian complexion to proceedings, the two contrasting protagonists emerge as one and the same identity. Hence, as if to underline the fated solipsism of 'modern man', it emerges as the autoimmune struggle of the introjected self with itself. The device witnesses the street-wise, dare-devil Tyler, a kind of self-styled, anti-corporatist law-unto-himself, trying to lure his therapy-seeking, insomniac counterpart Jack – suffering from the guilt of being aware his car company knowingly continues to sell critically flawed vehicles – toward self-seeing. Ultimately, as an underground operation masterminded by the two characters – essentially to sabotage American life so as to make it, and therefore the world, a better place – escalates into large-scale, spectacular terrorism, Jack discovers the elusive Tyler, whom he has been chasing across the country so as to put an end to the destruction, is in fact himself. To find a surviving identity with which he is at ease, he must kill off Tyler, whose excesses are threatening to destroy completely not only himself but life on earth. A conflict fought within the domain of the psycho-physical is, thus, indicative of a world at war with itself.

Brecht himself frequently made use of the dual identity as a device. Naturally, he always told you that was what he was doing: eyes on the course, not the finish (Willett 1978: 37). Its most obvious application is in *The Good Person of Setzuan* (1941) where one character (Shen Teh) becomes two (Shui Ta) in an examination of the capacity to be 'good' under capitalism (see chapter six). Even in a play like *The Caucasian Chalk Circle* (1944), though, two characters, embodiments of maternity, are essentially used as contesting instances of attitudes – the natural and the nurturing respectively – towards a single phenomenon, namely ownership rights. (Mother figures frequently feature centrally in Brecht's plays as vehicles for the exploration of the contradictions and options presented by material conditions. Or, *pace* Phelan, as maternal agents who 'allow us to glimpse how matter works, and to see what is the matter with us' [1993: 117].) However, as Wright has argued,

Brecht's concern was with operations at the level of (false) consciousness, showing the way social reality is constructed. What postmodern 'inheritors' like Heiner Müller – and we can add *Fight Club* to this category – recover is the complexity of subjectivity, the way material contradictions come to dwell in and affect the workings of the psyche, and the way that reveals itself in the 'troubled body' (Wright 1989: 135). We suffer – play out and repeat – certain scenarios of behaviour because ultimately we are inextricably implicated in the flawed mechanisms of expression, of *being*, immediately available to us. The closest Brecht came to articulating that was in his early plays, foremost his first, *Baal* (1918). Retrospectively he said of his protagonist's wildly immoral behaviour: '*Baal*'s art of life (*Lebenskunst*) is subject to the same fate as any other art under capitalism: it is attacked. He is antisocial, but in an antisocial society' (*Plays* 1: 370).

Crashing

Returning to car accidents, I've only ever been in one. I say *only* because car travel is so ubiquitous in modern life, and with it comes the widespread inevitability of failure both human and technological. It is in these terms that J. G. Ballard seems to be justifying his preoccupation with the phenomenon of accidents in the introduction to his novel *Crash*: 'a pandemic cataclysm that kills hundreds of thousands of people each year and injures millions' (1995: 6). As it happens my crash took place in Berlin on a visit in the summer of 1994, coincidentally at a crossroads a stone's throw from where I had lived nearly a decade previously. We were a small carload of people on our way to a wedding reception down at Wannsee in the south-west of the city, having just left the register office in Schöneberg. I had been chief witness, the nearest equivalent to best man in Germany. The young woman driving had just passed her test. I was sitting right behind her and saw the whole thing coming. Waiting for the signal to turn left at the crossing, she accelerated as a bronze, 1980s-generation Mercedes came towards us. It was only a light bang; no one was hurt. To this day, though, I don't know whose fault it was. The young woman's spontaneous response as we rebounded back into our seats was to say that she should not have gone. That was patently true, even if the oncoming Mercedes had shot the lights, which was distinctly possible. In other words, she may well have been fixated on her own traffic lights and, perhaps under pressure with a car full of strange people, had accelerated as soon as they had changed without double-checking that the road was clear. The courts couldn't sort it out either, so justice was pegged subsequently at equal culpability.

I was amused that day by the expansion of my allotted role as witness. In one case – the wedding – it was of a planned, ritualised event in which I could imagine or rehearse myself performing beforehand. In the other, it was of a chance occurrence. The latter was over in an instant but produced the greater impact (as it were). The terror of the moment – and there was a clear split-second where I could see it coming – became coupled with the pleasures of the aftermath, which involved both immediate relief at the relative mildness of the incident and a form of vanity at having a good story to tell, particularly a whole gathering of wedding guests. Most powerful, perhaps, was my own private taking of pleasure in the terror retrospectively; the recalling, as survivor, of the moment when you didn't yet know it was going to be alright. The chance incident made the ritualised event as a whole – with which it shared a temporal space – more memorable. Had its effects as an accident been more grave, it would have been a different story but nevertheless, memorable. Perhaps the crucial point is that the reality of the moment, its 'making strange of the everyday', not only marked it *as* a moment, but also called for you to take some form of stance towards what had occurred in your role as messenger: the one charged with passing on the news of what they had seen. That role is problematic, of course, because invariably there is a return to the proto-dramatic, to the clutches of language and the fictive – quite possibly cliché (see television news disaster survivors' accounts) – which cannot articulate the unspeakable part, the little encounter with death, that has occurred. In other words, it is something to which you resort in order to be *able* to speak, but also perhaps to 'cope' with what has taken place.[1]

It is a role Ballard addresses in the introduction to *Crash*. In his novel desire is shown to be alienated on to technology. As the author suggests, we live in a world in which any 'original response to experience' has been pre-empted by the television screen. It is a world ruled by the fictions of 'mass-merchandising, advertising and politics conducted as a branch of advertising'. The way Ballard sees it, '[t]he writer's task is to invent the reality' because the 'fiction is already there' (1995: 4). The novel opens strikingly with the protagonist, a 'nightmare angel of the highways' playing out his ultimate death-wish scenario:

> Vaughan died yesterday in his last car-crash. During our friendship he had rehearsed his death in many crashes, but this was his only true accident. Driven on a collision course towards the limousine of the film actress, his car jumped the rails of the London Airport flyover and plunged through the roof of a bus filled with airline passengers.

> *(1995: 7)*

Vaughan's extended rehearsal of self-destruction represents the last remaining possibility of experiencing the real in a 'sick world'. The climactic act emerges as 'his only true accident' because it contains the one element the narrative of which can neither be premeditated nor recounted: his death. It is the bleak but logical conclusion, as Damian Hirst might have put it, to 'the physical impossibility of death in the mind of someone living'.[2] Obviously that apotheosis simultaneously signals the end of experiencing. If Ballard's point is to portray the tragic double-bind of a mediated world – one in which the human body has been reconstituted post-organically, as it were, by technology – in the most extreme way, it is also to highlight the importance of the artist's introduction of shocks to the system or 'controlled explosions' as a means of at least approaching the real.[3]

Double-seeing

In his discussion of contemporary performance's preoccupation with producing witnesses as opposed to spectators, the writer and director Tim Etchells talks of a relationship to the artwork premised on 'feel[ing] the weight of things and one's own place in them [...] an invitation to be here and be now' (1999: 17–18). Ultimately, he invokes an image of us 'left, like the people in Brecht's poem who've witnessed a road accident, still stood on the street corner discussing what happened, borne on by our responsibility to events' (18). The Brecht poem he means is 'On Everyday Theatre'. It not only represents an early recognition of the performative nature of everyday life itself, but also argues for the imperative of art to seek a connection with the quotidian:

You artists who perform plays

In great houses under electric suns

Before the hushed crowd, pay a visit some time

To that theatre whose setting is the street.

The everyday, thousandfold, fameless

But vivid, earthy theatre fed by the daily human contact

Which takes place in the street.

(1976: 176)

Wittily Brecht identifies the stagehands as the true witnesses of the overblown spectacle that is the theatre. For they are the ones, positioned in the transitional space 'between dressing room and stage', who get a glimpse of the 'mysterious transformation' that occurs in that moment when 'an actor leaves the dressing room [and] a king appears on stage'. The performer on the street corner, by contrast, is 'no sleepwalker who must not be addressed [nor] high priest holding divine service' (178). Instead, as the witness to incidents on the street, s/he is a demonstrator who 'must not identify with the bearing of the other but must "quote" him so the audience will see the split between who speaks and who is spoken' (Wright 1989: 32). The poem served, of course, as the prototype for Brecht's foundational model for an epic theatre, the Street Scene (Willett 1978: 121–9). For Brecht it signified 'a big step towards making the art of theatre profane and secular and stripping it of religious elements', a move which encroached upon the daily life realms of the erotic, business, politics, law, religion and, not least 'the application of theatrical techniques to politics in fascism' (Brecht 1993: 115). As Etchells seems to be suggesting in his observation, the poem addresses the combined roles of both witness and reporter, of a spatio-temporal 'being here now':

Take that man on the corner: he is showing how

An accident took place. This very moment

He is delivering the driver to the verdict of the crowd. The

     way he

Sat behind the steering wheel, and now

He imitates the man who was run over, apparently

An old man. Of both he gives

Only so much as to make the accident intelligible, and yet

Enough to make you see them. But he shows neither

As if the accident had been unavoidable. The accident

Becomes in this way intelligible, yet not intelligible, for both

     of them

Could have moved quite otherwise; now he is showing what

They might have done so that no accident

Would have occurred. There is no superstition

About this eyewitness, he

Shows mortals as victims not of the stars, but

Only of their errors.

(1976: 177)

What appears to be at stake in the crash scene is less the truth of what occurred than a form of opening up of possibilities or alternatives which induce participation in the event. It is the replication of Sennett's forced engagement with disordered events, and the prelude to civilised and civilising social life (Fyfe 1998: 264), a notion endorsed by Robins, also in Fyfe and Bannister's citation: 'the readiness to be out of control, combined with a maturity to handle the consequences [forms] the basis of an urban public and political culture' (264). As Brecht explains in the Street Scene essay itself:

> The bystanders may not have observed what happened, or they may simply not agree with him, may 'see things a different way'; the point is that the demonstrator acts the behaviour of driver or victim or both in such a way that the bystanders are able to form an opinion about the accident.

(Willett 1978: 121)

Central to this mechanism operating successfully is that the 'demonstration admits it is a demonstration (and does not pretend to be the actual event)', in the same way that the theatre should not pretend *not* to be the construct that it is (122). Later in the essay Brecht establishes the relationship of the Street Scene model to the notion of *Verfremdung*, arguing that '[t]he direct changeover from representation to commentary that is so characteristic of the epic theatre is still more easily recognised as one element of any street demonstration' (126). Identifying the 'discontinuity which provokes the Brechtian shock' as 'a reading which detaches the sign from its effect', Barthes usefully reminds us that 'the originality of the Brechtian sign is that it is *to be read twice over*: what Brecht gives us to read is, by a kind of disengagement, the reader's gaze, not directly the object of his reading' (1989: 213 and 219).

Referring to the Street Scene model, Jameson describes the V-effect as the 'instant of intrusion into the everyday: it is what constantly demands to be explained and re-explained' (1998: 84). So, as witnesses of everyday life, but ultimately also of theatre, we are allotted positions not only of performing the act of distanciated seeing (or 'conceptual intervention') but, in a kind of double move, of recognising the performative nature of that act of performance, a 'looking-at-being-looked-at-ness' as Elin Diamond phrases it (1997: 52). Or, as Jameson reiterates: '[t]he theory of estrangement [...] must always estrange us from the everyday; the theory is thus itself an acting out of the process; the dramaturgy is itself a drama' (1998: 84). If the street scene is a model for anything it is, as Barthes suggests generally about Brecht's work, one which 'seeks to elaborate a shock-practice (not a subversion: the shock is much more 'realistic' than subversion); his critical art is one which opens a crisis: which lacerates, which crackles the smooth surface, which fissures the crust of languages, loosens and dissolves the stickiness of the logosphere' (1989: 213).

As the poem 'On Everyday Theatre' goes on to discuss, the street scene situation ultimately has implications related to social justice. The demonstrator 'Knows that much depends on his exactness: whether the innocent man/Escapes ruin, whether the injured man is compensated'. (Brecht 1976: 177). It is not simply a matter of establishing what may have happened but of allowing what may be at stake ideologically in a quotidian incident like this to emerge. In other words, the street scene encapsulates the form of the Brechtian *Gestus*: the 'pregnant moment' which crystallises social relations. And in doing so it sets up a clear link between the events of real life and their emerging or potential 'readability' as contradictory constructs, as revelatory of the way social processes can 'appear' in the detail of human behaviour. As Vaßen observes, Brecht's 'philosophy of the street' 'reworks sociological and cultural analysis in a way which attempts to develop anticipatory behavioural lessons from necessary forms of response to the new realities of the city' (1998: 78). The street scene model also underlines the intended 'usefulness' or 'applicability' of Brechtian production in its day. The spectacle of the 'accident' emerges not merely as an abstract model of an epic scene, a means of questioning the dangerously mesmeric 'traffic flow' of life as it is represented to us, but also as a significant marker for our personal experience of the street.[4] Hence, as a trope or *gestic* moment which encapsulates the unexpected rupturing of the habitual and familiar necessary in the process of 'seeing', it prepares us for our implicated role in the encounter with the 'shock' of alterity in the streets of the city.

There is a clear association to be made here with Lefebvre's concept of 'moments' as Harvey delineates it in the afterword to the former's *The Production of Space*:

> fleeting but decisive sensations (of delight, surrender, disgust, surprise, horror, or outrage) which were somehow revelatory of the totality of possibilities contained in daily existence. Such movements were ephemeral and would pass instantaneously into oblivion, but during their passage all manner of possibilities – often decisive and sometimes revolutionary – stood to be both uncovered and achieved. 'Moments' were conceived of as points of rupture, of radical recognition of possibilities and intense euphoria.
>
> *(1998: 429)*

Harvey goes on to mention Lefebvre's foreshadowing of 1960s situationist practice. However, where the former's 'moments' seemed to reveal a bias concerned with individual *perception* of the 'momentary' read as having social implications, the latter's contrivance of 'situations' possessed both a *creative-interventionist* impulse – prefigured by Brechtian practice as well as Benjamin's notion of consumers becoming producers, or readers/spectators turning into collaborators (1977: 85–103) – *and* a private turn (albeit within the public domain), owing more of a debt to the figure of the *flâneur*. Working off the key concepts of 'diversion' (*détournement*) and 'drift' (*dérive*), the Situationists envisioned a form of aesthetic remapping of the city, based on a performative practice of walking and interacting, which would reclaim its territory for the urban dweller. As Sadler suggests (citing the movement's most celebrated player):

> The constructed situation would clearly be some sort of performance, one that would treat all space as performance space and all people as performers. In this respect, situationism postured as the ultimate development of twentieth-century experimental theatre, the energies of which had been dedicated to the integration of players and audience, of performance space and spectator space, of theatrical experience and 'real' experience. 'The most pertinent revolutionary experiments in culture have sought to break the spectator's psychological identification with the hero so as to draw him into activity by provoking his capacities to revolutionise his own life', Debord declared.

> *(1998: 105)*

Despite clear Brechtian echoes of the requirements of the epic – 'arouses his capacity for action; forces him to take decisions' (Willett 1978: 37) – Guy Debord's statement contains a subjective turn ('revolutionising his own life') that recalls Benjamin's differentiation in his Baudelaire essay of *Erlebnis* as the 'lived through' experience lacking the 'weight' of *Erfahrung*. For Benjamin, '[m]oving through this traffic [of the big city] involves the individual in a series of shocks and collisions. At dangerous crossings, nervous impulses flow through him in rapid succession, like the energy from a battery' (1999a: 171). However, as Highmore explains, 'these moments of "shock experience" (*Erlebnis*) fail to enter into the shared discourse of experience (*Erfahrung*) that could give the modern everyday a voice that would allow for both critical attention and critical practice' (2002: 67).

Wo/andering

About the same point in history that Brecht was concerned with the articulation of the street scene model, the Austrian novelist Robert Musil was engaged in the writing of his unfinished *magnum opus, The Man Without Qualities*. Keith Tester identifies 'Musil's use of the devices of *flânerie*' in the novel and 'his tendency to connect them to global problems of existence in cities'. It is a generalising move which distinguishes his *flânerie* from the Baudelairean paradigm specific to nineteenth century Paris (Tester 1994: 10–11). Thus Musil's narrator declares of Vienna:

> Like all big cities, it consisted of irregularity, change, sliding forward, not keeping in step, collisions of things and affairs, and fathomless points of silence in between, of paved ways and wilderness, of one great rhythmic throb and the perpetual discord and dislocation of all opposing rhythms, and as a whole resembled a seething, bubbling fluid in a vessel consisting of the solid materials of buildings, laws, regulations, and historical traditions.

> *(Musil 1954: 4)*

Tester's motive is to elucidate a 'dialectic of flânerie' between a narrator who observes and defines, but still seems subject to the enigma of the city, and the action of the narrative itself, 'the wandering along a city street of two individuals' (1994: 11). There is a defining moment early in the novel, Tester maintains, when the two individuals are suddenly faced with an accident in the street:

> These two now suddenly stopped, having become aware of a crowd gathering in front them. A moment earlier the regularity had been broken by a sudden oblique movement: something had spun round, skidding sideways – the abrupt braking, as it appeared, of a heavy lorry, which was now stranded with one wheel on the edge of the pavement. In an instant, like bees round the entrance to their hive, people had collected round a little island of space in their midst. The driver, who had climbed down from his seat, stood there grey as packing-paper, gesticulating crudely, explaining how the accident happened. The eyes of those joining the crowd rested first on him and then were cautiously lowered into the depths of the enclosed space, where a man had been laid on the edge of the pavement, apparently dead.

> *(Musil 1954: 5)*

Having earlier credited Musil with bringing the *flâneur* figure into the twentieth century through the generalisation suggested above, Tester now extrapolates this fictional incident into an emblematic comment on the *flâneur's* fate. Essentially the twentieth century's introduction of technological urban rationalisation, of which 'the problem of traffic' is one effect, could imply the end of this form of 'knowing' the city given the threat posed: 'perhaps the man who is knocked down [...] is, in fact, the last *flâneur*' (1994: 13). Of course, as Tester acknowledges, Benjamin had already killed off the *flâneur* once in the streets of Haussmann's nineteenth century Paris. That was a death associated specifically with the demise of the arcades (interior streets) – which provided both mystery and protection for the idle observer – and, more broadly, with the rationalising impulse of a fast-moving modernity. However, Frisby points at the same time to Benjamin's essay 'The Return of the *Flâneur*', in which he reviews Hessel's 1929 book on *flânerie* in Berlin.[5] The supposed 'decline of *flânerie*' was shown to have 'lacked finality', according to Frisby (2001: 13), who adds: 'If we have witnessed a renewed discourse on the *flâneur* and the practices of *flânerie* in recent decades, then in large part this must be due to our rediscovery of Walter Benjamin's own analysis of this urban figure in the late 1920s and 1930s' (304). So, 'the *flâneur* was back', as Esther Leslie agrees. And this one 'was not just one man in the crowd, but was part of the crowd', she says, inserting the following quotation from Benjamin's review (Coles 1999: 85):

> For the mass – with which the *flâneur* lives – gleaming enamel sign-plates are as good or better a wall decoration as the oil paintings in the bourgeois salon. Firewalls are its writing desk, newspaper stands its libraries, postboxes its bronzes, benches its boudoir and the café terrace its oriel from where it observes goings-on.

'If', Leslie continues, 'the *flâneur* can be bothered to translate his viewing into reviewing, or his thought into theory, then this street furniture provides a bureau and drawing desk on which he can assemble the pieces of litter, the fragments of city lives, into images and narratives' (85).

The evident resurrection occurring gestures towards an understanding of the role as a changing one in history, one, as Frisby makes clear, which may be attributed not only to Benjamin's critique of the figure, but also to the practice of his own writings (2001: 34). As he indicates later in the same chapter, Benjamin's '*One-Way Street*' (1928) is itself a constellation or "construction" of aphorisms as a street', a conjunction of the acts of walking and writing – or, as I would have it, wandering and wondering – which invites the reader in turn to 'stroll along the textual one way street' (45).[6] Similarly, Leslie identifies the concern of 'Berlin Childhood around 1900' as one in which Benjamin 'dissolves himself into social spaces and speculations on things [...] writing less of people and more of objects there, and the spaces they inhabit' (Coles 1999: 59). The historical shift to which claims may be made, then, is from 'the negative conception of the dandyish stroller and producer of harmless physiognomies to the notion of the more directed observer and investigator of the signifiers of the city' (Frisby 2001: 35), indeed to the one who would bear witness. As Liggett suggests of Derrida's understanding of the latter role:

> If an issue for artists and intellectuals is what they should do, Derrida's notion that they are 'bearing witness' is a response that changes the nature of the question. It is

not what artists and intellectuals should be doing (that they are not); it is that bearing witness is what they do. As Derrida puts it, 'The responsibility, once again, would here be that of an heir' [*Specters of Marx*, London: Routledge, 1994, p. 91]. The situation in which we find ourselves (first) is one in which we are witness and cannot not respond. That position, to be a witness and to bear witness, is a form of deeply responsible action in the face of modernity. For some theorists and cultural producers in modernity this became a life work.

(2003: 97–8)

Benjamin can be given credit, then, not only for a specific kind of attention to urban detail but also for a method which Susan Sontag identifies as the slowness of the Saturnine, melancholic temperament: 'things appear at a distance, come forward slowly' (1997: 13–14). The speed of modernity is forced, effectively by the act of noticing, to slow down. It is a method that allows, as Benjamin himself puts it, 'the simultaneous perception of everything that potentially is happening in this single space. The space directs winks at the *flâneur*' (2002: 418–419). Hence, as Graeme Gilloch summarises:

For Benjamin, the buildings, spaces, monuments and objects that compose the urban environment both are a response to, and reflexively structure, patterns of human social activity. Architecture and action shape each other; they interpenetrate. The metropolis constitutes a frame or theatre of activity. The buildings of the city, and its interior setting in particular, form casings for action in which, or on which, human subjects leave 'traces', signs of their passing, markers or clues to their mode of existence.

(1997: 6)

In a similar vein of 'deceleration', Brecht's 'heir' Heiner Müller, who was also of course a long-time inhabitant of Berlin, seizes on the image of the pedestrian as a metaphor for the necessary process, as enacted by the writer, of slowing down contemporary life. Extrapolating in fact Brecht's use of the term 'pedestrian' with regard to the perception of German art in the latter's briefing to the actors of the Berliner Ensemble before its visit to England in 1956 (see chapter two, note two), Müller observes in an interview: 'in this modern, far more mobile society, the pedestrian – that's me – the pedestrian who, unlike the driver, has no bodyguard, is far more exposed to danger and has to be faster even than the cars in order to survive' (Müller 1995: viii–ix).[7] Paradoxically, it would seem, the pedestrian-writer of postmodernity has to be 'quicker' in order to bring about a deceleration that might produce space: 'The terrible thing at present is of course that all that remains is time or velocity or the passage of time, but no more space. What one has to do now is to create and occupy spaces acting against this acceleration' (Kluge/

Müller 1995: 80). Hence, the pedestrian's physicality or 'presencing' within the spaces of the city is analogous to a writing that proves obstructive as well as slippery within the fast, overdetermined flow of mediated experiencing.

Inflected through an understanding of the accidental Brechtian Street Scene, then, the Benjaminian street-walking figure, a 'new *flâneur*', takes its place 'here and now' as one which would seek, as implicated rather than idle witness, a connection with the unsettling 'dust and asphalt', as well as 'steel and glass' – not to say 'voids' – of the modern urban everyday. And, by telling of that encounter, rendering visible various tensions in the city – its 'growing pains' – as it undergoes transformation. That figure performs, moreover, a mapping of the 'idea of Brecht', a reading as well as a writing of the refunctioned Brechtian trace in its living relationship to an evolving Berlin, whilst also aspiring thereby to establish a form of temporary personal identification – of interim belonging – mediated by the moving body's unrehearsed experience of the material and premised, paradoxically perhaps, on the possibility of transformation produced precisely by such a *dis*placement.

Notes

1. An anecdote recounted by Barthes would appear to illustrate the point. Within the space of a split-second he seems to elide the roles of victim and messenger, imminently becoming the performing witness to the shock of his own accident as a means of dealing with the situation:

This morning, around eight, the weather was splendid. I had an impulse to try M's bicycle, to go to the baker's. I haven't ridden a bike since I was a kid. My body found this operation very odd, difficult, and I was afraid (of getting on, of getting off). I told all this to the baker – and as I left the shop, trying to get back on the bike, of course I fell off. Now by instinct I let myself fall *excessively*, legs in the air, in the silliest posture imaginable. And then I understood that it was this silliness which saved me (from hurting myself too much): I *accompanied* my fall and thereby turned myself into a spectacle, I made myself ridiculous; but thereby, too, I diminished its effect.

(1989: 367)

2. This is the title of Hirst's famous full-size tiger shark in a glass tank of formaldehyde solution (1991).

3. In his novel *Mao II* (1992), Don DeLillo explores the proximity precisely of the writer and terrorist. The narrative traces a reclusive novelist's gravitation, as he approaches death, towards the terrorist's desperate conditions of being (from the point of view of being the latter's hostage). As the protagonist suggests at one point on his journey, in a comment which has a particular resonance after 11 September 2001: 'Beckett is the last writer to shape the way we think and see. After him, the major work involves midair explosions and crumbled buildings. This is the new tragic narrative' (157). In *Leviathan* (1993) – dedicated to DeLillo – Paul Auster develops this convergence, his

writer actually turning into a terrorist who embarks on a project of blowing up the many replicas of the Statue of Liberty across the length and breadth of the United States. A topographical narrative of terror thus constructed leads inevitably to its creator's self-destruction.

Auster's novel is also pertinent to Ballard's intersecting of fiction and reality. One of the characters, an artist called Maria, is based on Auster's actual collaboration with the real-life artist-ethnographer Sophie Calle. However, as Kuchler reports, '[i]n the descriptions he made of Maria many elements correspond to Calle's life; but Auster has also introduced rituals that are totally fictional. In order to get closer to Maria, Calle decided to obey the book' (Coles 2000: 94). Maria/Calle's work involves devising some form of rule or condition, which she plays out in real circumstances whatever the consequences. In the novel the impulse for what became a conscious activity is shown to be rooted in an anonymous newcomer's whiling away of hours as a kind of *flâneuse* figure in the strange city:

She began following strangers around the streets, choosing someone at random when she left the house in the morning and allowing that choice to determine where she went for the rest of the day. It became a method of acquiring new thoughts, of filling up the emptiness that seemed to have engulfed her. Eventually, she began going out with her camera and taking pictures of the people she had followed. When she returned home in the evening, she would sit down and write about where she had been and what she had done, using the strangers' itineraries to speculate about their lives and, in some cases, to compose brief, imaginary biographies.

(Auster 1993: 62)

In a further reversal, Calle then went on to request Auster to write a narrative about a character called Sophie whose story she would then live out (Coles 2000: 94–5), thus emphasising the blurred proximity and interplay of art/life narratives.

4. It is worth just drawing attention to another, apparently irregular dimension to that notion of 'usefulness' from Brecht's private life. He himself had a crash once as a young man in the 1920s. Faced with an overtaking vehicle, he wrapped his car round a tree. It was a Steyr convertible, supplied to him gratis by the company in exchange for writing a little advertising poem. Now the car was a write-off. Brecht was desperate for a replacement. Fortunately for him the company came up with the idea of using the detailed events of the crash as a kind of cautionary tale whose real purpose was to advertise the reliability of their cars (Völker 1979: 91–2). Steyrs are better, even – or particularly – in the unlikely event of you crashing them. Brecht got his new car. Fuegi attempts to discredit Brecht for dealing with Steyr in particular, 'which made weapons as well as cars' (Fuegi 1995: 164). But in fact Brecht refers precisely to this fact in the opening lines: 'We were bred/In a weapons factory/Our little brother is/The Manlicher carbine' (*GW* 8: 318). Presumably the company would not have made use of the verse if it had objected to this being highlighted. By the same token, Brecht would not have risked anything subversive since he might not have received his payment in kind then. In fact both the original jingle and the post-crash cautionary tale are in themselves very candid pieces of writing. Brecht, moreover, was far from being against the advancement of mass technologies, so it is not difficult to see how he would have viewed his contribution as 'spin-free',

matter-of-fact publicity. Where the matter may be contentious is in Brecht's apparent exploitation of privilege.

5. The original title of Hessel's book was *Spazieren in Berlin*. It was reissued as *Ein Flaneur in Berlin* (Berlin: Das Arsenal, 1984) See Benjamin (*GS* 3: 194-99) for 'The Return of the *Flâneur*' (in German).

6. Eckhardt Köhn, one of a whole raft of Berlin writers preoccupied with *flânerie* in the early twentieth century suggests in his book *Strassenrausch* (Berlin: Das Arsenal, 1989) that the contents of Benjamin's *One-Way Street* are, as Frisby cites and translates, 'taken from the linguistic material of the street, or more precisely, mirror the written material of the street as it is offered to the observer in a stroll down a metropolitan street on name-plates, posters, advertising hoardings, house facades, shop windows and exhibition showcases' (2001: 45). This seems to echo exactly the psycho-geographical methodology employed by Iain Sinclair in *Lights Out for the Territory* (London: Granta, 1997), his book on walking a delineated route in London 'reading the signs'.

7. In a further reference to Brecht's predilection for going everywhere by car Müller adds wittily: 'Whereby you should mention that "Heiner Müller" hates to walk. Everywhere he goes he takes a taxi…you can add that as a footnote' (Müller 1995: ix).

Part 2

4. Oranienburger Strasse: the Space of Recurrence.

Being made finer, air becomes fire.

Being made thicker, it becomes wind,

Then cloud, then,

When thickened still more,

Water, then earth, then stones.

And the rest comes into being from those.

As our soul, being air,

Holds us together and controls us,

So does wind or breath and air

Enclose the whole world.

(Tacita Dean, The Berlin Project)

Collective memory, moreover, is a current of continuous thought still moving in the present, still part of a group's active life, and these memories are multiple and dispersed, spectacular and ephemeral, not recollected and written down in one unified story […] History on the other hand gives the appearance that memory persists in a uniform manner, being handed down from one period of time to another and passing successively from place to place. Disrupted from its original time and historic place, the past then reappears as a historical theatre, presenting its voice to the spectator through a series of images. Because this past is fragmented, it can be rewritten and recomposed into plays and theatrical scenes. Such a historical theatre acts out the past, little by little extending its power over the spectator's memory, slowly turning former events into an imaginary and fictional museum.

(M. Christine Boyer, The City of Collective Memory)

Firelands

Looking both ways twice, I cross the street. I'm outside Chaussee Strasse number 13 now, otherwise referred to as Borsig House. Recently renovated and housing smart dental practices, it was once the central administration block for the factories built and owned by Berlin's foremost railway magnate of the nineteenth century, August Borsig. His name is proprietorially embossed on the facade of this five-storey sandstone edifice. Immediately above the entrance is the centrepiece of an ostentatiously adorned frontage: the voluptuous figure of an iron foundry worker, striking a triumphant pose, of socialist-realist proportions in fact, with his leather apron and metal-pounding hammer for a staff. Good job he's not doing my fillings, I reflect, craning my neck to look up at him.

As a liberal Borsig was committed to the notion of a strong, united Germany, viewing industrialisation as the means to advance civilisation. Having bought a small piece of land just outside the city gates on Chaussee Strasse in 1836, he moved quickly to producing steam engines and locomotives. By 1858 the one-thousandth engine was rolling off the production line. The whole area around Chaussee Strasse became a centre for heavy industry, Borsig's complex alone being described as a small city (Richie 1998: 143). Popularly the quarter acquired the name *Feuerland* as a result, literally 'fireland', spawning, immediately to the west and north-west, the famous worker's districts of Moabit and Wedding.[1] By the time Walter Benjamin came to describe a visit to the factory complex during the later Weimar years it had long since expanded further and moved to the north western peripheries of Berlin (*GS* 7i: 111–117).[2] Situated next to Tegeler See, one of the city's many lakes, this permitted easy access for barges, which would transport machine parts for export to Hamburg via the Havel-Elbe river network. Trains, moreover, could trundle straight on to the compound, which, with its 65 metre high office tower, the Borsig Turm (completed in 1924), boasted the first piece of high-rise architecture ever built in Berlin (*GS* 7i: 112–113). Nowadays there's an Underground station called Borsig Werke (works) and the suburb around it – largely residential – Borsigwalde (woods).

The lower end of Chaussee Strasse, where the Brecht and Borsig Houses are to be found, edges on to the upper periphery of the so-called Scheunenviertel, the 'barn quarter', according to one of the most up-to-date travel guides to Berlin (Gawthrop and Holland 2001: 102–3). It's an area which has come effectively to span the entire northern band of what is seen as the city's centre. However, its exact delineation is disputed. The barns in question were built in the seventeenth century and were actually associated with a restricted area between what is now Rosa Luxemburg Platz and Rosenthaler Strasse towards the east of this band (Rebiger 2000: 186–9). Their purpose, according to Ladd, was to house animals (1997: 113). Being outside the confines of the city walls as they existed then, they conformed to a decree passed in the seventeenth century – perhaps even as an indirect consequence of the 1666 Fire of London – banning the storage of flammable hay and straw (intended for the animals) in the centre of the city itself. In its own way, then, Scheunenviertel too bears early historical testament to the presence and force of *fire*, coming about as a strategic tactic of avoidance. If there was going to be a fire, *here* is where it should occur rather than in the centre of the city. The quarter eventually became engulfed by a suburb of Berlin called Spandauer Vorstadt,[3] which began to develop beyond the city walls in the nineteenth century. Informally the area still bears that name.

And, just for the sake of creating further appellative confusion, this part of the city is *also* referred to by some as the Jewish Quarter, having as it does a long history of Jews living and working in it. Having been expelled from the Mark Brandenburg, and therefore Berlin, in 1573, Jews began to be allowed back in to the city in limited numbers and under strict conditions a whole century later (Rebiger 2000: 15–17). It wasn't until the middle of the nineteenth century, however, that a full-blown Jewish community might be said to have been populating Berlin again, Jews finally being accepted officially into public life rather than 'formally tolerated' (22). The 1866 inauguration of the Neue Synagoge (new synagogue) in Oranienburger Strasse, with its vast space for three thousand worshipers – making it Germany's largest (Enke 1999: 48) – underlined the community's growing self-confidence, as well as the location of its operative heart. The area's subsequent metamorphosis into a 'Jewish Quarter' or *Stetl* is, however, a matter of grave concern to some historians and commentators. Detlef Friedrich, for instance, sees it as a convenient rewriting of history, implying that it functions to portray the Jewish presence in the city as having been topographically marginal:

> Percentage-wise there were no more Jewish Germans living in Spandauer Vorstadt than in Charlottenburg, Wilmersdorf or Weissensee. There were synagogues in all districts. The term 'Jewish Quarter' belies the fact that before the Nazis the whole of Berlin was a Jewish city, in the same way that it was a Christian city.

> *(Friedrich 2001: 9)*

Friedrich has a point, moreover, because it is the Nazis who are credited with extending Scheunenviertel – effectively to duplicate Spandauer Vorstadt – precisely for the purposes of discrimination after 1933 (Enke 1999: 280). In

7.

other words, it became a useful extended euphemism for 'dodgy area containing Jews, prostitutes, homosexuals and other such criminal elements'.

Anybody would be hard-pressed, then, to demarcate precisely where the boundaries and overlaps of these various topographical identities lie or whether they can even be said legitimately to exist. Apart from anything else, they have shifted in time. Their spread and shrinkage is a measure of the extent to which the extreme winds of history have swept through them. Rosa Luxemburg Platz itself, situated in a part of what was the original Scheunenviertel, has been subject to rapid-fire change in the twentieth century, typifying the general tendency in Berlin toward trying to sign ideological supremacy through street names.[4] It was newly conceived in 1906 as Bülow Platz after Germany's fourth imperial chancellor, famous for his pre-World War 1 advocacy of the nation's 'rightful place in the sun' in the colonialist scheme of things. The Nazis renamed the square Horst Wessel Platz in honour of the notorious SA thug and pimp who died a protracted martyr's death at the hands of the communists in 1930, having bequeathed to the Nazis what became the '*de facto* German national anthem' of the time, known simply as the Horst Wessel song (Richie 1998: 393).

In 1931 a young Stalinist called Erich Mielke, later to emerge as the infamous director of *Stasi* operations in the GDR, shot dead two policemen on the occasion of a demonstration against the general 'miserable conditions of the times'. This took place in front of the square's Karl Liebknecht House, which had become the Communist party's headquarters in 1926. (These days it houses the Party of Democratic Socialism, formed in 1990 as the immediate successor to the GDR's Socialist Unity Party of Germany.) Incredibly Mielke was eventually put on trial for this act some 60 years and four regimes later. In 1993, at the age of nearly 85, he was sentenced to six years in prison with his various *Stasi* crimes still pending examination (Bose and Duerr 1998: 653).

One of the most extraordinary experiences I had in Berlin in 2001 was visiting the

Street Scenes: Brecht, Benjamin, and Berlin

former *Stasi* headquarters in Normannen Strasse (Lichtenberg), now a museum and research institute whose work attempts to uncover and reappraise the murky history of the organisation. I was the only visitor, and not a single attendant in sight. Perhaps any association with notions of security or guardianship were too painfully ironic to contemplate in this context. Instead, everything was openly accessible, there to be seen and touched. In the main it amounted to unbelievably crude surveillance devices: cameras hidden in flower-pots and tree trunks, jam jars containing samples of people's odours, microphones embedded in pencil-cases, handbags and purses. The state security apparatus concealed in the private paraphernalia of everyday life; secrets of the home, home-made secrets. *(Un)heimlich*. This place was so *deserted* it gave me the creeps.[5]

My spontaneous impulse: to check whether or not my every move was being watched on CCTV. Then, before I knew it, I was standing in Erich Mielke's old office. The building at Normannen Strasse was ransacked on 15 January 1990, but the theory – put out by the research institute itself – is that there were *Stasi* members amongst the demonstrators, leading others away from critical material, whilst also seizing the opportunity amidst the chaos to destroy important documents (Forschungs und Gedenkstätte Normannenstrasse 2000: 5–6). The mess was quickly tidied up. Now it looks as if Mielke simply put the phone down one day and said, 'Right, then, chaps. That's enough. Let's go home', and left. In fact, as Large reports, he tried perversely to reassure the East German people that he still loved them (2002: 531). As for telephones: awaiting trial in Moabit Prison, he appeared to have turned senile – though it could have been a ruse – 'barking orders to imaginary inferiors on a toy telephone kindly supplied by his guards' (570). First tragedy, then farce. The genie of state madness returning to torment the 'genius' that let it loose. Mielke was in fact released from prison in 1995 owing to ill health.

Returning to the Square in question: having functioned temporarily as Karl Liebknecht Platz after the end of the Second World War, it was renamed Luxemburg Platz in 1947 before the GDR authorities finally added Rosa in 1969, presumably to distinguish it from the principality (spelt the same in German). Famous as martyrs to the cause of the Spartacus uprisings in Berlin after World War 1, Luxemburg's posthumous *replacement* here of Liebknecht replicates in a sense the pattern of their respective fates in 1919: following Liebknecht's assassination by soldiers in Tiergarten, Luxemburg was similarly shot and dumped in the city's Landwehr Canal on the same day (Karwalat 1988: 18). Liebknecht, of course, has a highly significant street named after him instead (see chapter nine).

Transgressing the Street
At the Oranienburger Tor end of Chaussee Strasse – once a gateway to the city – I'm waiting for the lights to change. It's one of those little red fellows from the

former GDR who's preventing me from crossing. The ones wearing trilbies and flashing open their raincoats at whosoever's attempting to hurry by. That's one sure way of stopping pedestrians dead in their tracks. (Perhaps this is where Anthony Gormley got the idea for his giant sculpture *The Angel of the North* sited outside Gateshead and dubbed locally 'The Flasher of the North'. That and Benjamin's surveyor of history's wreckages.) As signifiers of the way life in the GDR was (or was supposed to be), these pedestrian lights – called *Ampelmännchen*[6] – are distinctly misleading: bourgeois, colourful, fun. Like cartoon figures. That's probably why they survived as one of the few formal relics of the East, contributing supposedly to myths of nostalgia – or *Ostalgie*[7] – and western fetishisation. They've not only been retained as far as practicable – so popular did they prove after 1989 – but they also seem to appear in places where there were no signals previously: the western side of Potsdamer Platz, for instance.

When the lights change, the green *Ampelmännchen* sets off with an urgency usually witnessed only in athletes doing a 100-metre sprint. Perhaps it's to encourage pedestrians to do precisely that, given that many of the wind-swept avenues in the eastern half of the city centre are so broad – running to four and five lanes in one direction – that you stand no chance of making it across both sides before the red chappie flashes you again. The city centre section of the old Stalin Allee, for

8.   9.

instance – the pride of the former East Berlin, renamed Karl Marx Allee the same year the Wall went up in 1961 (in response to the dictator's discrediting)[8] – is all of 90 metres wide. In an ideal world they would have had the green fellow chasing after his trilby, swept off his head by *a sudden gust of wind*.

Pedestrian crossings in Germany in any case possess a revealing psychology in practice. Strictly the law prohibits crossing when the lights are at red, and you can be fined if a police officer catches you doing so. Quite aside from those obvious occasions where there really isn't a single moving vehicle in sight, there is something fatally paternalistic – or panoptic – whatever the circumstances about trying to force pedestrians to comply with directives about how, where and when they may move within the common confines of a city. If, as de Certeau maintains, walking corresponds to a form of articulation within 'a space of enunciation' in which 'the act of walking is to the urban system what the speech act is to language or to the statements uttered' (1988: 97–8), then such controls are a bit like being told the poetry you write can only have proper value if it's in Alexandrines. Anything else is aberrant and will lead inevitably to the corruption of your soul. They are certainly anathema to the *flâneur's* untrammelled practice of 'distracted drift'. Revealing clear links with the Situationists' performative rearticulation of urban space (see Sadler 1998), De Certeau adds: 'The walking of passers-by offers a series of turns (*tours*) and detours that can be compared to 'turns of phrase' or 'stylistic figures'. There is a rhetoric of walking. The art of 'turning' phrases finds an equivalent in an art of composing a path (*tourner un parcours*)' (1988: 100).

What kind of poetry do these signals permit, then? Perhaps they are more like punctuation marks, veering between a full stop and a colon. It still happens that solid citizens – usually elderly ones – will grumble or grimace if you dare to cross when the street seems to you to be clear but the signal red. There's no question, though, as with the inclination of the younger generation to assume more easily the informal address *Du* over the distanced *Sie* in speech, that the general attitude has become more lax (a hopeful semi-colon). Perhaps this is particularly the case in Berlin, progressive place that it strives to be, though interestingly the eastern part of the city appears by my casual reckoning to be more conformist in this respect. The psychology of crossing frequently encountered involves a pattern whereby a gradual build-up of fidgeting pedestrians on either side of the street – in inverse proportion to the amount of traffic passing – leads to one person eventually breaking rank, followed by another and another, and then a gathering rush: a single person's triggering of a breach of the law, one which he or she has sensed – or at least is hoping – will be met with collective endorsement. If there is a risk involved, then, it is not of being knocked over, but of whether that calculation is accurate in the circumstances or whether it will be met with tight-lipped incriminations. The sacrificial hero's body language always speaks of self-conscious vulnerability, even if this expresses itself as exaggerated indifference. Schematically speaking, the procedure describes – when it succeeds – the pattern (or poetry) of mass revolution. Hence, in the same way as language proposes a proper way of being used, its words, though binding as currency, are inevitably subject to unforeseen, 'improper' use in their actual enunciation. As de Certeau suggests:

> The long poem of walking manipulates spatial organisations, no matter how panoptic they may be: it is neither foreign to them (it can take place only within them) nor in conformity with them (it does not receive its identity from them). It creates shadows and ambiguities within them. It inserts multitudinous references and citations into them (social models, cultural mores, personal factors).

(1988: 101)

The New Synagogue

Turning now, halfway between Brecht's house and his former theatre, into Oranienburger Strasse, I'm following one of the main arteries into the heart of Scheunenviertel. The imposing centrepiece of this street, otherwise bustling with a profusion of bars and restaurants, is, as I've indicated, the Neue Synagoge. It replicates Moorish architectural style – its entrance modelled specifically on the Alhambra in Granada (Cobbers 2000: 80) – the most distinctive feature being its vast golden dome. This was authorised to be given a new gilding in 1988 in one of the last acts of the East German government,[9] one not finally completed, though, until well after reunification. Despite its name, it's actually an *old* synagogue. Since 1995 it has functioned as a museum and cultural centre (*Centrum Judaicum*) for Jewish life in the city. In fact, it is only the front section of the building that remains, the GDR authorities having dynamited the vast hall of prayer in 1958 for unspecified reasons (Rebiger 2000: 78). But it effectively ceased being a synagogue on the 9 November 1938, the infamous *Kristallnacht*. SA men set it on fire along with countless other Jewish installations in Berlin. Thanks to the swift intervention of a local police officer, Wilhelm Krützfeld, who alerted the fire service and, along with a couple of colleagues, chased away the SA, the damage was limited. It was five years later that the synagogue finally succumbed to flames, those produced by allied bombing. However, in a blatant attempt to falsify history photographs of the burning building were released in the world's press after the war attributing the act to the Nazis in 1938 (see Valgren 2000: 69 and Rebiger 2000: 77–8). Ladd doesn't mention the police heroism but confirms 'this grand building escaped from *Kristallnacht* in 1938 with only minor damage' (1997: 114).[10]

So, from the nineteenth century firelands of Borsig's factories in the north-west, pumping out great blasts of optimism over the progressive potential of the industrial revolution, to the anxious seventeenth century transplantation of flammable agricultural hazards to the periphery of the urban centre in the north-east, to the destructive effects of fascism at its core in the twentieth century, *fire* has raged both literally and symbolically through the foundations of this quarter's past. Between the world wars the area was a melting pot of radical activity. During the Weimar period it was implicated in the rich, bohemian culture of the city (Von Eckardt and Gilman 1993), with an accompanying image of seediness (and the fertile setting, of course, for Döblin's celebrated expressionist novel *Berlin Alexanderplatz*, later filmed by Fassbinder). Eventually it gave over to the brutal street fighting of the dawning Nazi era and the simultaneous dismantling of its Jewish infrastructure. But if the winds of history have blown hot here, they have also blown cold. After the Second World War and until reunification in 1989 the area appears to have lain more or less dormant, a ghostly silence descending for some 40 years on its decrepit and abandoned streets. Police officers stand on permanent guard now outside the Neue Synagoge, indicative both of the continuing threat of anti-Semitic attacks on Jewish installations across the city and a living symbol of Krützfeld's intervening act. The plaque exhorting visitors or passers-by to 'never forget' was put in place on the centenary of the synagogue's completion in 1966, whilst another less exhortatory one was added on 9 November 1988, 50 years after *Kristallnacht* and one year to the day before the Berlin Wall was breached.

New Nazis

Ironically the Nazis themselves, or some of their latter-day acolytes ensconced in the ranks of the Nationalist Party of Germany (NPD), have taken to heart the message never to forget at precisely the symbolic site at which it is expressed. On Saturday, 1 December 2001 the Neue Synagoge segment of Oranienburger Strasse played host to street battles between so-called lefties (*Linke*) or independents (*Autonome*) and police, as the former attempted to penetrate a cordon preventing them from reaching an estimated 3,500 neo-Nazis marching from Friedrich Strasse up Chaussee Strasse (past Brecht's house) to the railway station Nordbahnhof. The NPD is the largest extreme right-wing party in Germany. One of its strongest sources of recruitment is the so-called skinhead scene, above all in East Germany where there are organised formations openly propagating anti-bourgeois proletarianism, violence, anti-intellectualism, xenophobia and male supremacy. At the time of writing, the NPD itself has three major banning order applications filed against it at the federal constitutional court in Karlsruhe. One is by the German government on the grounds that the party propagates violence and anti-Semitism, as well as being a breeding ground for right extremists. A second is by the lower house of the German parliament on the basis that the NPD shows a clear historical kinship with the former Nazi party, the NSDAP. The third is by the upper house, again based on the NPD's links with violent skinheads and neo-Nazis (Averesch 2001: 6).[11] The protest, which amounted to the largest gathering of nationalists since World War II, was against a controversial exhibition showing

10.

Wehrmacht crimes: the alleged murder of innocent civilians by regular German soldiers on the eastern and south-eastern fronts between 1941 and 1944.[12] It had opened that week in a gallery space in August Strasse immediately behind the Neue Synagoge. Originally the NPD march was to have passed provocatively through the 'Jewish Quarter' – past the synagogue – in protest at the exhibition's supposed besmirching of national socialist history.

Cobblestones and bottles had been thrown, bins and skips set on fire; water cannon and tear-gas had responded. The battle had raged for an hour. When I arrive at the Neue Synagoge, having spent two hours attempting to enter the area in question from its western and southern sides, only to find it hopelessly sealed off by police, an anxious hush has descended. It's a lull in the aftermath of threatening events the final outcome of which no one is sure. A mass of people mill around, mostly moving up to the police cordon to the left of the synagogue to see what is happening and ambling back when there doesn't prove to be much to behold. The street is drenched. Twitchy police stand around in small clusters, a line of their vans stretching the full length of Oranienburger Strasse towards Hackescher Markt. One water-cannon carrier waits ominously in the wings along with several armoured cars, whilst another forms the centrepiece of the police barrier. At one corner I can see two demolished police vehicles, wrecked by the *Autonomen* when they had become hemmed in during the battle. The press made it four in all, one turned upside down. Counter-demonstrators had plundered equipment and relayed joke-messages through the megaphones (*Tagesspiegel am Sonntag* 2001: 9). After a while there is a flurry of activity at the police barrier as photographers and television crews cluster round a politician chatting to protestors. There are calls for a megaphone so he can be heard by all those present. The crowd wants something decisive to happen. Eventually, half hauling himself up onto one of the water-cannon carriers, we are addressed by Gregor Gysi, one of the leading figures of the leftist PDS.[13] The anti-demonstration will make its way round to the location of the exhibition in August Strasse. That is where the counter protest will be registered, for it is vital to show the NPD that they are not welcome in the city of Berlin. But, please, no more stone throwing.

There are cheers. The tension is diffused. I circle back to Friedrich Strasse to try and get an idea of what the neo-Nazis are up to. The police cordon has moved further up the street. The demonstrators, apparently congregated at the bottom end of Chaussee Strasse but still well out of reach, are singing Nazi songs and being addressed at intervals by men with rasping voices. Later, at Alexander Platz, in the gathering gloom of an early December dusk, I see a teenage gang of lads chase after two young skinheads. One runs off, the other falls squealing to the ground and is kicked a couple of times in the stomach. Before I know it, all concerned have vanished into the shadows of the coming darkness. A little later, as I wait for the U2 train on the platform of the Underground (U-Bahn) at Alexander Platz, there's a slogan video-projected on to the wall opposite. It's part of an interactive installation called *Urban Diaries* – seen as 'a new form of writing the story of the city' – which permits anyone to relay anonymous text messages: 'You're better off down here, cos up there it's started raining again', it says.[14]

11.

12.

Seventy odd years ago, I reflect later, it might have been those lads' great-grandfathers getting involved in similar left-right skirmishes. Richie gives a vivid account of the astonishing, everyday extent of hand-to-hand factional combat in the streets of Berlin in the latter years of the Weimar Republic. Beginning in 1927 Goebbels waged a campaign against German communists (the KPD), which eventually moved from containment in working-class districts to more central areas of the city. At the same time, of course, he organised beatings of any Jews or anyone 'of Jewish appearance' found in the way (Richie 1999: 387). However, the KPD itself was quite capable of indulging in similar activities, not least against the ruling Social Democrats. The left split, motivated by Stalin on the communist side, is commonly held to have paved the way for Nazi ascendancy. As Richie writes:

> Much has been made of the street fighting between the Nazis and the KPD and there is no doubt that much of it was brutal; even so the brawls were often by both sides for cynical publicity purposes. Christopher Isherwood noted that there was something false and ritualistic about many of the attacks; the short, violent conflicts would last 'fifteen seconds, and then it was all over and dispersed'. Both sides enjoyed the violence, both wanted to prove that anarchy reigned in Berlin and that the republic had lost control of the streets.

(403)

One of the confusions of the day that I witnessed was produced by the neo-Nazi march's re-routing. Police officers I asked professed not to know where it was heading. Later it emerged an alternative route had already been agreed with the organisers a month beforehand (Emmerich 2001: 15). The speculation in the press in the days preceding the march, and by the Jewish community, whose leaders had declared their commitment to a sit-down protest barring the neo-Nazis' way, was all so much wasted breath. The violence appears to have erupted in part out of a sense of disappointment on behalf of the counter-demonstrators – numbering some four to five thousand – at not being able physically to register their disapproval of the NPD. The latter's rally, whilst being the largest nationalist one since the Second World War, also effectively took place in a vacuum. Jewish community members, having just emerged from their Sabbath prayers as the battle broke, felt compelled to go ahead with the staging of their sit-down protest in the street. As one of its elders was quoted as declaring: 'We cannot allow those who would protect us from the Nazis to be beaten up' (Bommarius 2001: 3). A significant reversal has occurred in this perception, wherein the upholders of peace and justice have metamorphosed into violent supporters of fascism: 'The Nazis receive protection from the police, whilst those who try to help us, get battered' (3). Naturally, the police would maintain it had merely asserted its disinterested priority of keeping the peace by preventing a direct confrontation between factions. Subsequent to the demonstrations the police officers' union criticised the Jewish community for allying itself with criminally-minded troublemakers (*Berliner Zeitung* 2001: 21).

The tenor of such post-event exchanges, as reported in the press, begins to take on a programmatic tone – echoing Isherwood's view of 1920s street fighting as 'false and ritualistic' – right down to the local politician responsible remorsefully apologising for somehow neglecting to disclose the re-routing of the march earlier (Krause 2001: 13). There is also a clear sense in which the police's 'impartial pragmatism' in its handling of the event itself emerges as the dominant discourse, one which largely *neutralises* by paradoxically reinforcing polarised circumstances: the NPD ended up performing only to themselves (no significant media images were even released); the counter-demonstrators supposedly shot themselves in the foot by being seen to initiate violence, thereby giving the police the opportunity to demonstrate its 'efficiency' at handling such extreme situations. A few smashed up police vehicles only contribute as effects to a perception of the heroic intensity of the challenge to the security forces, as well as usefully stoking the antipathy of conservative taxpaying citizens who are reminded that they will ultimately foot the bill for the damage. Under such circumstances it is highly questionable whether the democratic process is being permitted to run its course. The police's strategy is pre-emptive. The trouble that occurs is predictable – deliberately provoked precisely so as to be so – and therefore containable. Alone the extent of the police's presence, similar in size to the numbers of counter-protestors, suggests smothering tactics. One policeman I asked about access points to the neo-Nazi rally said I should consult one of his Berlin colleagues, implying extra forces had been drafted in from outside the city. On the other hand, the performative resonance of the confrontation is not entirely cancelled out. For instance, a minority like the NPD knows exactly what it must do and where it should target its operation in order to induce maximum provocation. It does not even have to declare a vague intention to bring about a 'repetition of the past'; choosing the location it does allows that particular possibility to be produced as a matter of course. The counter-action is inevitably trading in the same currency, if to distinct ends.

In the 1920s Brecht wrote a poem, the third of the 'city-dwellers' cycle, essentially concerned, as Vaßen maintains, with 'the (mythological) liberation from the child-devouring father, the destruction of oppressive tradition and the dawning of a new age' (1998: 80). Originally entitled 'To Chronos', this odd, clunking poem encompasses the notion of the father as both (an older) time and the thwarter of revolution.

> We do not want to leave your house
>
> We do not want to smash the stove
>
> We want to put the pot on the stove.
>
> House, stove and pot can stay
>
> And you must vanish like smoke in the sky
>
> Which nobody holds back.
>
> [...]
>
> The cities are allowed to change
>
> But you are not allowed to change.
>
> We shall argue with the stones
>
> But you we shall kill
>
> You must not live
>
> Whatever lies we are forced to believe
>
> You must not have been.

(1976: 133–4)

Benjamin attributes retrospective significance to the poem, asserting that '[t]he expulsion of the Jews from Germany was (until the pogroms of 1938) carried out in the spirit described in [it]'. Above all the poem 'shows very clearly why National Socialism needs anti-Semitism. It needs it as a parody'. What Benjamin means is that national socialism copied the form of a revolutionary situation, casting Jews as the oppressors of the masses: 'The Jew – Hitler ordains – shall be treated as the great exploiter ought to have been treated'. However, because it is a treatment that 'is not really in earnest [...] the distorted mirror-image of a genuine revolutionary action', it emerges as parody, 'a mockery of the historical proposition that the expropriators shall be expropriated' (Benjamin 1977: 62).

Both Brecht and Benjamin recognised the actual 'application of theatrical techniques to politics in fascism' (Brecht 1993: 115), a reversal, as Buck-Morss puts it, of 'the avant-garde practice of putting reality onto the stage, staging not only political spectacles but historical events, and thereby making "reality" itself theatre'. The use, for instance, of the Nazi slogan *'Deutschland Erwache!'* ('Germany, Awaken!'), represents not an 'awakening from recent history, but recapturing the past in a pseudo-historical sense, as myth' (Buck-Morss 1989: 36). Arguably, then, the neo-Nazis' nostalgic protest against the 'besmirching of the national socialist past' can be said to take the form of a parody of a parody, or myth-making of myth, copying as it does the trappings of Nazism in a doubly 'distorted mirror-image'. Moreover, as Burgin says: '[t]he rhetoric of neo-fascism, by no means unique to Germany, sounds familiar – but it now resounds in a different space' (1996: 156). It is not so much the threat of history actually recurring, then, as the stimulation precisely of that idea – the return of the repressed in the form of a remobilised *Doppelgänger* – that is in operation. As Krause concludes sardonically: 'An NPD demonstration which fails to let itself be fought and beseeched on the basis of it being a repetition of "the" past really is a bitter disappointment' (Krause 2001: 13). In the same way, though, as Nazism is not adequately described in terms relating to formal rhetorical devices, but was at the same time something that really and terrifyingly occurred, so the emergence of the latter-day phenomenon poses an actual socio-political threat.

New Weimar

Since the events of 1989 this section of the city – Scheunenviertel, Spandauer Vorstadt, 'Jewish Quarter', whatever you may wish to call it – has experienced an extraordinary revitalisation, one which has certainly sought to reconnect in some way with the variety and spirit of its Weimar identity. This includes 'rediscovering' its artistic and Jewish communities, its commercial nightlife, as well as going in for extensive renovation of buildings. Some of the work carried out in this latter respect is highly contentious, being viewed as part of a falsifying process of urban gentrification not untypical of first world metropolises generally in the 1990s. The narratives of history – the what and how of its writing – are contested in the very fabric and construction of buildings.

None encapsulates these tensions more than the former department store Tacheles, which is situated a little further up Oranienburger Strasse from the Neue Synagogue, back towards Chaussee Strasse. It was once part of a huge arcades complex, the Friedrich Strasse Passagen, built at the onset of the twentieth century. Suffering damage during the Second World War it stood abandoned, like so much of the area, until the early 1990s when it was squatted by a group of artists and turned into a form of alternative centre for culture. Functioning as a multi-purpose venue, including a theatre and cinema, and providing artists' studios and a café-bar, the building teemed with life. As a result of the interest generated, it actually set in train the widespread programme of regeneration that has occurred in that part of the city. As eager speculators swarmed all over the Spandauer Vorstadt, it seemed only a matter of time before the rough and ready dilapidation of Tacheles would succumb to their development plans. However, despite – or perhaps because of – its forbidding presence, which, with its glassless windows and crumbling stairwell would have been enough to give any health and safety officer a heart-attack, the occupiers were able in 1998 to strike an interim deal with an investor that was

13.

satisfactory to them (Enke 1999: 50). The building would remain intact, though in reconstructed form, and would continue to function as an arts centre. In the meantime, its vulnerable rear facade, much of it swathed in graffiti, has had large panes of glass inserted where previously there were only cavernous gaps. In fact, most of it isn't a rear facade at all – or wasn't – but an internal wall which has lost its rump. Resembling bitten-off biscuits the continuity of the floors has been abruptly interrupted on each level. Now it can have the unsettling appearance of a double exposure in certain lighting conditions, two buildings in one. Actually it's several buildings in one, a succession that the glass serves both to magnify and preserve. The word itself, *Tacheles*, is Yiddish for 'plain speaking' or, in German, *Klartext*. The only thing that's clear about this text, though, is that the story it would tell is by no means over.

Whilst the jury is still out, then, on the final outcome of Tacheles, the solution so far certainly contrasts strongly with the majority of developments that have taken place in the remainder of the area. These have tended towards smart, full-scale renovation and refunctioning. It's a familiar process, which has affected several parts of Berlin. For some, such as the journalist Uwe Rada, it amounts to the 'far more exciting legend of colonialisation and discovery', as he observes sarcastically. It is the story of an invasion, claims Rada – citing his colleague, André Meier – which has shamelessly constructed an attractive narrative of continuity between the 'golden twenties' and the 'colourful nineties'. In doing so it has suppressed not only 50 years of local community history but also the critical events of some 50 years ago (Rada 1997: 226–9).

Situated at the other end of Oranienburger Strasse from Tacheles, Hackesche Höfe provides an interesting counterweight to the former's recent developmental history. What has taken place in Hackesche Höfe is what might have been foreseen for Tacheles. It is a hugely popular complex of early twentieth century courtyards, housing upmarket small businesses, smart apartments, craft workshops and artists' studios, as well as bars, cafés, cinemas and a theatre. In the 1990s it became a kind of epitomising focal point in Berlin

14.

for the potential residing in the discovery and restoration of original buildings, a process through which 'new life' would be generated. Presumed by its discoverers to be the largest cohesive grouping of courtyards in Europe, it was deemed a 'jewel' for urban developers and conservationists alike (Rada 1997: 227). Above all the facade of the first of eight courtyards represents an impressive recovery of its art nouveau origins. Rada's resistance seems to be less to that kind of material rediscovery and 'dusting off' than the gentrified *ersatz*-culture it has spawned in and around it. This he sees, first, as suppressing the history of the locality such as it was. Specifically he is referring to the phenomenon of the *Kiez*, which occupies a special place in Berlin life as the location of a communal, neighbourhood identity, one nurtured by the widespread system in the city of tenement blocks. The Berlin *Mietshaus*, as it is called, is an eighteenth century innovation, a block of several adjoining five-storey apartment buildings, each with side and rear wings (the renowned *Hinterhäuser*) grouped around an inner courtyard. Striving to house a mix of social classes, it became widespread in the latter part of the nineteenth century, forming the highest metropolitan population density in Europe at the time (Haubrig 2001: 77). In fact, though, the history of the *Mietshaus* is mixed. Also known as rental barracks (*Mietskasernen*) they began life, as Benjamin explains in another one of his radio broadcasts for children (*GS* 7i: 117–124), as military accommodation designed to allow soldiers to live with their families. Far from amounting to most un-Prussian-like magnanimity, this was actually to prevent the high instance of desertion by soldiers owing to the extreme discipline of army life. Effectively the *Mietskasernen* functioned like self-contained detention camps for all concerned. The principle began to be transferred to the civilian population under Friedrich the Great, though there was actually no shortage of land space necessitating this. By the mid-nineteenth century the city authorities saw blanket development of *Mietskasernen* as a cheap, convenient form of city planning in the coming age of industry, a move which mainly appeased landowners. By its pre-World War 1 height, however, it began to be acknowledged as being very far from an ideal solution to housing a large, mainly poor, population. As Ladd observes: 'A wide consensus condemned the *Mietskaserne* as an unhealthful place to live [...] It was the overcrowding in the apartments and the poverty of their residents that gave the *Mietskaserne* its dismal reputation' (1998: 103). It was only much later, in the 1970s, by which time many had been knocked down, that the solidly-built tenements enjoyed a revival of interest in both East and West Berlin: 'Planners and urban critics began to praise the old buildings as incubators of neighbourhood identity and attractive urbanity' (105).[15]

Rada's second objection is based on what he views as a spurious, self-replicating historical mythologising, one that implies this 'new culture' always existed here, there and everywhere: 'I keep entering new bars which resemble one another without anyone actually knowing who created this style that everyone keeps copying. It's a quarter without authorship' (1997: 227–8). On the other hand, it can also take the form of a spurious authorship such as the one which has turned it into a 'Jewish Quarter'. As Large observes:

> Rather than promoting a living Jewish culture, Berlin cultivated a nostalgia for the lost era of pre-Nazi Jewish vitality. Oranienburger Strasse, once lined with Jewish businesses, now became a kind of Jewish theme park. In addition to the New Synagogue [...] there was an upscale kosher restaurant where tourists in search of an authentic Jewish experience could eat vegetarian blintzes and listen to piped-in klezmer music.
>
> *(2002: 576)*

Boyer sums up the process of myth making as a general tendency in the memorialisation of modern metropolises:

> In this desire to solidify the traces of the past into a unified image, to restore an intactness that never was, the designer focuses on the context of a landmark or a historic district, thus becoming the architect of theatrical stage sets that have little to say about the memory of place. By borrowing art forms moulded in the nineteenth and early twentieth centuries, the structure of repetition becomes more important than innovation. The reproductive mould rises above the production of city space: a mould that now incorporates hollowed-out pieces of the city recently deprived of their usefulness and patiently waiting to be filled with contemporary fantasies and wishful projections.
>
> *(1998: 373)*

Rada's book as a whole is about the process of *Verdrängung* detectable in Berlin's evolution since 1989. That is, that which has been systematically suppressed, denied and falsified out of existence. On the one hand, one can sympathise wholly with his concern at a perceived 'neo-Weimarist' artificiality – driven, of course, by profit and consumerist motives – arising in an area like Spandauer Vorstadt. In the same way as the Nazis were able to redesignate the area to their own discriminatory ends, and neo-Nazism attempts to profit from restaging the effects of that particular move, so business speculation strives to 'naturalise' certain topographical narratives to suit its selling priorities. (Any Rip van Winkles waking up in Berlin these days and seeking to orientate themselves via a recent Falk-Plan – for many years the standard, folding map of the city, publishing its 62nd edition in 2000 – could be forgiven for thinking the hamburger chain McDonald's was a civic amenity comparable to a church, hospital or WC. The company's logo pinpointing all its outlets appears to lay strategic claim to the city like the advance guard of a colonising army.[16]) On the other hand, there is also the suggestion of rather too blithe a recourse in Rada's critique to stable notions of 'realities', 'pasts' and 'origins' in his comments. His sardonic question 'What does reality matter?' (226) – whose? his? – coupled with the implicit yearning for the hand of authorship to be established, can begin to sound like a form of idealisation as contrived and (n)ostalgic for an idea of 'what was' or 'might have been' as the *ersatz*-culture he would prefer had not replaced 'it'. In a sense Rada falls into the trap of believing there is a fixed or natural 'truth' of the locality being masked by a form of false consciousness. How cohesive and 'authentic' was the quarter that he perceives is being left behind?

The tension is between two ideological standpoints – naturalisations of history – both of which insist upon the sanctity of their positions. If there is a 'reality' in operation, it is surely messier. A phenomenon like Tacheles, for instance, reveals a relationship to the past and/or identity – which is ultimately what is at stake here – that is, if you will, profoundly at one with its incompleteness. It conveys a sense of 'liminality' or 'continuous becoming', an unstable state which speaks of its various locations in time as ones that have not only shifted ground but are still doing so as the building continues to perform a role in the life of the city. To use Benjaminian terminology, then, it is a building whose 'truth' is not merely manifest 'in ruination' but also in the fact of its 'afterlife', in the way it changes (see Gilloch 1997: 196). And, as Caygill says in discussing Benjamin's specific preoccupation with the Parisian arcade: '"in the process of becoming and disappearance" [it] discloses and conceals aspects of itself. As an origin, the arcade does not possess a fixed character, but reveals different aspects of itself through the passage of time' (1998: 133). Hence, Tacheles articulates rupture and disappearance *as well as* continuity. It is not that every edifice should or indeed can 'be like it', but by making manifest this ongoing process of transformation, the building issues a challenge to the many other building projects of the new Berlin, one that contests their role in the general forging of a refunctioned identity for the city.

Notes

1. The area was also referred to as 'the Birmingham of (the Mark) Brandenburg' (Enke 1999: 52).

2. The Borsig account is one of a series of radio broadcasts made by Benjamin for young people in Berlin between 1927 and 1933. Resembling in content his *flâneur*-friend Franz Hessel's reports on aspects of the city, collected in *Ein Flaneur in Berlin* (1984), they are described by Susan Buck-Morss as pedagogic in their purpose, teaching audiences 'to read both the urban landscape and the literary text generated within it as expressions of social history'. In this regard she points also to the influence of Brecht, likening the broadcasts' combined form of entertainment and education to his practice (1989: 35).

3. Spandau itself forms a large borough in the western-most part of Berlin. *Vorstadt* means 'suburb', literally 'pre-city'.

4. As Large reports, a 1985 West Berlin ruling on street names was extended to include the whole city after reunification. It stipulated 'the removal of those street names from the period 1945 to 1989 [honouring] active opponents of democracy and also intellectual-political precursors and defenders of Stalinist tyranny, the GDR regime and other unjust Communist regimes'. Seventy-five changes in the eastern half of the city were duly made without resistance, '[b]ut as time went on, with more and more Communist heroes losing their places of honour on the municipal map, East Berliners with ties to the old system began to complain that the Wessis were trying to rob them of an important part of their collective identity'. When conservative politicians in the city proposed a blanket removal of communist-related names, legislation had to be introduced which stated 'that communists who had died too soon to help bring Weimar down, or the GDR up, should not be purged, thus sparing Marx, Bebel, Luxemburg, and Liebknecht' (Large 2002: 560–1).

5. In 1997 the British artists Jane and Louise Wilson made a video installation entitled *Stasi City* based on their experiences of both the Normannen Strasse headquarters and the *Stasi* prison at Hohenschönhausen. The latter was a sizeable complex buried within the confines of a residential neighbourhood in which no one had been aware of its activities. As such it embodied in concrete form the notion of the lurking presence of the secret state within the everyday. For photographic documentation by the artists and critical analysis of this piece see Doherty and Millar (2000).

6. *Ampelmännchen* literally means something like 'lights (or signal) chappie', but it also cross-refers to *Hampelmännchen*, a jumping jack. In fact, an appropriate translation for *Ampelmännchen* might be 'jumping jack flash'.

7. *Ostalgie* is a popular coinage which coalesces the notion of nostalgia for the east (eastalgia, if you like). As Richie points out in the introduction to her history of the city, the phenomenon has serious implications: it 'has become the new scourge of Berlin, turning the city into a battleground over the history of the GDR' (1998: xli).

8. More precisely, the GDR leader Walter Ulbricht authorised the removal of Stalin's name as a mark of gratitude to Khrushchev for getting the Warsaw Pact countries to sanction the erection of a wire fence between East and West Berlin, presaging the eventual Wall itself (Large 2002: 449–50). A massive statue of Stalin outside number 70, once a site of high veneration, was simultaneously removed. Stalin Allee, which had previously been called Frankfurter Allee, was renamed Karl Marx Allee as far east as Frankfurter Tor, another former gateway to the city where it turned into Frankfurter Allee again (Enke 1999: 244).

9. Rebiger points out that the GDR's sudden interest in the restoration and acknowledgement of Jewish installations at the time was an opportunistic foreign policy tactic, a last ditch move, as history testifies, to stimulate trade relations with the USA (Rebiger 2000: 79).

10. Richie, however, maintains that the whole event, though ostensibly a reprisal for the killing by a Jewish youth of a German diplomat in Paris, had been pre-planned by Goebbels and succeeded in its execution:

The fire brigade was on full alert to prevent damage to adjoining 'Aryan' property [...] Nine out of twelve large Berlin synagogues were plundered and destroyed that night, including the magnificent synagogue on Oranienburger Strasse, which was consumed as Berlin fire-fighters stood by and watched.

(1999: 430)

Given that Krützfeld was subsequently inexplicably sidelined and retired early by the Nazis (Rebiger 2000: 77), to say nothing of the fact that his act of heroism was later brought to light and commemorated in 1995 with a plaque on the facade of the synagogue, it is difficult not to conclude that Richie has believed the version of events peddled by the international press after the war.

11. Connolly reports that 'Germany's constitution allows those parties to be outlawed which are deemed to be undemocratic [...] Like other recognised parties in Germany it [the NPD] receives state funding' (2002: 4).

12. The *Wehrmacht* exhibition's Berlin opening was actually a re-launch after a two-year interval. Originally the exhibition, curated by the Hamburg Institute for Social Research, had begun touring German towns and cities in 1995 amidst criticism that its principal message, implicating the ordinary footsoldier in atrocities, was misleading. Provoking heated debates in parliament, the exhibition was eventually pulled on a technicality: the incorrect titling of certain photographs. The re-opened Berlin exhibition had been thoroughly revised, growing to twice its size and concentrating on explanatory texts rather than photographs, whilst retaining its central thesis. Amongst the criticisms originally articulated was that it had been put together by sociologists rather than historians, a point taken seriously by its curators in the reworking, with a panel of historians being commissioned to verify its authenticity (Geithe 2001: 72–3).

13. The PDS is the eastern-based party of democratic socialism, which effectively replaced the old GDR socialist unity party (SED) and at the time was rapidly gaining ground as the only political party in Germany that would truly represent the concerns of the eastern populace. After Berlin elections in October 2001 it eventually emerged, following protracted talks, as the partner in a grand 'red-red' coalition with the SPD, the German social democratic party. Though there are profound reservations about the PDS's lingering links with unreconstructed ideologues of the old GDR regime – Gysi himself has been outed as a *Stasi* informer – many feel that an exclusion of the PDS from local government would have represented a dangerous escalation of the ongoing alienation perceived by the eastern half of the city, 48 per cent of which voted for the PDS.

The considerable success of the party in the capital was felt at the time to have significant implications for the national elections to be held in September 2002. If it forced itself into the limelight, it would prove a thorn in the side to a returned SPD, the latter having stated its refusal to enter into a similar coalition at national level. The PDS still held 'awkward' leftist views such as resistance, after 11 September 2001, to prosecuting a terrorist witch-hunt in Afghanistan. As it happens, the fear proved unfounded. Gysi resigned from his post in the summer preceding the elections for curiously 'mild' reasons. Admitting that he had inadvertently put air miles acquired on business trips to private use, he attempted to bow out with the dignity of the 'honest, repentant man, doing the decent thing'. Whether there were 'other' reasons, such as his being fed up with trying to resolve Berlin's dire financial problems, or some more substantial 'skeleton' from which he may have been distracting attention, is unclear.

14. *Urban Diary* was organised by Friedrich von Borries. It ran for 100 days with all messages sent being logged on the Internet. The original idea stems from a collective of Berlin architects, artists and designers called rude_architecture (see *Zitty Berlin*, no. 24, 15–28 November, p. 8).

15. See Irina Liebman's *Berliner Mietshaus* (Berlin: Berliner Taschenbuch Verlag, 2002), for a documentary account of the varied lives of one particular tenement building in East Berlin's Prenzlauer Berg district during the early 1980s.

16. In fact, looking at an older Falk-Plan, its 42nd edition, which has no date but probably appeared some time in the late 1970s, 'colonialist advertising' is already in evidence in the form of the Mercedes Benz logo, indicating showrooms and garages in West Berlin. It's safe to assume that during the Cold War, this kind of practice would have played its part in the general ideological points-scoring that went on between the two halves of the city. Both 'sides' happily used any excuse they could find to underscore the superiority of their respective systems, not least in their building programmes. The TV tower is a clear example of that in the east, whilst the 22-storey Europa Centre – with a rotating neon Mercedes star on its roof epitomised western competitiveness (see chapter six).

5. Grosse Hamburger Strasse: the Space of Disappearance

Identity freezes the gesture of thinking. It pays homage to an order. To think, on the contrary, is to pass through; it is to question that order, to marvel that it exists, to wonder what made it possible, to seek in passing over its landscape traces of the movement that formed it, to discover in these histories supposedly laid to rest 'how and to what extent it would be possible to think otherwise'.

(Michel de Certeau, Heterologies)

Benjamin writes: '[…] There is no document of civilisation that is not at the same time a document of barbarism' (1999: 258). The monument is precisely such a 'document'. [It] is doubly mythic: in its evocation of a false history and in its proclamation of its own permanence. The monument is petrified myth. To break its spell, it must be critically unmasked as a historical form, embodying particular articulations of past and present.

(Graeme Gilloch, Myth and Metropolis)

Void Space

Approaching Hackescher Markt, Oranienburger Strasse – for the most part a broad boulevard with glistening yellow trams gliding up and down it – takes a slight zig to the left and becomes an awkward little one-way street. On one occasion, to get some relief from the continuous straggle of pedestrians bumping and grinding its way through the bottleneck produced by narrow pavements, parked cars, building work, boutiques and café-bars, I take a left turn down an innocuous-looking side-street. Grosse Hamburger Strasse it says at the corner. My Falk map of the city tells me there's a corresponding *Kleine* Hamburger Strasse nearby, the 'big' street's little counterpart. No indication on the map of a McDonald's outlet, though it would surely present itself as the ideal location to colonise or, indeed, rename (Big Mac Strasse). Instead, not far up the street there's a police officer to be spied once again, seemingly standing guard. My curiosity aroused I approach a large, off-white building enclosed in heavy-duty iron fencing with closed-circuit television cameras

15.

covering its perimeter. Number 27, the former Jewish *Knabenschule* (boys school), as the inscription over its portal declares. It became mixed in 1931 but only returned to being Jewish after reunification, although, befitting of its location on what was once known as 'Tolerance Street', it accepts other denominations, too (Herzogenrath 1990: 84). Does the security just become a way of life, the police officer you pass at the gate as unseen to you as the images privately picked up on CCTV? I didn't see the lollipop lady who used to halt the traffic for me twice daily outside my school till she was knocked down one day (by someone else who didn't see her), and then I never saw her again. But that hardly seems the same. When I begin to take photographs, the police officer watches me closely and I stop, not because I am afraid of what she might say or do but simply because I feel guilty. Everyone, it seems, wants to have a piece of this 'Jewish reality'. What exactly am I photographing? The spectre of history looking to repeat itself?

Directly opposite the school there is a gap in the neo-baroque block of tenement buildings, a house-size gap, which nevertheless has a number. Or two, in fact: 15–16. When the twin towers of the World Trade Centre in New York were destroyed, one of the witnesses, whose balcony overlooked the scene from a safe distance, described the effect graphically as reminding him instinctively of the time as a child when he had had his two front teeth knocked out. This is more like a missing molar. Numbers 15–16 took a direct hit in the spring of 1945. In 1990 the French artist Christian Boltanski chose the void as the site for an installation which he entitled *The Missing House*.[1] Wander into it and you see, running vertically up the walls on either side, sutures of exposed brickwork where the tenement's basic structure has been ruptured. It's like a searing wound that's been stitched. On each of the blank walls there are large plaques with the names and occupations of the building's last inhabitants, situated at the point where their apartments used to be: G. Jacobi, salesman; A. Porteset, clerk; H. Budzislawski, poultry merchant. (There's even a J. Springer, salesman.) This is Boltanski's installation. Not all the occupants were Jews, but most. In Samira Gloor-Fadel's documentary film *Berlin – Cinéma* (1999), which is about the film director Wim Wenders' relationship to film-making and the changing city, the latter refers to Boltanski's installation as a wailing wall. His own wail is that these walls offer precisely the kind of memorial no longer available to Berlin citizens in relation to *the* Wall, of which there is virtually no trace now. It came down too quickly and comprehensively, according to Wenders. You could say it is a void that doesn't exist. There is no recovering wound, neither stitching nor scar. It's an undesirable monument, erased and the space of its absence filled.

Boltanski's *Missing House* is effectively the aesthetic inverse of the piece that was Rachel Whiteread's *House* at 193 Grove Road in Tower Hamlets, London. Whilst Boltanski makes his mark by drawing attention to the curiosity of vacant space presenting itself unexpectedly in a heavily built-up residential part of the inner-city, Whiteread marked the interior space of a terrace house by filling it with concrete and removing its exterior walls. Thus she emphasised both the absence *around* her house – the other houses in the terrace that had disappeared – and the dense, continuing presence of what was previously enclosed space. In a sense it was the inverse of what was *once* there, homely air made solid, a plasticised negative. What is 'there' in Whiteread – including the 'air' that is the rest of the terrace – is 'not there' in Boltanski, but both are offering the same kind of contemplative staging of a mourning for something which has gone, a memorialising process of making strange. Since *House* was removed and the area turfed over on the orders of Tower Hamlets council in 1994, there really is nothing tangible left to remind you either of the original house or Whiteread's installation. So a form of double voiding has occurred there. Whiteread's *House* has itself turned into a missing house, remembered only as part of an event which passed.[2] A missing house that is missed, like the people in Grosse Hamburger Strasse. As Jon Bird suggests: 'Memorials freeze-frame historical narrative, cutting through the web of events to single out a moment (an incident, an individual) which then becomes the personification of memory itself' (Lingwood 1995: 117). (Perhaps the bomb-aimer who successfully saw off numbers 15–16 used to live at 193 Grove Road, Tower Hamlets.) Going on to suggest that 'the only viable forms of public memory are those that embody paradox and the ephemeral', Bird might be describing the Brechtian *Gestus*, or what Benjamin came to refer to as the 'dialectic at a standstill' (Benjamin 1977: 13). Moreover, Bird contrasts memorials with official public monuments which 'tend to speak the voice of authority [...] a representation of power in symbolic form, documents of a culture's historical experience, [providing] instruction into the official narratives of the past' (1995: 116–17). Hence, where the latter proceeds from a closed perspective of supposed 'full seeing', the former draws attention to that which would disturb this gaze.

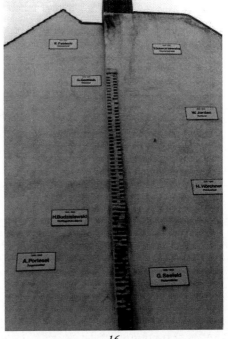

16.

It's productive in this respect to compare Boltanski's *Missing House* to the Neue Synagogue merely a stone's throw away. Not many in Berlin would deny the Jewish community its right to restore the historical centrepiece of its presence in the city and memorialise the stark truths of its destruction. Even if it no longer functions as a place of worship, its symbolic parameters have simply shifted. It now stands as an open site for the preservation and promotion of Jewish culture generally. Perhaps the most important feature of its current presence, then, is the *fact* of its rehabilitation, the taking place of some form of regenerative *movement*. My concern here lies with the situating of the visitor or spectator. If there is one thing that is noteworthy – paradoxically – about Boltanski's installation, it is its discreet quality. Grosse Hamburger Strasse continues to function as an ordinary street with residents and local amenities, ranging from cafés and newsagents to a hospital and church. I nearly walked past the *Missing House* without registering it. And it is not even particularly accessible. Frequently when I have visited, the gate, which serves also as the entrance to apartment buildings on either side, has been locked. The special quality the piece has is the way it produces an unsettling effect initially, one in which the rationale for the piece eventually begins to *dawn* on you. But before that moment even, it is a site you must *locate*. This occurs on the one hand by happening upon it and being willing to pursue its allure, a phenomenon which the Jewish academic James E. Young refers to as a *Stein des Anstosses* or 'stumbling block' (1994: 29).[3] On the other hand it implies being prepared to go off the beaten track a little in the first place. Both experiences produce the sense of an encounter with something out of the ordinary. Citing Pierre Nora, Young underlines the prerequisite for this procedure as the 'will to remember' without which 'the place of memory "created in the play of memory and history [...] becomes indistinguishable from the place of history"' (23). It is not that the Neue Synagoge is indiscreet, then, it is more to do with the way it attempts to assert rather than facilitate presence and memory: 'Never forget'. The message projects a perception of memory as an object rather than a medium or process, a fixed phenomenon, even a metaphorical cane with which to whack you. No room for manoeuvre there, except to run away. Or, as we have seen in the case of the neo-Nazi rally, to interpret it perversely from your own extremist perspective. In both instances its performative intention is contradicted.

Moving Monuments

As a member of the architectural jury charged with choosing an appropriate design for a Holocaust memorial in the centre of Berlin, Young warned of the dangers of 'the finished monument that suggests an end to memory itself, puts a cap on memory-work' (Wise 1998: 154). Of course we're not really talking here exclusively about a Jewish issue at all. What Young seems to be identifying are effectively two forms of monument, one 'static' – an object – the other 'in motion', an event. The categorisation of a monument as either of these depends on a range of variable factors. For one, there is the degree to which designated monuments offer a kind of excess space around themselves. Those that do presuppose that what they present relies on a relationship with an interlocutor. Monuments that do not afford space are essentially fixed in their conception, representations that desire a single thing to be thought or felt about them. The obvious – crass – examples here are those old socialist realist monuments of revolutionary heroes with which the whole of Cold War Eastern Europe was adorned. They've caused considerable controversy since 1989, not only regarding the political question of whether or not they should remain but also the practical one relating to the sheer cost of removing them. In fact, the latter concern can easily outweigh the former. The ambiguous GDR hero Ernst Thälmann – the loyal Stalinist leader of the Communist party in Germany in the 1920s and 30s, who became a victim of the Nazis – is a case in point. His huge, bombastic monument on Greifswalder Strasse was left in place in the end because of the prohibitive costs of its demolition (Ladd 1998: 201–3).[4]

17.

Particularly pertinent, though, as Michael Z. Wise points out, is the tendency, not only in the old East but in Germany as a whole, towards 'simplistic semiotic equations' in which 'the symbol [is taken] for the reality itself' (1998: 19), the signifier for the signified. Wise suggests that 'the debate itself [is] far more effective than any physical monument' (154). And Laura Mulvey's citation of Musil's verdict on monuments warns of the paradoxical *forgetting* or disappearance that a lack of significant interactivity can induce. (It recalls, moreover, Benjamin's reference to objects 'looking back', in this case withholding their gaze.) Thus: 'The most striking feature of monuments is that you do not notice them. There is nothing in the world as invisible as monuments [...In fact] we should say that they de-notice us. They withdraw from our senses' (Leach 1999: 220). Young, too, talks of the significance of dialogue in the actual constitution of any aesthetic memorialisation: the 'art consists in the ongoing activity of memory, in the debates surrounding these memorials, in our own participation in the memorial's performance' (1994: 39).

Ironically, though, the exhaustive to-and-fro of discussion can also produce fatigue it seems, as the Holocaust memorial project in which Young himself participated as a consultant adjudicator testifies. Actually a broader memorial to the murder of European Jews, it was initiated as long ago as 1988. Since then it has gone through two competitions – Chancellor Kohl did not approve of the original winner – and multi-faceted debates which take in its positioning, size, funding, aesthetics, subject-matter and, not least, its necessity. In 1999, after a debate in parliament that produced only a narrow majority, the memorial was given approval on condition it add a public information centre. Boasting the size and dimensions of several football pitches it will occupy a prime position between Brandenburger Tor and Potsdamer Platz. The second round winners were named in 1997 as the architect Peter Eisenmann in collaboration with the sculptor Richard Serra. The latter soon withdrew, however, over adverse criticism particularly of its monumental scale. Other points of contention are its failure to include other groupings subject to Nazi persecution and the fear that, given its prominent location, it will simply serve as a meaningless 'dumping ground' for the commemorative wreaths of visiting VIPs (Rebiger 2000: 154). The last point in particular begins to gesture towards the dangerous potential of inertia creeping in: not only of it being one Holocaust memorial too far, but also of the protracted wrangling producing public indifference.[5]

What's interesting about the Thälmann monument – to return to it for a moment – is the way it's been 'set in motion' since the fall of the Wall by becoming swathed in graffiti. Whilst it still carries the trace of its former celebratory function, it has been 'interfered with' and thus refunctioned for a new era, now standing as a monument of wounded discontent. Moreover, a discernible shift in the graffiti's expressive tenor seems to be indicative of the political mood as the decade since 1989 has worn on, swinging from public indignation to a form of private resignation. Ladd provides evidence of early 1990s counter-propaganda on the monument. On the one hand, this revealed a graffiti of protest, summing up in terms as one-dimensional as the monument itself embitterment over the state's handling of both Thälmann himself and the memory of him: 'imprisoned – murdered – besmeared'. On the other hand, he cites a strategy of resistance based on sarcastic fun-poking at the sheer, vainglorious scale of the monument: 'Don't you have it in a larger size?' (Ladd 1998: 202). All there is now is the nihilistic smear of personal signatures. Involuntarily, then, as a consequence of events in history, the Thälmann monument has spawned interlocutors who have forced a change in its identity. Monolithic as it may be, it now stands – or wobbles – as a signpost of existing political instabilities. In fact Rachel Whiteread suggested a similar interpretation of graffiti's purpose on the occasion of the unveiling of the controversial *Holocaust Memorial* at Vienna's Juden Platz in October 2000: 'A few daubed swastikas would really make people think about what is happening in their society, their culture. I certainly don't want to encourage it, but if it happens, it happens' (Searle 2000: 12). Here, it is the deconstruction of the symbol that produces – to invoke Wise's terminology again – a 'debate' which you might call 'the reality'.

Whilst Thälmann has been given a new identity, other former GDR monuments were systematically removed after reunification. It has been a process of 'memorial undoing' recorded by the artist ethnographer Sophie Calle in her collection of texts and photographs entitled *The Detachment* (1997) or *Die Entfernung* in German (literally both the 'removal' or the 'distance'). The work is based on visiting locations in the former East Berlin where the iconography of GDR history has been effaced. There she would photograph the absent space, ask passers-by and residents to describe the missing object concerned, and substitute descriptions of their memories in its place. Superficially, then, Calle's work is about the fading memory of the GDR, lost objects or symbols which remain alive only in the collective recollections of its former populace. However, as Griffin observes, the monuments in question related to the 'various legitimating narratives of the GDR, in particular, the myth of the GDR as a state founded on anti-fascism [in which] the Holocaust was simply an episode in the Nazi oppression of international communism'. The East Berliners' descriptions reveal the extent to which the removal of those official displacements of memory has produced its own form of withdrawal for its former citizens, a psychological distancing 'arising from a population's collective memory that has been undone' (Griffin 2000: 169). The void addressed by Calle's publication 'circumscribes [...] not the absence left by a state's demise but the absence of a murdered people. In the displaced causality at work in the GDR, the ethnic specificity of the Holocaust is sublimated by the fiction of anti-fascism' (170). Framing the detached (removed) monument in this way brings to light the historical detachment (distancing) that has taken place as well as the resultant vacuum produced for those implicated in the reconfiguration.

The Space of Encounter

Unlike the Neue Synagoge in Oranienburger Strasse, Daniel Libeskind's Jewish Museum is not 'merely a stone's throw' from Grosse Hamburger Strasse. It is, though, similarly a gathering point for the historical existence of a Jewish presence (as well as absence) in the city of Berlin. But where the axes of history appear to come to a dead stop under the vast gilded dome of the former synagogue, Libeskind's building looks to function as a transitional node, an asymmetrical crossroads within a complex continuum of spatio-temporal and textual 'lines'. In fact, the museum suspends itself, and therefore directs us, between those lines – in accordance with its formal 'subtitle'[6] – as they converge and cross, and carry on. And it is not simply Jewish culture that is at stake here but, as some commentators have hinted, the identity of the city as a whole. If there is a single architectural project relating to the reconfiguration of the 'New Berlin' of the late twentieth century that would seem to epitomise the transitional status of the city 'as void in relation to memory and history' (Huyssen 1997: 75), it is Libeskind's construction. It offers 'an emblematic reading of the city itself' (Balfour 1995: 183), one which also seems to crystallise many if not all of the issues I have been raising so far in this chapter with regard to specific installations or institutions. Moreover, if it is a reading – and therefore a writing – of the city, its methodological principle corresponds to the Benjaminian encounter with the traces of history within the walked space of the present that similarly informs the practice of this book. The building also replicates the recurring theme of 'porosity' in Benjamin's writings. Emerging in his observations of 'Naples life' (1997: 167–176) as blurring the boundaries between indoor and outdoor existence, an interpenetration of the room and the street, here, as Schneider suggests, 'it is an urban spatial experience that can be gained [...] only from the inside of this building [...]: the experience of the building not merely as an extension of the museum, but as an extension of the city; as a city within the building' (Libeskind 1997: 124). In fact, the building's reference to Benjamin is quite direct; his oblique textual topography of the city in *One-Way Street* served as one of the structural mappings underpinning Libeskind's overall architectural conceit. The irregular zigzag outline of the museum – a lightening bolt which takes its cue from a distorted Star of David – is made up of a continuous sequence of sixty sections 'each of which represents one of the "stations of the star" described in the text of Walter Benjamin' (Libeskind 2001: 26). It's a text which adopts the form of a speculative meander, each section 'frequently beginning', in Köppler's suggestion, 'with the description of something seen, to then consistently go over to free reflections of a philosophical, historical or political nature' (Museumspädagogischer Dienst Berlin 2000: 109). So, as Vidler concludes, 'there is in the Jewish Museum an implied architectural reading of Benjamin' (2000: 238).

Traversing the zigzag husk from within is a straight but interrupted line of 'voids'. Visible only through internal windows, it is an inaccessible, enclosed vacuum which refers to the ruptures and gaps of the Jewish presence in the cultural evolution of the city, ultimately of Germany. Two lines, then,

> [o]ne straight but broken into fragments; the other tortuous but continuing into infinity. As the lines develop themselves through this limited-infinite 'dialectic', they also fall apart – become disengaged – and show themselves as separated so that the void centrally running through what is continuous materialises itself outside as ruined, or rather as the solid residue of independent structure, i.e. as a voided-void.

(Libeskind 2001: 29)

The built form of both lines takes its place within a conceptual network that has traced connections on a street map of Berlin between the one-time addresses of both Jewish and non-Jewish luminaries in the cultural history of the city: Heinrich Heine, Mies van der Rohe, Heinrich von Kleist, Paul Celan to name a few; an invisible topography of artistic and intellectual life. Libeskind draws an analogy with the mythical *Berliner Luft* – that heady, world city atmosphere of chaos and invention (generally associated with the Weimar period): 'These people constitute the *Berliner Luft* – the air across Berlin which mixes with the air of history to shape the city. For those who are aware of it, it is extremely palpable; however, for those who are unaware of it, the air is there nevertheless' (Libeskind 2000: 21). Effectively Libeskind takes up Brecht's proposal in his poem 'Of Poor BB' – that 'Of those cities will remain what passed through them, the Wind!' (1976: 108) – delineating the traces of this memorial air in Berlin. Overall the joined coordinates allow an elongated Star of David to emerge, a fixed form, but the lines of continuity extend through and beyond both the concrete manifestation or 'evidence' of the museum building and the imagined Star itself. One-way streets.

A further conceptual overlaying witnesses a similar matrix of addresses being drawn. In this case it is based on the homes and final destinations of deported Berlin Jews, culled from the *Gedenkbuch*, two volumes containing 'lists and lists of names, dates of birth, dates of deportation, and presumed places where these people were murdered [...] in Riga, in the Lodz ghetto, in concentration camps' (Libeskind 2001: 26).[7] These 'deathlines' slash across and into the armour of the museum's zinc-clad husk at various points and angles. The wounds that remain, irregular cuts and gouges, form windows which bleed daylight into the interior in an ever-changing play of natural illumination. Libeskind's inspiration for this idea, as well as that of the 'void', has its source in his witnessing of the vast but blank marble slabs of family tombstones at Berlin's largest Jewish cemetery, Weissensee. Not only was there 'no one left to visit' but there was 'almost no evidence of Hebrew letters or symbols [...] it was built, somehow, for the future of a community which hardly had any future' (Libeskind 2000: 37). Like Boltanski's *Missing House*, in which the names of a disappeared community have been restored (by chasing up archival records), effectively as gravestone epitaphs marking a void, Libeskind has looked to inscribe the 'traces of the gone' in his building, 'an absence which is structured in the city' and, finally, 'in the topography of a country' (Libeskind 2001: 204). At the same time his concern is with the 'traces of the unborn': to those who might have been, to the discontinuities of history. Picking up the tab of that voided potential points restoratively to a future, one that might be better. Similar to Gilloch's observation of Benjamin's work, so Libeskind's building can be said to strive to be 'situated at the intersection of immanence and redemption'. And 'from forgetfulness, remembrance is to be won' (1997: 183–4).

Originally – shortly before the Wall came down – the Jewish Museum was commissioned as an extension to the existing Berlin Museum, concerned with portraying the cultural history of the city as a whole. That had been founded in West Berlin in the 1960s as a counterpoint to the Märkisches Museum, which performed a similar function but had ended up in the eastern sector of the city. As was typical generally after 1989, Berlin found itself with two institutions replicating one another's practices. So a decision was taken in 1995 to give over entirely the then Berlin Museum building, a former Prussian courthouse on Linden Strasse, to the Jewish Museum initiative. In doing so, its conception shifted to encompass the

18.

evolution of Jewish culture in Germany as a whole, viewed through the optic of Berlin history (Museumspädagogischer Dienst Berlin 2000: 25–6).

As I stand across the street from the museum for the first time – in the summer of 2000, when it is still completely empty but open for viewing – the crass disjuncture of well-preserved, proportional baroque on the one hand and 'neurotic' late-twentieth century blitz on the other, is all too apparent. There is a narrow gap between the two buildings, as if the latter had been repelled by the former: static electricity in search of a home, the present looking for somewhere to let the past go – not to say, *let go of the past* (in the sense of processing it). In Benjamin's notes based on conversations with Brecht in 1934 – when they spent extended periods of time together in Denmark as exiled friends – he argues that 'the true measure of life is memory. Looking back, it traverses the whole of life like lightening' (1977: 112). Here the lightening bolt has been momentarily frozen: Benjamin's 'dialectic at a standstill'. Or, to invoke its Brechtian correlative in the form of the *Gestus*: an unexpected 'zigzag development' of contradictions and instabilities of circumstance arising in social relations and experience (Willett 1978: 277). The theatrical analogy is appropriate; Benjamin suggests in his 'Berlin Chronicle' that 'memory is not an instrument for exploring the past but its theatre' (1997: 314), and that is precisely the premise for the visitor's interaction with Libeskind's museum. It is a heuristic encounter in which spectators importantly become aware of their place in a retroactive drama. Embedded in this process a particular relationship to history is implied. As Gilloch points out, for Benjamin the

dialectical image 'is rooted in [a] rejection of historicism'. It is 'a pause, a moment of interruption and illumination, in which past and present recognise each other across the void which separates them'. It is when, quoting Benjamin from his *Arcades Project*, 'the Then and the Now come into a constellation like a flash of lightening [...] The Then must be held fast as it flashes its lightening image in the Now of recognisability' (Gilloch 1997: 113). Hence, memory is associated with an active moment of awakening or insight. And, as Burgin formulates it, it is a return that implies change:

> Forward movement in life is achieved through a backward movement in memory, but one that is more than a simple temporal regression. In place of the blocked nostalgia or nausea of the perpetual return, the past is transformed in such processes as 'working through' and 'deferred action'. This is what must be involved in Bhaba's '*performance* that is iterative and interrogative – a repetition that is *initiatory*, instating a differential history that will not return to the power of the Same' [...] We are accustomed to believe that *forgetting* is precisely that which it is most important to resist. (Are we to forget slavery, forget the Holocaust?) But if we understand Benjamin's 'forgetting' to correspond to the unbinding of the 'signifying sequence' that has become symptomatically knotted, to a process of reinscription of the past in the present, then we may allow that nothing is *lost* in the process.
>
> *(1996: 273–4)*

I'm still standing opposite the museum when, like a theatre foyer's three-minute call to enter the auditorium, a harsh bell suddenly rings out. But this one persists and sends the audience in the opposite direction. Figures come crawling out of unexpected chinks in the zinc-work and within minutes there are a dozen wailing fire engines blocking off the street, hoses at the ready. This is a high-voltage

19.

emergency. How can empty space burn, I find myself wondering. On the other hand, memory is there to be extinguished. Libeskind's design is attributable to an early installation work of his entitled *Line of Fire*. And according to one commentator, the museum is like 'a branding or tattoo that has burned a fireline into the location' (Museumspädagogischer Dienst Berlin 2000: 28). Imagery of physical scarring rightly abounds in relation to the building. It is surely no coincidence that its external appearance also seems to replicate the 'classic' aesthetic style of jagged, silvery graffiti. So prevalent in the cityscape of Berlin, graffiti can also be said to be performing a kind of poetics of disappearance (see chapter six). Fortunately it is a minor incident of no consequence – visiting electricians in the basement – merely a dramatic prelude to entering this highly performative space.

Libeskind's building has no visible doorway. Entry is gained via the former courthouse: 'Programmatically, it is important to enter the baroque Berlin with all its rich history and then descend through the entrance void to the underground connections' (Libeskind 2001: 26). It is a descent into the dark, distorted realm of twentieth century experience, a Benjaminian labyrinth 'pushed back from the normal distance of vision, in a collapse or multiplication of the point of view that seems coordinated to a parallel collapse of perspective in the world' (Vidler 2000: 240). Memory is the performative medium of past experience 'as the ground is the medium in which dead cities lie interred. He who seeks to approach his own buried past must conduct himself like a man digging' (Benjamin 1997: 314). Thus, the visitor's descent into the depths of the Jewish Museum is, as Gilloch says of Benjamin's approach to the city in his 'A Berlin Chronicle', like the archaeologist's dig, 'delving beneath the surface of the modern city and the modern sensibility it engenders' (Gilloch 1997: 70). Empty as it is, its interior functions almost like a ruin before its time: a raw concrete edifice that looks as if it's got a past when officially it hasn't even been born. A pre-life that appears as an after-life. And it is a subterranean city that presents a series of shocks or, to recall Young's terms, 'stumbling blocks'. On this day, the first is the strict security frisking, manual and electronic, before entering. As visitors we are all terrorists until proven innocent. Again, I think: this building is empty. But it does remind you of the regular attacks that have occurred on Jewish institutions in the city. A contract is thereby made; our minds are concentrated.

Arriving underground there are three 'one-way streets' from which to choose, corridors representing annihilation, exile and continuity, each with a certain destination. The axis of exile is the dialectical pause – a displacement – between death (annihilation) and life (continuity). It leads to a dense, square forest of 49 leaning stelae with olive willows growing out of their tops. The ground on which you tread is awkwardly sloped and framed by odd perspectival angles to effect the disconcerting experience of topographical disorientation. *Terra incognita*. It's also called the E.T.A. Hoffmann garden, he being one of Berlin's most renowned (nineteenth century) writers. (Freud's theory of 'the uncanny' is based on his short story 'The Sandman'.) As it happens he was also a lawyer who lived nearby and practised in the *Kollegienhaus*, the baroque court house that is now one part of the Jewish Museum.[8] The E.T.A. Hoffmann garden of exile, a disconcerting crowd of concrete pillars, a labyrinth affording little elbow room to the 'out of place' wanderer.

The axis of continuity by contrast leads up a steep staircase, six flights altogether, the light growing steadily brighter as you ascend. From the foot it looks as if there is no end to it; as you reach the top and turn left into the upper exhibition area, a few steps, leading nowhere but a blank wall, carry on. The future is an unmarked space; all you can believe is that it will happen. Our group – for on this visit it is a requirement to be guided round – shuffles first along the right-turning axis of annihilation. As we approach a large, black door, the angled dimensions of the corridor literally begin to close in. It is getting darker. Something appears to be shutting down. Not merely a one-way street, then, but a dead end. You could say all our group would need now would be overcoats with yellow stars and battered suitcases to complete the picture. But this is precisely not some spurious empathy with the past with which we're being invited to identify, a hypothetical stepping-into-the-shoes of victims in some highly ephemeral play-acting scenario devised so as 'to really feel what it was like'. Just before we enter through the heavy steel door of the

20.

so-called Holocaust tower, I notice another barred door immediately to the left. It has a sign, which translates as: 'Escape exit. Security alarmed. Open only in case of emergency'. A staggering irony – all the more so for its lack of intention – which you might condemn retrospectively as insensitive, but which poignantly suggested to me the distinction between a past moment when that was *definitely not an option* and the apparent theatricality of the present event. An everyday detail or 'slip', that which would be marginal or incidental – between the lines of the primary text – actually brought into focus what the space of the building was trying to frame for me; but it was the framing itself, the invitation to *sense*, that permitted the detail to emerge resonantly in the first place. The lines produce the space between.

Our guide tells us we will spend three minutes in the tower. In that time no one in the group of fifteen moves or utters a word. It is 24 metres high, a four-sided but irregular enclosure of raw concrete walls. Its only source of light is a narrow, open-air slit high up at the western-most end of the blackened ceiling. Coupled with its being unheated, the tower is thus subject to the elemental fluctuations of daily and seasonal cycles. Muffled sounds resonate from the outside: children playing, the rush of city traffic, a squawking crow. They sound distant in time and space, yet are actually near, like Benjamin's 'Then in the Now'. As my eyes accustom themselves to the gloom, I can make out the rungs of a ladder attached to one wall. It is there for maintenance and technical purposes, but there seems to be only one thought you can have: escape. Appropriately the rungs begin too far up to be reached. Ultimately, we stand still and silent in little more than an unlit, bare concrete tower, but the *weight* of the moment is palpable. The space invites us to accord it poignancy. But it is only an invitation. On a later visit, when parts of the empty museum have become closed to the public to make way for exhibits to be sited, guided tours are no longer obligatory. Large numbers of Japanese tourists roam freely on this day, excited to be 'safely not home'. A friend and I spend about fifteen minutes in the Holocaust tower. It might have been longer but for the repeated intrusion of visitors entering, visibly wondering what on earth they were supposed to be looking at, and leaving again quickly. Perhaps it was because it was too dark to take pictures. The failure to capture via photography threatens the emergence of a narrative void within the economy of the touristic order, one that cannot be tolerated. Photos evidence presence, even conquest; if you cannot produce them, you were not there, or: where you were was not significant. I rationalise my irritation as over-preciousness: with my admiration for the architecture, with 'my historical inheritance'. Why should those from another culture care? When I get home and begin to write in my diary, I realise it is 6 August, 55 years exactly since Hiroshima.

Potentially, then, the Holocaust tower is a 'thinking space', effectively a monument that has been turned inside out. We look at it, but from within; it envelops us in a way that induces us to contemplate our presence there. In a sense it performs in the inverted manner of Whiteread's London *House* or her *Holocaust Memorial* in Vienna: negative space. But where Whiteread solidifies the unseen or departed – thickens the air of history – Libeskind evokes it through enclosing absence: a voided void. In that respect it is an anti-monument, one which counters the stability and outright *visibility* of fixed imagery (and/or ideology) through movement, through its fluid dependence on an interactive, differentiated relationship with its viewer. As Libeskind provocatively (and with a nod to the turn-of-the-century Berlin art historian Karl Scheffler[9]) states in his original competition proposal, which was written between the notational lines of music paper: 'The Museum ensemble is thus always on the verge of Becoming – no longer suggestive of a final solution' (2001: 29).

As a brief postscript to the short-lived circumstances of experiencing the building as an empty space, one feature which astonished me on visiting the completed museum in 2001, with its exhibition of German Jewish History, was an 'interactive' device posing a question requiring, literally, a yes/no push-button response: 'Do attacks on Jewish cemeteries and synagogues arise out of an enduring flaw in the German character?' Well, if they do, there isn't really much hope, I thought. And before I even encroach on the question of nationhood and who might consider themselves to be included under the rubric 'German' – an issue I address elsewhere (see chapter eight) – let me dismiss the question as being precisely of the kind that stops thinking. Seduced into a spurious binarism (as if it were that simple), you punch in your knee-jerk response – and it has to be quick because there are people waiting behind you in the queue – which gets recorded and processed as a percentage statistic. So-and-so many of the visitors to the

21.

museum for or against. (On my visit the responses stood about even.) Like the poll finds of public opinion we are led to make a spontaneous decision without responsibility. In fact, we are positively relieved of it. It is rather about playing the game, a virtual participation that mocks Libeskind's performative template, as well as implicitly dooming its project to redeem the positive from the catastrophic.

Thinking Space

In German there are several words for public monuments, but two in particular would seem to encapsulate what is at issue in the function of memorials. Both are literal in that spade-is-a-spade way which is not untypical for German compound nouns, and which underpins Wise's semiotic observations mentioned earlier. And both contain the word *Mal*, meaning 'mark'. (That in itself is revealing perhaps if related to Whiteread's remarks on graffiti, inasmuch as the latter phenomenon also corresponds to a form of mark making.) The one, *Denkmal*, is literally a mark at which you think (denken). *Mahnmal*, on the other hand, has clear connotations of exhortation, the verb *(er)mahnen* meaning simultaneously to admonish and remind.[10] The space of thinking versus the pointing/wagging finger. It's interesting too perhaps that Brecht was frequently accused of the latter: the prescriptive didact, seeking to convert his audience into committed communists. But, as I've already argued, the writer encouraged various forms of thinking which you could sum up as being positively 'lateral' or 'awkward'. Above all he was keen to situate the spectator, who would perform the reflective part of 'pensive art'. In essence, he sought to implement a mechanism whereby alternative possibilities – of acting otherwise – revealed themselves through the pinpointing of the complex, contradictory nature of situations.

Brecht's own bronze in front of his theatre at Schiffbauerdamm is instructive in this regard. Perhaps it ought to have been entitled 'He who laughs last'. It's a creation fashioned in 1988 by the sculptors Flierl and Cremer shortly before the GDR's last gasp. Cremer in particular is well-known for his idealised portrayals in the 1950s of *Aufbauhelfer*, the strapping workers of East German reconstruction. An inflated Brecht sits upright on his bench meaning to exude global stature, but looking for all the world like death propped up. A *Totenmal* or 'death mark' perhaps. As it happens Cremer produced a death *mask* of Brecht, which seems to have served as the model here (Schumacher 1981: 342). The eyelids have been prised open slightly but the man is clearly in the back of beyond. His bland peasant clothes flap and fold around his body as if it were outsize burial garb in which some undertaker's assistant, who didn't know his size, has dressed him. Oddly enough, Cremer was also responsible for making the steel coffin in which Brecht was buried. Heiner Müller recounts a tale of the sculptor's anxiety over whether Brecht would fit into it since he'd forgotten to take measurements – 'as in the case of [Schiller's] Wallenstein whose legs had to be broken by his conspirators because the coffin was too small' (Müller 1992: 231). Cremer's worries were unfounded as it turned out; they got one of the attendant workers who roughly matched Brecht's height to lie down in the coffin. He fitted, so, Müller quips, '[t]hat was The Measures Taken 1956' (231).[11] But it seems he over-compensated 30 years later when faced with a similar proportional dilemma. Only a slight, wry grimace on Brecht's lips leads you to imagine a hint of mischievous amusement on the writer's part at this portrayal of him. It's unintentional but it redeems the sculpture. A sign of life, like a mummified body whose pierced heart still has a bit of bleeding to do. As Schumacher suggests of the look, it is 'in acquiescence with something that remains secretive, ambiguous' (1981: 313). Brecht is having some kind of cryptic little joke with us from behind death's mask.

In one of the self-contained scenes in Brecht's *Fear and Misery of the Third Reich*, set in 1935, the Jewish wife of a surgeon nervously rehearses the speech she intends to deliver to her Aryan husband on the eve of her departure to Amsterdam. Four times she stops herself and attempts a fresh tactic. Before the audience's eyes, she adopts 'attitudes' – accusatory, self-incriminatory – each one designed in its own way to perform a charade of persuasion. Ultimately, she knows it is a matter of hitting the note which will make it appear there is no choice in the situation but to leave. Her fifth attempt is a *tour de force*, which pulls no punches. She denounces her husband – and the Aryan intelligentsia generally – as hypocritical and lays bare the possibility of this being a leaving which simultaneously marks the end of their relationship. It is the speech her husband should have been subjected to but is not. As she imagines her husband's treachery – 'So don't go telling me, "After all, it's only for two or three weeks", as you hand me the fur coat I shan't need till next winter' (*Plays* 4iii: 51) – he returns home. When the actual conversation ensues, platitudinous as it may be, you are led to wonder whether the husband's integrity hasn't been rather unfairly maligned as the absent 'other' in his wife's rehearsed portrayal. The scene closes, however, with the wife asking her husband to hand her the fur coat. He obliges with precisely the words she predicted. It is an empty gesture, but as a *Gestus* it encapsulates the fatal and inextricable link between the private and political at that moment in history. The betrayal is

22.

one perpetrated by both a husband and a social class, paradoxically couched in caring concern. Symbolically the fur coat represents the antithesis of a wedding ring, a pledge of disloyalty as well as cowardice.

For all the eventual predictability of the husband's response, the scene not only takes you through the process of ordinary but intricate lives and relationships being subtly dismantled before your very eyes – prior to the wife's 'rehearsals' of her speech she has been making farewell phone calls of varying truth to a range of acquaintances – but also places you before the question of alternatives. What if the husband hadn't behaved as forecast? What might he have undertaken? Why, indeed, does the wife not deliver the devastating speech she rehearses? What has she got to lose? And, finally, at what point does resistance begin? In broad terms, history tells us things occurred roughly as the scene portrays them (although the Jewish Museum in Berlin foregrounds prominently the statistic that some 15,000 Jews survived as a consequence of being ensconced in mixed marriages). By the same token (West) Germany has spent over half a century trying to come to terms precisely with the haunting matter of the culpability of its citizens' actions during the Third Reich. (The furore over the *Wehrmacht* exhibition – see chapter four –

is indicative precisely of the extent to which this remains a highly sensitive issue.) The importance of Brecht's scene – and the play as a whole – lies also in its description of the everyday, the effects of Nazism on ordinary folk, Jew and gentile alike. They are the ones who might have lived in Boltanski's house. As Richie argues:

> More than anywhere else in the world Berlin can contribute to an understanding of the Holocaust and of the other crimes committed by Nazi Germany by exposing the insidious nature of evil. Visitors should be encouraged to understand how it crept into the city slowly, into hearts and minds, into cafés and *Hinterhöfe* and side streets and entire districts. So many of those who worked in Berlin were not for the most part inhuman monsters but ordinary people who made the wrong choices.

(1999: lviii)

In fact there's an outdoor installation at the top end of Grosse Hamburger Strasse, at Koppen Platz, which is probably more directly apposite to Brecht's living-room scene. It's called *Der Verlassene Raum* (1996), the abandoned room – or, more abstractly-speaking, the space of disappearance – and depicts simply a bronze table and two chairs, one of which appears, arrestingly, to have been knocked over in a hurry. The installation, originally commissioned by the GDR authorities in 1988, is by the artists Biedermann and Butzmann (Rebiger 2000: 153). Around its edges

23.

Street Scenes: Brecht, Benjamin, and Berlin

there is a quotation from a poem by the Jewish Nobel prize winner Nelly Sachs: 'Oh these dwelling-places of death,/Enticingly arranged...'.[12] A Brechtian *Gestus* without actors or characters. The piece could also have been entitled 'All that is left'. Like a ruin it records a moment which, in Gilloch's words, was for Benjamin 'the pause between life and death', a dialectical image that 'captures the last fleeting moments of the afterlife of the object, the precise instant of demise in which illusion withers and truth becomes manifest' (Gilloch 1997: 127). Benjamin, as we have seen, entitled his characterisations of cities *Denkbilder* or 'pensive portraits' (see Preamble). This too is a *Denkbild*, a liminal image that opens up a space in which we can think about what we think.

Marking Disappearance

Next door to the secondary school opposite the *Missing House*, at number 26 Grosse Hamburger Strasse, there was once an old people's home with a Jewish cemetery immediately behind it. Not content with annihilating the living, the Gestapo did the same to the dead, removing some 3,000 graves from it in 1943. That's sacrilegious enough under any circumstances, but more so since Jewish graves mark their particularity as sites laid down for eternity. So now the graveyard, which has become a park, represents the memorialisation of a memorial site. Ironically, the old people's home – that last place before death – is where many Berlin Jews, 55,000 of them, were rounded up for transportation. Of course a lot of them were *young* people, some boys and girls who would have attended the school. For them the walk between the two front doors ended up being emblematic of their short journey from birth to death. After being rounded up, the deportees would have been sent to what is now Grunewald S-Bahn station in the west of the city, part of the overland suburban rail network. If you go there these days, you'll be taken aback as you wander through the underpass by a sign for platform seventeen, since there's no call at this station for more than two platforms now. Should you venture on to it, you find the track culminates in a small cluster of recently-planted silver birches. Running down either side, etched into the edge of either platform, are the exact dates, destinations and numbers of Berlin Jews transported daily to the camps between 1941 and 1945. Lodz, Riga, Minsk, Lublin, Bergen-Belsen, Auschwitz and others. Sometimes over a hundred people, getting less as the war wears on. Platform seventeen, in the idyllic setting of the Grunewald forest, was the last piece of *terra firma* they felt under their feet in the city.[13]

As you enter the park that was a cemetery, which you do from Grosse Hamburger Strasse, there's a memorial stone on the left marking the former location of the old people's home. Like Heiner Müller's grave, it's piled high with small stones placed there by visitors. It has an inscription which refers to 'bestial murder' – as if murder by itself were not bestial enough – ending with the ever-wearing entreaties: 'never forget this, resist war, preserve peace'. The living's dead message. To the left

24.

of it, almost buried in the bushes, is Will Lammert's 1957 maquette for a sculpture originally intended for the concentration camp at Ravensbrück near Berlin. It depicts a group of women and children, waiting as if on a crowded platform. Blackened figures, anxious and innocent. Lammert, who died the same year, presumably failed to complete the sculpture itself, so the prototype has appropriately assumed its place at the beginning rather than end of that final journey.

There's an installation by George Segal entitled *The Holocaust* (1984) at Lincoln Park, San Francisco which could form the temporal counterpart to this piece, the true destination and fate of Lammert's purgatorial figures: behind a solitary ghost of a man, standing with one hand clasping a barbed-wire fence, lies a random heap of whitened corpses. Lammert's doomed figures knocked over like ninepins into a Pompeian sprawl of anaemic plaster cast-offs. Segal's motivation to accept the commission was driven by what he perceived as the utter indignity suffered in death:

> In any culture, if a human being dies, there's an elaborate, orderly ritual that accompanies the burial. The body is laid out in a straight line. Hands are crossed. There's a burial case and a prescribed, almost immovable succession of events that involve the expression of grief of the family, the expression of love, the expression of the reli-

gious beliefs in whatever civilisation. It's a prescribed order, and if a modern state turns that order topsy-turvy and introduces this kind of chaos, it is an unthinkable obscenity. I determined that I would have to make a heap of bodies that was expressive of this arrogance and disorder.

(Young 1994: 86)

Finally, before entering the park proper, perhaps the most arresting of signs: 'Do Not Trust Green Areas' (or 'parkland'). Apparently it's the opening line of a novel entitled *Herr Moses in Berlin* by the contemporary writer Heinz Knobloch, who was coincidentally the person who ensured the posthumous recognition of the policeman Wilhelm Krützfeld's *Kristallnacht* heroics at the Neue Synagoge (see chapter four). Of course, it's a reference to the Gestapo's desecration of the cemetery in 1943: 'civilised cities protect the right, upheld by the Jewish faith, of the dead to eternal ownership of their graves', the sign says. Only the grave of the renowned and revered enlightenment philosopher Moses Mendelsohn – Herr Moses – remains, resurrected in 1962.[14] Young refers to the phenomenon of the *Yizkhor Bikher* or 'memorial books' which, as narrative text – or words – rather than stone, glass or steel, formed 'the first memorials to the Holocaust period'. As he goes on to explain, citing one of the prefaces, reading these books is intended to replicate the sense of standing next to the graves, denied the victims by their murderers:

> The stetl scribes hoped [...] the *Yizkhor Bikher* would turn the site of reading into memorial space. In response to what has been called 'the missing gravestone syndrome', the first sites of memory created by survivors were thus interior, imagined grave sites.

(1994: 22)

Part of the centre to be added to Eisenmann's as yet unbuilt Holocaust Memorial will contain a 'House of Remembrance' with a twenty metre high 'Wall of Books' designed to emphasise the notion of reading as the performance of memory. As Large writes: '[t]he books, a million tomes in all, would be open to consultation to scholars, thereby accommodating the ideas that the Holocaust memorial should not be just a thing to gaze at, or to get lost in, but an 'interactive' center of education and research' (2002: 634). The two volumes of the *Gedenkbuch* (meaning 'memorial book'), on which Libeskind drew for his Jewish Museum design, also fulfil this memorial function; ultimately his building, as well as Boltanski's *Missing House*, which was sourced from various municipal 'texts', represent the spatial articulation of such readings. But the words on the sign in question also draw attention to the fact that some 2,500 civilians and soldiers who died in the final battle for Berlin were buried here in 1945. In 1970 these graves were flattened by the GDR authorities and the park created in their place. The park itself, encircled by age-old trees, affords an extraordinary tranquillity. Again there is that rippling wind. In one of his late Svendborg poems, 'To Those Born Later', written between 1936 and 1938, Brecht famously bewailed the fact that calamitous times meant '[A] talk about about trees is almost a crime/ Because it implies silence about so many horrors' (1976: 318). Here, to one born later, it has synthesised into its opposite. It is the trees marking this space of disappearance, which seem to talk. A mute eloquence which I do not mistrust.

Missing house, missing people, missing gymnasium, missing gravestones. Even missing teeth. Or the black hole of Helene Weigel's open mouth: that well-known image of her as Mother Courage in the 1949 Berliner Ensemble production of the play (or its 1961 filming) at the point when she hears shots ring out and realises she has haggled too long over the price of her second son Eiliff's life, and he has been executed. She turns her head and *mimes* a protracted scream of absolute agony, witnessed thus by George Steiner in Elin Diamond's citation:

> The sound that came out was raw and terrible beyond any description that I could give to it. But in fact there was no sound. Nothing. The sound was total silence. It was silence which screamed and screamed through the whole theatre so that the audience lowered its head as before a gust of wind.

(Parker and Sedgwick 1995: 162)

It is the scream that tells of people sacrificed at a poignant moment in history; private loss as the expression of immediate collective experience. It is also, as Diamond suggests, invoking Walter Benjamin's definition of the Brechtian *Gestus*, the scream of 'dialectics at a standstill' in which 'what cannot be thought – death – becomes the felt other [...] The fully extended mouth [...] stands for the terror of the unseen in the seen' (163). For Diamond, seeking a Brechtian link with Lacan via Benjamin, the dialectic emerges through the mysterious 'blot in the visual field', or through 'that which would threaten the seamless unity of the real', for which she invokes Holbein's famous painting of 1533, *The French Ambassadors*, with the blurred skull in the foreground (155). In other words: the way the 'spectator's imaginary identifications – the plenitude of full seeing – are interrupted by the contradictory relations of the symbolic' (160). Staging a mechanism of looking, as Brecht did with his V-effect, with estrangement or distanciation, produces for the spectator a sense of 'feeling seeing' (155), of noting your own desire as well as anguish at trying to see something you cannot quite catch sight of because it is not given to be seen.

Notes

1. Documentation of the project, one of several citywide interventions by a range of renowned international artists, is to be found in Herzogenrath *et al.* (1990: 71–86).

2. Full documentation of the events surrounding *House* is contained in Lingwood (1995).

3. There are many such art works as 'stumbling blocks' to be found in Berlin. Perhaps the epitome is Norbert Rademacher's 1994 installation at one of Sachsenhausen's former satellite concentration camps in Sonnenallee (in the Neukölln district of the city). It involves pedestrians unwittingly setting off the projection of a slide on to the pavement by walking through a light-beam tripwire. The slide provides information about the camp.

4. Although Thälmann fought a vigorous campaign against the Nazis and was finally executed by them, he was seen as an ambiguous hero in the GDR because his Stalinist commitment led him to do battle above all with the SPD, thus producing the 'left-split' which enabled Hitler to come to power in the first place. At the same time there was a suggestion that he could have been rescued by Stalin after 1933 but was left in the lurch (Buse and Doerr 1998: 993; Ladd 1998: 201–3). Ironically, the massive monument is the work of a Russian artist and was bequeathed to the GDR by the Soviet Union. Its size led to it being jokingly referred to as the GDR's bronze reserve (van Treeck 1999: 55–6).

5. The start date for building was finally set at the summer of 2001, with completion projected to be early in 2004. By the summer of 2003, however, the memorial was still two years away from being finished. For full documentation of proceedings, see Cullen (1999).

6. Unusually for a building, but in keeping with a perception of it as being closer to a performative installation in its conception, Libeskind gave the Jewish Museum the title 'Between the Lines', referring specifically to 'two lines of thinking, organisation, and relationship' (Libeskind 2001: 23).

7. See *Gedenkbuch – Opfer der Verfolgung der Juden*, Koblenz: Bundesarchiv and Avolsen: Internationaler Suchdienst, 1986.

8. According to Shields, only Hoffmann 'is accorded the status of a true *flâneur*' in Benjamin's *Arcades Project* (Tester 1994: 79). As Benjamin himself writes, Hoffmann's story 'The Cousin's Corner Window' 'probably is one of the earliest attempts to capture the street scene of a large city' (1999: 169).

9. In a conclusion drawn in the early 1900s and often quoted since the fall of the Wall because of its uncanny applicability to circumstances nearly a century later, Scheffler declared that Berlin was condemned 'forever to become and never to be' ((1989), *Berlin – ein Stadtschicksal*, Berlin: Fannei und Walz, p. 219).

10. For the sake of comparison other forms of *Mal* are *Ehrenmal* which is a commemorative monument such as those celebrating heroic acts of war (a mark of honour) and *Merkmal*, a distinguishing feature (literally a mark that you notice or remember). *Muttermal* (mother mark) is a birthmark, whilst *Brandmal*, which has been applied as a metaphor for the Jewish Museum, means branding. *Gedenkstätte*, meanwhile, is the popular term for memorial site.

11. Müller later used this anecdote as the basis for a scene in his play *Germania 3 Ghosts at Dead Man* (Weber 2001: 203–9).

12. '*O die Wohnungen des Todes,/Einladend hergerichtet...*'.

13. *Gleis 17* – in Germany you refer to the track rather than the platform number – is by the artists Hirsch, Lorch and Wandel and was installed in 1998. Interestingly it is referred to officially as a *Mahnmal*, though there is nothing apparently exhortatory about it.

14. Mendelsohn was the inspiration for Lessing's character Nathan the Wise in the play of the same name (1779). In it Nathan pleads for tolerance of other religions. Mendelsohn himself urged Jews to adopt the customs of the country in which they had chosen to live and to practice the use of German as a secular language.

6. Niederkirchner Strasse: Wall Wounds

For this splendid Mahagonny

Has it all, if you have the money.

Then all is available

Because all is for sale

And there is nothing that one cannot buy.

(Bertolt Brecht, The Rise and Fall of the City of Mahagonny)

No one who had seen this city when it was divided could ever forget what it had been like. Not forget, not be able to describe it, not be able to tell the real story.

(Cees Nooteboom, All Souls' Day)

The Last Station Stop

Without really giving it much thought, I always assumed, when I lived in West Berlin in the mid-1980s, that one of the city's disused railway stations, the Anhalter Bahnhof at Askanischer Platz in the district of Kreuzberg, was called that because it had been a terminus station. *Anhalten* in German is the infinitive 'to stop' (or, for that matter, 'halt'). So for me this particular *Bahnhof* (station) was where the trains not only used to stop but where they literally came to a stop because they could not go any further. Perhaps the misconception was strengthened subconsciously by the fact that the station was only a stone's throw from the Berlin Wall, the anti-fascist protection barrier, as it was called in the east, which really did bring everything to a grinding halt. Somehow, then, in the muddle of my assumption, a conflation of images had occurred in which it was a station at which trains stopped – as they do – as well as one which stopped trains finally, thereby rendering passengers 'stoppers' (*Anhalter*). In other words, it was where they got off because they had to. For some reason it didn't occur to me that, logically, it could also have been the point at which one might *begin* one's journey, and that the

25.

station might therefore just as easily be called Abfahrer Bahnhof. Illogically, though, the notion of travellers stopping the trains to get *on* was mixed in there somewhere, since I was familiar with the German *'per Anhalter fahren'*, which means to hitchhike. Fortunately, I don't appear to be the only one who's wandered into a speculative labyrinth over this. In Wenders' 1987 Berlin film *Wings of Desire* the 'Colombo character', Peter Falk playing Peter Falk, stalks past the relic of Anhalter Bahnhof muttering something about being told it was the only railway station at which *it* rather than the trains could be said to have stopped. And Walter Benjamin, who harboured vivid turn-of-the-century childhood memories of Anhalter, also makes a little joke about it being the station 'where the trains must stop' (*GS* 4i: 246).

As I came to realise in the course of time, the station was called what it's called because Anhalt is the name of the region south-west of Berlin – part of the former GDR – to and from which the trains would travel.[1] The private railway company which operated the line, and so built and owned the station, was the *Berlin-Anhaltische Eisenbahngesellschaft*. This pattern of stations serving specific places was replicated throughout Berlin in the nineteenth century. Hence, Hamburger Bahnhof, Stettiner Bahnhof, Potsdamer Bahnhof and so on, dotted strategically around the city. Lehrter Bahnhof, too, followed this trend, though Lehrte itself is one of those places that invariably provokes queries as to its whereabouts. In fact, it's a small town a few kilometres east of Hanover. But, as Hessel observes on one of his strolls in the 1920s: 'one of the most pleasant of the older Berlin stations', it

128 Street Scenes: Brecht, Benjamin, and Berlin

didn't actually send its trains to Lehrte 'but mainly to Hamburg' (1984: 127). As a consequence of its positioning near the political and commercial heart of the new Berlin, the location of the former station – just a stop for the S-Bahn until the summer of 2002, when it was demolished – has been chosen as the appropriate intersection for a single main station for the city.

The rapid development of the railway industry and the extensive network fanning out from Berlin were of course absolutely central to the way the city began to seek to assert itself as the capital of a unified Germany in nineteenth century Europe. Richie points out that its eleven radiating main lines made it the prime rail node, the city looking on rail maps of the time 'like a contented fat black spider perched in the centre of a dense web extending the length and breadth of Europe' (1999: 140). A single central station never materialised at the time because of the *old* city wall, the customs one that used to protect and unite rather than divide and threaten the inhabitants of the city. Eventually it was pulled down in the 1860s to accommodate the new S-Bahn.[2] Work on the massive new Lehrter Bahnhof began in the mid-1990s but won't be completed until well into the first decade of the twenty-first century. Although it will form the principal station, its construction has been conceived as the convergent interchange in a whole network of national, regional and urban rail connections and services. Owing to the shape this produces in outline, it has come to be termed the *Pilzkonzept* or mushroom-concept (*InfoBox: der Katalogue* 1998: 18–19). Join the dots along the contours of a northern 'arc', a central, east-west S-Bahn 'band', as well as a north-south 'stem' of stations and that's what you end up with. Metaphorically, then: animal to vegetable. Once again the Berlin rail network is projected to form a prime node in European travel and communications, not least in its strategic capacity between east and west.

Changing Stations

When I arrived in West Berlin in the 1980s, trains had long stopped stopping at Anhalter Bahnhof. The station was badly damaged during the Second World War and, though temporarily revived afterwards, was finally demolished in 1961. Apart from its northern portal, that is, which remains in place to this day as a strangely imposing ruin. The striking fact about Anhalter, though, is that amongst the profusion of stations in Berlin, it came to enjoy the status of being the main one, positioned as it was very close to the heart of the city. In fact, less than a kilometre away Potsdamer Bahnhof was even more central, flanking the city's main square, Potsdamer Platz. But Anhalter offered a more grandiose presence both in terms of the ultimate destinations of its trains – essentially 'south', which eventually came to include other European cities such as Rome, Vienna and Basle – and the sheer expanse of its hall. In Walter Ruttmann's 1927 film Berlin – *Die Sinfonie der Großstadt*, a silent, orchestrated montage of the rhythms in a day in the life of 1920s

Berlin, Anhalter is seen to feature centrally as the vibrant focal point for the flow of the city's vast commuting populace, as well as travellers from further afield. It also became renowned for its capacity to stage 'appropriately ostentatious' receptions of dignitaries, most notably Kaiser Wilhelm II's formal welcoming of the King of Italy in 1889 (Maier 1987: 243–7). Arguably its prime importance previously is precisely what rendered it so dramatically obsolete when historical circumstances changed radically. A similar fate befell nearby Potsdamer Platz. Once the Piccadilly Circus of Berlin, it ended up in no-man's land after the Second World War and, after partition, in the frontier exclusion zone between the two walls that existed in the centre. But that's for the next chapter.

Anhalter's demise also correlated exactly with the sudden, brutal imposition of the Wall. It could have been restored after the war but wasn't because partition between East and West made it unclear how it would function. Its location no longer represented the beating heart of Berlin but anaemic non-land, effectively on the *edge* – albeit an inside edge – of West Berlin. Trains would have arrived 'nowhere', effectively grinding to a halt at the Wall. So, in 1961, the very year the Wall went up, the station finally came down, an event predicted by the architectural historian Hoffmann-Axthelm to 'rest in the memory of this city as one of the great acts of self-mutilation' (Baehr 1984: 107). Only the portal was left in place as a memorial, baring all the scars of its amputation. The severance when it occurred really was arbitrary it seems. No neat retention of archways or smoothing of edges, the vernacular yellow brickwork mercilessly hacked at and cracked. As I stand now in

26.

the shadow of the ruin that remains, my body reels in its presence. Later, tracing its outline on an old photograph of the whole building, I can see how vast it must have been. To this day the space of the former station hall, measuring some 170 by 60 metres, remains undefined, empty terrain. In 'Berlin Childhood around 1900' Benjamin refers to the expanse of its hall 'where locomotives are at home' as *die Mutterhöhle der Eisenbahnen*', literally 'the womb of the railways' (*GS* 4i: 246). Clearly he was laying claims to Anhalter being some kind of ultimate sanctuary. The force of what he was meaning to express is probably best translated these days as 'the Mother of all railway stations'. But just to nudge that into a further perspectival light: the new Lehrter Bahnhof platform hall is projected to extend 430 metres – not far off half a kilometre – east to west (Balfour 1995: 321). And that's just one of three levels.

Periodically proposals have been extended suggesting uses for the Anhalter site, but for a range of reasons agreement has never been reached throughout both Cold War and post-reunification times. It's not exactly wasteland. Temporary installations – circuses and other such tent-events – come and go, and saplings line its eastern and western flanks.[3] It's not just a building gradually falling down either but a designated monument, an official ruin. That's the revised function it now performs as an edifice. Paradoxically, then, the arbitrariness of its demolition was deliberate. It's *meant* to look like a ruin.[4] Again, though, its precise identity in this respect is unclear. As I wonder across the abandoned terrain towards the portal, a taxi driver from the rank on the forecourt is just relieving himself against the

27.

28.

straggling fence that encircles it provisionally. If the fencing hadn't been there he probably would have pissed on the brickwork itself.

So if the Anhalter ruin is a memorial site, what act of remembrance does it perform? Is it only the one supposedly attached to it, simultaneously a celebration of its pre-war grandeur and an exhortation not to forget the destructive effects of fascism? Or does the clue to its force lie more in the scars of its hysterectomy, the visible rupture of its fabric, and in the troubled indefiniteness of that which surrounds it? Surely the ruin itself stands, like Tacheles on Oranienburger Strasse, as a representation of the transition of identity of a building. Perhaps that's why the question of the area behind its portal, the missing rump, has never been resolved. Somehow the fragment of the station needs the empty space of its phantom other in order to function as a monument, as a continuing testament to what (it) *was*, as well as to what *has gone on*. That is, it indicates the event of transition of the building and, consequently, the city as a whole, not to say the fate of a people. The station's transition – literally its *de-motion* from a functional place of maximum activity to a symbolic relic – is staggering, but then so have been the events in history which have produced the dynamic of that movement. Coincidentally the infinitive *anhalten* can also mean the opposite of 'stop': to 'continue' or 'last'. Thus, it is a station that has *stopped* functioning one way in order to *carry on* in another. As Gilloch says of Benjamin's view of ruins as monuments, they have 'an "afterlife" which negates the original intention' (1997: 73). If Anhalter is a monument, then, it is one which performs the ceaselessness of change, functioning according to a continuing process of displacement; a series of historical superimpositions – stopped moments which in their plurality produce continuity – each of which bears the trace of that which it would supersede, of a Berlin that is both left and being left but that has certainly not arrived.

Wall Stories

On Niederkirchner Strasse, halfway between Anhalter Bahnhof and Potsdamer Platz, lies one of the few remaining stretches of the Berlin Wall. As it happens it borders the grounds of the former Gestapo headquarters from which the Holocaust was masterminded. They were housed in Prinz Albrecht Palais, which was demolished in 1950. The street used to be named Prinz Albrecht Strasse but changed to Niederkirchner the following year because of the association of the

29.

former name with the Gestapo.[5] As with Anhalter, there's wire fencing strung round the Wall, as if its identity were in abeyance, though the intention now would seem to be to retain it as a memorial site. In fact, it is barely recognisable as the Wall I once knew. On the western side that meant serving as a canvas for tourists and West Berliners alike to daub graffiti as it graduated through successive 'generations' to become the 'longest graffiti surface in the world' (van Treeck 1999: 101). That wasn't permitted to occur in the same way on the eastern side, of course. Draconian punishments were in force and, though the will to transgression was doubtless given amongst many members of the populace – how could it not be – they didn't in any case possess the optimum equipment: spray cans were not a known quantity in the GDR.

A less-known fact is that the western side of the Wall also came under the jurisdiction of the GDR, so what appeared to be permitted was strictly not (van Treeck 1999: 101). The problem, obviously, was one of enforcement, which would have been virtually impossible. Remembering that there were two walls enclosing the security buffer zone, the *Todesstreifen* or death strip in the centre of the city, GDR frontier guards themselves would not normally have come within touching distance of the western one, let alone its other side, without raising suspicions of an intended defection on their part. The willingness of border guards to monitor one another is documented in the well-publicised case of Rudolf M. who was charged and convicted in 1998 with shooting and killing his colleague Reinhold

30.

Huhn at Checkpoint Charlie (Flemming and Koch 2000: 74). However, Ladd reckons that there were concealed doors in the Wall through which guards would slip occasionally to make arrests (1998: 26). And one of the most renowned Wall artists, the Frenchman Thierry Noir, makes claims to a close call in 1984 when four armed GDR guards suddenly jumped over the Wall to attempt to nab him as he drew on the western side (van Treeck 1999: 128).

Now, the street-facing side of the Niederkirchner Strasse Wall has been desecrated, the rusting iron rods of its structure protruding like the ribcage of some ravaged beast mercilessly stripped by vultures of its flesh. But this used to be the *inward* side of one of those two walls. In other words, it was within the unreachable death strip, so its desecration represents the post-fall work of souvenir hunters – dubbed 'wall-peckers' – incorporating those simply seeking a private memento as well as those intent on selling what they have mined. The latter variety could be seen openly spraying untainted sections of the Wall like this one with aerosol cans after the event of its fall, and hacking off small pieces to sell as the 'real thing'. They didn't even have to be inventive with what they sprayed since they were dealing in small fragments.

As such, this relic of the Wall is perhaps far less a document of its life in the period of the Cold War than of what has *become* of it since 1989 and, by figurative extension, of the implications of reunification generally. It is an open wound, a publicly performed inscription, which tells many stories. Chronologically, these begin of course with the brutal partition of a city and its peoples on ideological grounds, moving in the aftermath of its hauling down to opportunistic profiteering and the desire for private ownership, and ending – though the performance must go on – as the unresolved (eye) sore of cultural discord. Traffic belting past on one side and, amidst overgrown foliage, visitors respectfully picking their way through the terrain of the outdoor Topography of Terror Holocaust exhibition on the other,[6] encapsulates what the writer Heiner Müller referred to as a 'time-wall between two speeds'. Back then he meant 'acceleration in the West [and] deceleration in the East' (Herzogenrath 1990: 9). It is frequently maintained now that this time differential has been reversed, which implies there still is a wall of sorts. What is meant is that the extent and urgency of change, involving as it does the making up of 40 years of stasis as well as the adjustment to new norms, is naturally all the greater in the East. Superficial as it is, that view tends to assume that the task in hand for the former GDR is simply to catch up by copying. In fact, as Calle's piece *The Detachment* was shown to reveal in relation to the renegotiation of historical narratives (see chapter five), the ground that requires to be crossed is actually a yawning chasm with no easily discernible 'other side' to reach.

It is also a view that masks the degree to which West Berlin, too, was locked into its own form of dependent stagnation, artificially sustained for strategic purposes by a range of socio-economic subsidies and exemptions, and strictly under the three-power allied protection of the French, British and Americans (Large 2002: 463–6). So, whilst East Berlin is popularly portrayed as the half of the city where not a lot happened, West Berlin – or Rest Berlin as some jokingly called it ('rest' being the term for 'rump' as well as embodying the English sense of the word)[7] – nurtured a paradoxical sense of ongoing, introspective emergency.

Effectively West Berlin was on a life-support machine, and nothing set the tone for that more than the truly extraordinary pre-Wall airlift of 1948–1949. With the Soviets seeking to squeeze the allies out of the city, they had completely sealed off the entire western half. The only way to provide inhabitants with the necessary food and fuel supplies was to stage an exhaustive daily airlift involving a continuous turn-around of British and American planes landing and taking off from the two western airports at Tegel and Tempelhof. The statistics of the famous operation are staggering: not only was it successfully sustained for over a year but in that time 2,325,000 tons of food and other supplies were transported in on some 277,500 flights. On Easter Sunday 1949 alone 1,398 flights – one every 62 seconds – descended on Berlin in what was intended as an allied show of strength. Although Large draws attention to the blockade's deliberate 'leakiness' – since 'the Soviet sector in Berlin was no less dependent on trade with the West than the western sectors were on trade with the East' (2002: 402) – in the face of such resolve, the Soviets eventually gave up.[8] The conditions of the airlift functioned as a microcosmic precursor to the 28 years that followed on from the sudden, overnight erection of the first generation Wall on 13 August 1961, a move which Khrushchev had hinted at to Kennedy as being an exercise in 'squeezing the testicles of the West to make it scream' (Richie 1999: 714). It was time to 'lance the boil' of Berlin, he said apparently, seemingly seeking to crush the fledgling US president with the power of mixed metaphor. As Large suggests, however, following up his observation regarding the airlift's leaks:

> Politically the Russians might talk tough, but economically they could not afford to stand on their own. Their tactic of building a barricade and simultaneously undermining it was emblematic of the fundamental structural weaknesses in the Soviet empire that would remain in place until its collapse.

(2002: 402)

The airlift not only portended the committed tenacity of both the western allies and the citizens of West Berlin to hang on to its designated territories come what may, but also produced that prevalent sense of bizarre singularity that was to characterise the city during the Cold War years. Nothing seemed to happen in quite the same way as elsewhere, least of all the Federal Republic. Everyday practices were infused with a sense of extra-ordinariness. At the same time the extraordinary – the palpable tendency towards 'display' or spectacle, but also the need simply to resort to unusual measures as a means of dealing with what was essentially an emergency situation – was commonplace. Ultimately, of course, what appeared to be unique in the west of the city was, despite a certain blithe acceptance of the circumstances of partition, entirely dependent for that quality precisely on the phantom presence of the alien 'other' in the east. In its own way, the same applied in the east: though inhabitants had freedom of movement beyond the immediate confines of the city, they could not but define the limitations of their existence by the contaminating western parasite in their midst.

The many ideological acts of antagonism – some simply mythical or unproven, of course – whether expressed through competing architectural constructions, media propaganda, diplomatic confrontations or whatever, have been variously documented and many are popularly recounted orally. Nothing epitomises the symbiosis between east and west, and the near-farcical functioning of the ordinary-within-extraordinary-context, to a greater degree than the Wall itself: ultimately the most basic and crude 'unit' of architectural practice, performing here the most loaded of roles. A more resonant *gestic* phenomenon there could not have been; banal grey concrete pregnant with the contradictions of a protracted historical moment of global significance. On the one hand it was an example of architecture that negated its own purpose in being constructed against humanity. A city and people divided. Relating it to the Sophoclean myth of *Antigone* – which Brecht takes up, setting it in Berlin in the final phase of the Second World War[9] – Leach sees the building of the Wall as:

> the triumph of the unnatural over the natural, the state over the family. Antigone therefore becomes the emblematic motif of the Berlin condition: the family torn apart and denied by the state [...] Yet the Wall was not only an architecture of denial, it was also a denial of architecture. The Wall became a form of anti-architecture, a grotesque denial of the very social value of the art of building.

(1999: 216)

On the other hand it arguably prevented – or stood in for – the prosecution of a nuclear war, though if one had broken out, it wouldn't have taken place in Berlin. As such, the divided city was more a symbolic 'frontline', a kind of Cold War surrogate or deterrent buffer zone which bought time. Moreover, as Ladd poignantly reminds us, in their desire not to capitulate over Berlin, the western allies were actually relieved when the Wall went up because it represented for them the resolution to a crisis which had looked increasingly like it 'could not be solved by any means short of war' (1998: 21). In view of the escalating haemorrhage of GDR citizens into West Berlin, the Americans displayed sympathy, Kennedy himself privately 'musing that a border-closure might be a reasonable solution', and Fulbright, the chair of the Senate Armed Services Committee, expressing a similar view in public (Large 2002: 449).

At the risk of misrepresenting him, Baudrillard would probably regard the Berlin stand off as embodied by the Wall as an instance of hyperreality or, as he says of nuclear deterrence generally, 'the apotheosis of simulation' (1983: 58). That is, it functioned in the last instance to *make us think* that without it there would be a nuclear war and, thus, that it was a necessary security valve: 'just as prisons are there to conceal the fact that it is the social in its entirety [...] which is carceral' (25). For both east and west the Wall rested, then, on the myth of imminent invasion, a feigned statement of intent, in the former's case underpinned by the legitimising tale of resisting anti-fascist contamination. As Ladd also points out, the unsustainable nature of that particular narrative rampart was ultimately the undoing not only of its physical counterpart (in the shape of the Wall) but also the communist state as a whole (1998: 31). The Wall would have served its purpose for the western allies too in the perpetuation of the supremacist myth of capitalist ideology against an inadequate communism. That is why it would have been important to portray emphatically the Wall's fall as the ineluctable victory of the former. History and ideology were dead at last, 'let's go shopping', as Naomi Klein puts it. What she also draws attention to is the vacuum this produced, a factor that has been thrown into relief since the events of 11 September 2001 through the discovery of a new, 'uncivilised other' in the shape of 'medieval Islam' and an 'axis of evil':

> [H]istory's end also turned out to be a hollow victory for the United States' cold warriors. It seems that since 1989, many of them have missed their epic narratives as if it were a lost limb. Without ideology, shopping was...just shopping [...] During the Cold War, consumption in the US wasn't only about personal gratification; it was the economic front of the great battle. When Americans went shopping, they were participating in the lifestyle that the Commies supposedly wanted to crush. When kaleidoscopic outlet malls were contrasted with Moscow's grey and barren shops, the point wasn't just that we in the west had easy access to Levi's 501s. In this narrative, our malls stood for freedom and democracy, while their empty shelves were metaphors for control and repression.

(Klein 2002: 12)

Of course, before we get entirely carried away in the eddy of Baudrillard's endless 'precession of simulacra', which mask the absence rather than the reality,[10] it is worth holding on to a sense of the very immediate effect of the Wall's presence for those inhabiting the city itself. Part of the pleasure of living in West Berlin was premised on the enforced artificiality of the situation, in *knowing* that there was a constant and patent dissembling in operation between the two sides. But it was a tension that also conveyed a real danger. A kind of dramatic irony prevailed, particularly in direct encounters with eastern officialdom: as witness you knew what the unstated score was in the action unfolding before your eyes (see chapter one).

A further parable that exemplified the symbiotic machinery in operation is Brecht's *Good Person of Setzuan*. On a mission to locate a good human being, the Gods are pleased finally to find one in the shape of the prostitute Shen Teh, who, despite her destitute circumstances is the only person willing to give them shelter when they descend on the town of Setzuan. They reward her with a lump sum of money with which she is able to set up a tobacco shop. News of her fortune travels fast and she is besieged by all manner of parasitical 'relatives' and 'friends'. Naturally benevolent, she indulges their greed but eventually is forced to reinvent herself as her cutthroat, capitalist cousin Shui Ta, who mercilessly drives away the spongers and keeps the business ticking over profitably. Shen Teh makes a return but Shui Ta continues to lurk as a weapon to be invoked in case of need. Two contrasting identities in one, as symptomatic of the divisive nature of capitalist relations. From an audience perspective the situation takes its force precisely from knowing the game that is being played by Shen Teh/Shui Ta where the other characters do not. At the same time it is not a satisfactory solution that can be sustained. It is a temporary construct which ultimately must give way to *something*. The play does not resolve the conundrum – pathetic as they are, the Gods are happy for Shen Teh to bring her cousin into play on an occasional basis (the consensus politics of welfare capitalism) – and it acknowledges as much in its epilogue: 'don't feel let down:/We know this ending makes some people frown [...] Indeed it is a curious way of coping:/To close the play, leaving the issue open' (*Plays* 6i: 109). Brecht's idea, clumsy as its execution is here, was that the audience should decide what measures were best to deal with the problematic relationship between altruism and money. Since two into one plainly won't go, the imperative is that things must change. In a sense the central dilemma with which the play leaves you – how to deal with the competitive, self-orientated conditions of capital without giving up your sense of a moral identity based on compassion – was in general terms the one confronting the GDR once the Wall had come down. Whereas before the ideological split had been held artificially if not farcically at bay, now it was there to be faced directly.

'I have a paper'

When, in 1989, the turning point in the Wall-farce came, it was appropriate that it should be precipitated by a casual error, the accidental introduction, metaphorically, of a lethal, uncontrollable virus. Pressure had been mounting for some time, of course, not least with huge public demonstrations and an exodus of GDR citizens to the West German embassies in Budapest and Prague. In a September 11 landmark that will no longer carry quite the same resonance now, the Hungarian government declared its border with Austria officially open, paving the way for unrestricted passage to the West for those with passports. Finally, on 9 November, Günther Schabowski, a member of the GDR Politburo, the whole of which had resigned that morning, held a press conference at which he read from a piece of paper handed to him shortly beforehand. It declared that 'private journeys abroad can be applied for without presenting conditions, reasons for travel or names of relatives' and that 'permission will be granted at short notice'. This applied, moreover, 'at all crossing points of the GDR into the Federal Republic or West Berlin'. Questioned as to when the directive would come into force, Schabowski replied hesitantly, 'Well, as far as I can see…straightaway, immediately' (Flemming and Koch 2000: 66). The rest is history, but the point was that Schabowski should not have read from this piece of paper at all.[11] As Flemming and Koch explain:

> [The] GDR leadership had seen no alternative but to liberalise travel conditions, which in effect meant opening the border. However, this was supposed to happen under the strict control of the regime, according to a planned time-scale and fully safeguarded by GDR state sovereignty.
>
> *(70)*

The GDR did not intend to yield its status as a nation state but simply, under intolerable pressure from the populace, facilitate travel regulations concerning 'permanent exit' and 'personal travel':

> This was intended to prevent people making short trips and visits from being at a disadvantage in comparison with 'emigrants' […] If such people had to jump over bureaucratic hurdles this would lead to further unrest among the GDR population at large. At the time only four million people (out of a total population of seventeen million) were in possession of a passport and this was now to be a general require-ment. In this way they thought they could put a stop to a sudden mass uprising.
>
> *(70)*

The document from which Schabowski read was intended for release the *following* day as part of a controlled response by the government, a detail of which he himself was not aware. Border guards at crossing points to West Berlin were themselves caught unawares but hardly felt able to open fire on thousands of people. Later they expressed their anger at what appeared to them to be the lack of a formal directive from their superiors when in fact it had all been a mistake, the effects of which the GDR authorities were subsequently still prepared to try and reverse. Central border command was mobilised on 10 November to seize 'measures for strengthening border security and raising battle readiness to an operational level capable of securing the border and fulfilling battle and mobilisation tasks' (70). By January 1990 border troops had been reduced by half, however, and from June 30, there were no more passport controls between East and West Berlin. If Schabowski's unwitting slip typified the kind of ordinary-but-critical moment that partition could produce in bureaucratic terms – a gestic or monadic moment in which the detail contains not only traces of the socio-historic totality but also the seeds of its downfall (the *Ende* part of an inevitable W*ende*) – Richie's account of passing through the breached Wall on 9 November describes its physical enactment and is worth repeating. It was 'quite banal [...] one simply walked a few metres past a large, ugly structure and into another district'. At the same time 'it meant so much [...] everyone sensed that this was a moment they would savour for the rest of their lives' (1999: 835). Later, she reports how in March 1990, as the run-up to the first elections in the East since 1949 was in train, she was handed a 'particularly colourful piece of Wall' by a GDR border guard at Brandenburg Gate: 'to be offered a piece by such a man on the eve of the destruction of his state was too surreal an opportunity to pass up' (843).

East Side Stories

The most dramatic piece of the Wall epic is 'missing', as it were, and that is the very social and physical act of its rupture and removal. Niederkirchner Strasse tries to tell that particular story by simply embedding a copper strip in the street's surface along its former course, with an engraving of the dates of its existence, 1961–1989. Paradoxically, the strip is significant above all for the mildness of its impact. Most people, I'm sure, do not register it. In a way, then, it draws attention to the invisibility of the Wall, to its disappearance *per se*, by *not* doing so. It is a fact bemoaned by many Berliners because its rapid vanishing is viewed as indicative of a change that occurred too quickly and comprehensively. Richie's graffitied Wall-fragment represents the post-1989 souvenir *par excellence*. The incidental circumstances in which she was given ownership of it add a particularly delicious sheen of the sort that such sudden and monumental reversals of culture are likely to produce in myriad ways. For Berlin the moment of that transition was just the next stage in a century of continuous living through exceptional states. Richie's innocent acquisition will have been replicated many times over. I too have my five little pieces of Wall – collected for me by friends the day after the fall, since I wasn't there myself – including subtle differentiations of concrete mix and texture relating to distinct sections and/or generations of it. The fate of a wall. Some of it ended up being refunctioned to pave new roads in the eastern half of the city. A humdrum destiny, not comparable to the post-World War II heaping of city rubble on to a great pile to form one of the few raised areas in the Berlin landscape, the Teufelsberg in the Grunewald forest. One commercial entity in the east, getting quickly to grips with western-style opportunism, sold off large chunks of the anti-fascist protection barrier (van Treeck 1999: 112). These were subsequently auctioned off in Monte Carlo, mainly to American buyers paying outrageous sums, but not before the pieces had been nicely restored and 'legitimised' with certificates bearing the date of 9 November 1989 (Herzogenrath 1990: 100).

Apart from Niederkirchner Strasse and a formalised tourist shrine at Bernauer Strasse, there remains of the Wall only the East Side Gallery at Mühlen Strasse. It's a 1.3 kilometre stretch on the eastern bank of the Spree, beginning at the point where the river is spanned by the former border crossing at Oberbaumbrücke (a redbrick, gothic bridge, which once formed part of the old customs wall). Following the suggestion of the British cultural attaché in East Berlin, it was turned into an outside gallery in 1990, each individual segment of Wall serving as the canvas for the work of some 100 invited artists from across the globe. As you'd expect most of the contributions take a satirical form, running the full gamut from poignant to trite. One of the more resonant images shows a replication of a famous photograph depicting Brezhnev embracing Honecker with one of those full-on kisses that (male) eastern-bloc leaders were in the habit of giving one another. Doubtless fuelled in part by conditioned homophobia, seeing these images as an adolescent in the 1970s would always send a shudder down my spine. Far from being contrary evidence of 'a loving warmth amongst men' behind the chilling might of the Iron Curtain, they evoked bloodless brotherhood and hard-lipped duty. Stern bushy eyebrows that would scratch and vodka breath. The piece at East Side neatly replicates the style of Warholian silk-screen printing. Brezhnev and Honecker are portrayed ironically as the popular, comic-strip icons of a heroic eastern-bloc alliance. Like the Wall itself, the sad remnants of which they grace, it's a surface masking emptiness. A genuine fake. The artist, Dmitry Vrubel, has entitled his work *The Mortal Kiss* and its caption reads: 'God help me survive this deadly love'.

Much later, in October 1989, there was another embrace for Honecker. This time it was from his visiting uncle Gorbachev. Thirty years earlier it had been Khrushchev warning Kennedy of his intention to crush the testicles of an enclosed allied Berlin, now it was the

31.

GDR's turn to be squeezed, by its own. But, as the novelist Cees Nooteboom suggests in a detailed analysis of the images this *gestic* moment produced, it happened with a velvety kiss:

> In the second photo you can see that [Honecker's] hand is resting on the right shoulder of his opposite number and that his eyes really are closed. It's not a Judas-kiss; that's obvious, too. And yet this kiss seals the demise of the one, or possibly that of the other. Within the circumstances of the moment, nothing is out of the question, and it is a moment that may persist for a while.

> Human beings are the ones enacting the kiss, but it is states, strategies and political philosophies that are kissing one another. The country that was inconceivable without the Soviet Union is being kissed by the country that makes the demise of the GDR, such as it is, conceivable. The orthodoxies inherited from Lenin and Stalin are being kissed by the heretics. The philosophy that set everything in train is kissing the philosophy that clings to the old. [...] One of the men embodies one of the greatest adventures history has known, a revolution which the other perceives as the betrayal of revolution. Invisible in the picture are the others, those whom all this concerns.

(1991: 92–3)

Famous as some of its subjects might be, East Side Gallery probably wouldn't qualify for what graffiti taggers deem a hall of fame. For the purists amongst them that is in any case a derogatory designation these days; halls of fame have become those urban surfaces officially sanctioned by the authorities to serve as graffiti canvases: 'If you must, then here, please'.[12] As any parent of adolescents will recognise, that defeats the point of the exercise, although there are artists, those more preoccupied with the aesthetics of their mark-making than the *fact* of it, who may seize the opportunity. East Side Gallery isn't graffiti of the clandestine variety, it's simply 'alfresco art' whereby, of course, the canvas predominates. In existence for over a decade now, much of it has faded or crumbled, though some artists conscientiously rework their contributions. Even if its impact has receded in the meantime, it certainly represented an important outlet at the time of reunification, not only as the manifold, celebratory expression of spontaneity and democracy but also as the first visible eastern marking of the Wall.

32.

Writings on the Wall

Although graffiti had always featured in West Berlin, soon after 1989 great swathes of it began to adorn the entire Berlin cityscape. The great 'writing' plague had begun. As the Wall disintegrated, its infectious graffiti-microbes migrated east and west to the other districts of the city, nesting and breeding wherever they could. Mostly they occupied dangerous and dilapidated terrain where others dared not go. This was neither the legal art of East Side Gallery nor even the surreptitious intervention of a self-proclaimed artist like Six who, since 1995, has been leaving the numeral '6' painted discreetly but abundantly all over the city (Hooper 2001 and Schlör 2001). This was – and still is – hardcore tagging carried out by 'writers' or 'sprayers' known only within the confines of their specific tagging community. Cresswell refers to the practice as 'night discourse': 'subversive messages which appear in the morning after the secretive curtain of night has been raised' (Fyfe 1998: 268). Supposedly the work is not intended to impress – or offend – the general public, but to gain the 'respect' of fellow writers. In itself it isn't even particularly territorial, in the sense of demarcating a 'home patch' within the city, though it does sometimes cover vast expanses of surface, be that building or train. Its value to its executors lies more in a combination of quantity and risk, the latter being defined by both daringness of location and length of time spent completing a piece (which is consequently why quantity is prized). Strict stylistic rules apply within the city as a whole, as they do in other cities, not least New York. Hence, it is the features of a 'Berlin school' that cement a sense of identity or of belonging to a particular urban 'scene' (van Treeck 1999: 152–155). Territorialism seems to function, then, in a more general way: I tag (the city), therefore I am.

If graffiti-spraying of this sort can be called art – which according to van Treeck is a label writers themselves tend to reject (139) – surely it is one of performance rather than fine art. Surprisingly, considering his self-proclaimed enthusiasm for the practice, van Treeck himself seems to collapse nervously back into traditionalist evaluations based on skill and potential art historical significance. In an 'is it art?' debate he conducts with himself the conclusion is that some works are simply qualitatively better than others (135 and 139). Nothing could upset the impulse of the practice more than seeking to validate it on such a two-dimensional basis. For the impact of what writers leave behind is far less resonant for its intrinsic aesthetics (of painting or drawing) – though its stylistic features remain significant as signs of a specific metropolitan identity – than for the mystery of its executors' invisibility. You never see them. They're out there somewhere because their tags say they are, but you don't know who or where they are. So, what their pieces evoke – or *scream* might be more accurate – is the performance of their disappearance. That is the true moving force – perhaps threat – of their activity: their elusiveness.

I would argue, then, that writers *are* performing for the 'benefit' of a general public, as much as for their peers. Because, whilst the fact of their mark-making, its illegality in itself but also its execution in inaccessible, high-risk, forbidden locations, seeks an escape from surveillance, it nevertheless requires to be witnessed after the event. It must be sanctioned, if you will, as transgressive by those – everyday citizens – considered to be within the law. It has to be *dis*approved. As writing it *hurts*: it is both the outlaw's expression of the pain of exclusion and dispossession, and it wounds what is 'in law'. Ultimately the act is, as Berger says of the misunderstood terrorist or suicide martyr, 'a way of making sense of and thus transcending despair' (2001: 7). It is no coincidence, then, that taggers utilise the vocabulary of the terrorist: 'bombing' is to spray the whole expanse of a designated surface; we've all seen the 'wholecar bombing' of trains. As such, it has been criminalised, of course, subject in Berlin to a comprehensive implementation of New York-style zero tolerance.[13] A special police commando unit of 50 officers was formed to deal with the city's supposed 15,000 taggers. For Rada this signals police involvement in precisely the kind of social issues of which the force repeatedly claims to strive to steer clear (1997: 178). Above all, this sort of move carries the potential of effectively outlawing what is actually a significant 'intercultural communication network' (168–9). The initiative has reduced some activity but for the hardliner only raises the stakes. Zero tolerance cuts both ways in other words.

It is doubtless one of the ironies – some would say logics – of the situation in Berlin that New York remedies are being applied to a 'disease' so unashamedly characterised by New York symptoms. Van Treeck identifies Berlin as having become the 'secret graffiti-capital of Europe' in the 1990s, adopting a style which follows 'well-worn New York guidelines'. His glossary of Berlin writers' terminology is almost exclusively American (van Treeck 1999: 12, 152 and 275).[14] The proximity of style gives pause for thought: on the one hand it may be the creative adoption of a cultural form known to make its subversive mark effectively; on the other hand a vacuous duplicating of style which speaks of enslavement to the trappings and values of a dominant global Americanism. In the latter's sense the writer's tag can begin to betray affinities with the 'lifestyle branding' of corporate logoism, something copied out of context whose value to its emulators relates more to identification with Americana than a culture of anarchy. A tourist-eye's view of the decorated city will confirm who is winning the war of zero tolerance. Graffiti writing has in any case always had ephemerality – the continuous play of presence and absence – built into its very form. Nothing spurs the committed, way-of-life writer on to more spectacular exploits than to see their work removed. The Thälmann monument on Greifswalder Strasse, covered over and over with graffiti for more than a decade – as we have seen (see chapter five) – was finally cleaned in 2001 at great expense met, highly ironically given the man's status as a communist icon, mainly by private finance. Within days of its makeover, it had been bombed. One exasperated councillor disbelievingly asked how it was that the perpetrators *never ever* seemed to get caught (Raabe 2001: 25).

In spite of its non-specific territorial function within the context of the city, there is nevertheless a kind of necessary laying of claim to the built environment in operation in the application of graffiti. It is an irritant, an unwanted autograph or tattoo anonymously etched on to the body of official urban culture, reminding it that all is not well. Berlin has experienced an explosion of new and restored building since 1989. The city has been besieged by architects and developers fixated by the fresh and clean. Many of the drab old *Plattenbauten*, the systems-built blocks in the East, have been given rejuvenating facelifts, particularly in the more central areas. It is striking how the transformation occurring during the 1990s has seemed to emanate outwards from the new nucleus of the city, like a rubber glove gradually being turned outside out again. In the course of time the fingertips too will pop out, but they are not

33.

the priority. There are many who exist on the peripheries, who do not feel addressed by or included in the changes taking place. It has not improved their lives, appearing to be a centralised spectacle for 'other people'. It is no coincidence, to invoke another popular tactic in the tagging war, that the chances are virtually impossible of locating a single carriage-window of the U-Bahn or S-Bahn that has not been scratched over. The S-Bahn from Bahnhof Zoo to Friedrich Strasse takes you on a perfect viewing excursion along the coordinates of the 'new Berlin', following the central contour of the rail network's 'mushroom concept'. West to east, past the band of new government buildings, Foster's dome at the parliamentary Reichstag, Jahn's Sony Centre at Potsdamer Platz (in the background), and the unfinished Lehrter railway station to name a few recent markers. But you can't quite see them properly, and maybe that's the unthought intention. Why should you have the pleasure? *We smear buildings, we impair your privileged view and, when we get close enough, we'll scratch your retinas because why should you have what we cannot?* Perhaps this is a kind of evocation of the Lacanian 'blot in the visual field', the distorted gaze threatening seamless unity, which forces us to look again, 'differently'. In the East Berlin of old it always was a common complaint of the populace that western tourists would come for a day of rubbernecking at (the failure of) real existing socialism in action, a voyeurism it could do little about, particularly since its own government encouraged it. Graffiti

34.

35.

is effectively the revenge of the gawped-at, though I hasten to add that I'm not thereby ascribing its presence here solely to the eastern population. If you want to *read* the writing on the wall, it says: see *this*, you cannot afford not to. Signed: the disappeared.

'*Berlin ist käuflich*' announced large-size posters, prominently displayed all over the city in the summer of 2000. Another form of 'writing on the wall'. It was an advertising slogan for so-called Berlin porcelain – renowned and exclusive, delicate and whiter-than-white – and it testified to German advertisers' new-found dalliance with ironic word-play: 'Berlin can be bought', it said, meaning Berlin (porcelain) is affordable but, above all, 'Berlin is for sale', as it juggled with the indirect sense of the corruptible city willing to sell itself down the Spree river. If zero tolerance's solution is to wipe the problem of graffiti from central view, pretending thereby that it does not exist, graffiti writers continue to lay down their wreaths of mourning, embroidering the edges of the zero degree exclusion zone that remains. It is the space of ownership that is being contested, over which hang the age-old questions of justice and equality. Brecht's Caucasian circle, chalked on the ground as if some children's street game were being played. To whom shall belong the child? To the mother who would not wound it and make it scream in pain. To whom shall belong the mother-land? To those who are good for it.

Notes

1. The state of Anhalt joined with Sachsen (Saxony) in 1947 producing Sachsen-Anhalt, which continues to form one of the German *Länder*.

2. For West Berlin's 750 birthday celebrations in 1987, a section of the old customs wall very close to Anhalter Bahnhof, on Stresemann Strasse, was excavated and reconstructed.

3. In fact, the concert venue Tempodrom, which had floated between sites in the city for years whilst it sought to establish itself permanently at the far end of the Anhalter terrain, finally opened its doors there in late 2001 in a new building.

4. This seems to have been the characteristic fate of the architect Schwechten's buildings. He also constructed the Kaiser-Wilhelm Gedächtniskirche, the ruined church in the centre of the old West Berlin, which, as a relic of allied bombing, was one of the Cold War city's more famous landmarks. Ironically, Hessel, who cannot disguise his utter contempt for the church (by an architect 'whose name we would do well to forget'), prays in the 1920s for 'this cathedral with the long name at least to age and fall into ruin a little' (1984: 135).

5. Käte Niederkirchner was a communist resistance fighter killed in 1944. That fact, in turn, produced problems after the fall of the Wall when the municipal parliament reconvened in a building on the same street. After a vote in favour of retention of Niederkirchner Strasse as the name, right-wing and liberal politicians simply left the street off their letterheads (Ladd 1998: 158, 213–14). Later, Large reports, 'because the Berlin municipal parliament had taken over the former Prussian House of Deputies, which is located on this street, the small piece of the road directly in front of the parliament was renamed Platz vor dem Abgeordneten Haus. This way the Berlin legislators would not have the name of a Communist on their letterhead' (2002: 561).

6. Topography of Terror is temporarily sited outside whilst a permanent building is constructed for it on the foundations of the former Gestapo headquarters. Having lain untouched as wasteland since the immediate post-war years, the terrain was 'rediscovered' in the 1980s – not least its Gestapo interrogation cells – and plans for an exhibition site formed. For a detailed description of the location's evolution see Ladd (1998: 154–169).

7. The eastern part of the city was never formally called East Berlin by the East Germans. Officially

it was Berlin, capital of the GDR. The western half was never seen as anything other than a provisional allied protectorate. It appeared on maps as a blank space (*terra nullius*) described as Westberlin, which gave the impression of it being just a district of the city. Strictly the GDR and Soviet authorities broke four-power agreements made in 1944–45 which stipulated that the whole of Berlin should remain a non-integrated zone.

8. For a detailed account of the circumstances of the Berlin airlift see Richie (1999: 663–73) and Large (2002: 400–11).

9. As Leach summarises: 'The "crime" of Antigone had been to disobey manmade law. It was a case of the classic Greek dilemma between manmade and natural law, between *nomos* and *physis*. Antigone's two brothers, Polynices and Eteocles, had both been killed in battle, Polynices attempting to overthrow the city of Thebes and Eteocles struggling to defend it. Creon had decreed that in retribution the corpse of Polynices was to remain on the battlefield to be devoured by vultures, whereas Eeteocles was to be accorded a full state funeral. Antigone, however, defied Creon and buried Polynices, setting in motion the tragedy that was to consume them both. Just as Antigone became a martyr for obeying the natural law, so too Creon came to suffer for committing the ultimate *hubris* of overstepping the mark and overruling that law' (1999: 215).

Brecht adapted the play in 1948. Two sisters find their brother hanged as a deserter by the SS as the allies advance on Berlin. One of the 'missing GDR memorials' in Calle's *The Detachment* (see chapter five) commemorated the hanging by 'dehumanised SS-thugs' of two German soldiers, summing up, as Griffin suggests 'the GDR's position towards the Third Reich, which was that the Holocaust was simply an episode in the Nazi oppression of international communism' (Griffin 2000: 169).

10. For Baudrillard the decisive point in the inauguration of an 'age of simulacra and simulation' is the transition from signs which dissimulate *something* to signs which dissimulate that there is *nothing* (1983: 12).

11. The extent to which fortuitous messages on pieces of paper have figured in modern German history is amusing. Apart from Chamberlain's infamous guarantee from Hitler of peace in Europe in 1938 – which the latter later dismissed as 'really of no great importance' (Richie 1999: 479) – an impatient Bismarck crucially doctored an inoffensive telegram to him by Kaiser Wilhelm. Its subsequent publication in the press unavoidably precipitated war with France and the emergence of the first German Republic in 1871 (Richie 1999: 196–8).

12. There was a time, however, when halls of fame were spaces designated by taggers themselves as reserved for the best amongst them, known as 'kings' (van Treeck 1999: 275).

13. Uwe Rada reports on the visit to Berlin in 1997 of New York chief of police William Bratton to lecture Berlin police on zero tolerance methods in the fight against street crime (1997: 173–203).

Van Treeck provides an outline of what criminal law in Germany actually states and implies (1999: 172–178).

14. The other marginal influence van Treeck identifies comes from Paris and relates specifically to the phenomenon *pochoir*, stencil graffiti (1999: 190–203).

7. Potsdamer Platz: White Noise

I knew that cities were being built

I haven't been to any.

A matter for statistics, I thought

Not history.

What's the point of cities, built

Without the people's wisdom?

(Bertolt Brecht, 'Great Times, Wasted')

Great Babel vomited and it sounded like FREEDOM! and coughed and it sounded like JUSTICE! and farted and again it sounded like PROSPERITY!

(Bertolt Brecht, 'Great Babel Gives Birth')

City Centres

In the year 2000 Berlin suffered its first loss of a post-reunification piece of architecture. In fact it had only been in place since 1995. It was the Info Box at Leipziger Platz, a brilliant red, oblong construction which for five long years served as a kind of beacon of hope and calm amidst the chaos of building exploding all around. Sited just off Potsdamer Platz in the former territory of the death strip, it presented on three levels comprehensive high-tech displays of the various plans for the area (and beyond), involving not only the built environment but also the less apparent subterranean logistics of energy – water, gas, electricity and the like – communications and travel. Resembling a deluxe, jumbo-size portakabin – an elegant, temporary residence fit for a federal president – Info Box rested on angled black stilts which both elevated it above the confusion of 'Europe's largest building

36.

site' and gave it the appearance of an imminent getaway. Offset external staircases attached like stabilisers on either side functioned as fire escapes as well as leading to and from the flat roof. Here a raised platform afforded an all-round view of proceedings to visitors. The 'outside' experience the building gave, relating to the present state of play of the evolving city, was the perfect antidote to the 'inside' one, which sucked you into the rush of where it was all supposed to be heading.

It was entirely appropriate, then, that a construction which held the present and future in tension by design should eventually outlive its purpose and disappear once the distance between those distinct time-frames had been spanned. That was how it had always been intended. In contrast to the 'act of mutilation' committed with Anhalter Bahnhof in 1961, *not* permitting Info Box to go scampering off to find its own death-niche would have been to impede the building in its natural life-cycle.[1] If the temporary permanence of Info Box embodied the transition to the future, it invariably performed a discontinuous relationship with the past. Positioned where it was in the one-time non-land of the Wall, it had raised its head above the parapet and formed an antithetical bridging structure, a way station between east and west. Its role, then, was to symbolise as well as document the intricacies of rejoining the city. And it is worth remembering how the Wall cauterised the circulation not only of streets and people but also, for example, gas and water mains, and both over and underground train networks. But if it was about the process of east-west reconnection, it was also looking in one direction only: towards a new, westernised Berlin.

In his reflections on Tokyo in *Empire of Signs*, Barthes ponders the performative function of city centres. For the (European) occidental sensibility the notion of a holistic urban core to which one ventures and returns in a psycho-geographical playing out of a process of 'finding' or 'inventing oneself' has become established.[2] Cities have come to lay themselves out concentrically, their 'downtowns' representing the location of a socialising 'truth': the values of civilisation as articulated through the built embodiments of spirituality (churches), power (offices), money (banks), goods (shops) and general language flow (cafés and malls). Barthes' concern is to contrast this portrayal of space-filling *plenitude* with the oriental practice exemplified by Tokyo of having a large void at its core, the forbidden residential parklands of the emperor who remains unseen. Far from being an expression of power, having nothing more than an 'evaporated notion' at its heart has the purpose of 'giving the whole movement of the city the stabilising benefit of its central emptiness, permanently forcing traffic to be diverted. In this way [...] the system of the imaginary circulates via detours and return trips around an empty subject' (1982: 30–2).

As an inhabitant of West Berlin it was never really clear where the centre of the city was. The Kurfürstendamm was seen as the main shopping avenue, but it tended toward the exclusive and, with its broad pavements, it was really mainly a promenade for window-shoppers. Bahnhof Zoo was the principal railway station but the area around it was filthy and tackily commercial. Immediately to the east of it, heading in the direction of Wittenberg Platz, rose three of West Berlin's most renowned landmarks. First there were the neo-Romanesque remains of the bombed out Kaiser Wilhelm Gedächtniskirche (memorial church) – popularly referred to as the hollow tooth – sandwiched between its 1960s modernist supplements of a nave and bell tower. Then there was the Europa Centre complex of shops with its 22-storey high-rise building, topped by a giant gyrating Mercedes Benz star which, luminous as it was, dominated the night sky. Finally, there was the monolithic turn-of-the-century Kaufhaus des Westens, or KaDeWe for short, which was the only one of several such department stores in Berlin to have survived the war intact. Not unlike Harrods in London in its interior style, it gives a good idea, in terms of its architecture and presence of what Tacheles (discussed in chapter four) will have been like in its day. Along with the Europa Centre it played a significant part in the mythology of Cold War one-upmanship – not least through the provocative fortuity of its name, which means 'department store of the West' – supposedly epitomising the plentiful splendour, the sheer breadth and quality, that a free market could provide for the (relatively) ordinary citizen. It is amusing that these key players in the East-West competitive stakes should have been situated on a street named Tauentzien; referring to a heroic Prussian general of the Napoleonic Wars, it carries, again coincidentally, a distinct trace of *Tauziehen*, which is German for tug-of-war.

37.

As an area, though, it was not a particularly enticing one in which to dwell. It certainly did not produce the sense evoked by Barthes of a city centre fulfilling the needs of a citizen's self-seeking. For the inhabitant of West Berlin it was rather an area to circumvent and leave to the tourists. This did not result in the redirected flow of the oriental stabilising void, of course, more in an agitated displacement. West Berlin was characterised by the random dispersal both of its socio-cultural institutions and the living habits of its populace, creating small pockets of self-identifying activity. On the one hand you would have a sense of belonging to the specific district or perhaps street in which you lived, corresponding to the neighbourhoodly phenomenon of the *Kiez* (see also chapter four); on the other you might have attended the Free University in the city's southern periphery, visited the world class Egyptian Museum in the western Charlottenburg, or gone for a night of bar-crawling in the depths of Kreuzberg within a stone's throw of the eastern Wall. The point about West Berlin was that there was precious little, if anything, of the pre-war centre that fell within its jurisdiction. So the Wall did not engineer a neat severance down the middle but actually emasculated the west, effectively sending the notion of central cultural and civic institutions madly caroming in all directions. There was no town to which to go up or down.

To imagine that the east therefore ended up with all the 'juicy bits' of a ready-made centre isn't accurate either, however. Although many prized establishments – notably the various state museums grouped together at the eastern end of Unter den Linden – remained in the hands of the GDR authorities, the areas immediately bordering the Wall were effectively no-go zones, as Ladd indicates:

> Apart from official ceremonies, Easterners were discouraged from approaching the Wall and even taking note of its existence. Those East Berliners who lived in the streets next to the Wall had to adjust to special restrictions, intrusions and inconveniences. Friends from outside the neighbourhood could never just drop by, for example: permission had to be obtained from the police.

(1998: 14)

As we have seen with Spandauer Vorstadt, these abandoned areas, coupled of course with the broad band of the death strip itself, formed considerable expanses of liminal non-land in what had been the heart of the city. The east, however, was far more successful at effectively turning its back on the Wall and relocating its core concentrically around the vast, wind-blown space of Alexander Platz.

Without doubt the most striking instance of the voided centre produced by partition was Potsdamer Platz. Like its near-neighbour Brandenburger Tor, it formed one of the gateways to the city, providing passage through the old customs wall surrounding the centre until the 1860s. It was, thus, peripheral to the true centre, but once that wall had disappeared and Berlin began expanding in the latter half of the nineteenth century, Potsdamer Platz rapidly took on the status of principal junction in the general urban traffic of people, trains, buses, cars, trams and, of course, commerce. One of its distinctions, in fact, is to have been the location for the very first traffic light in Europe in 1925. So, although Friedrich Strasse, for example, will have held similar significance as a place for shopping, with its renowned arcades, it will not have functioned with that same sense of a throbbing hub that Potsdamer Platz had acquired as a *thoroughfare*, albeit one that appeared off-centre. In fact, as Ladd points out again, the latter never really was a square as such – leaving that role to the adjoining Leipziger Platz – more an intersection characterised 'above all by the bustle, speed and motion of the modern metropolis' (1998: 116). That was a perception which metonymised the image of Potsdamer Platz: the square '*was* Berlin because Berlin was the city of bustle and speed [...] the visible embodiment of the hypermodern urbanity [Germans] associated with the United States – thus it was an "American city", or a "German Chicago"' (117), or 'Chicago on the Spree' to invoke Mark Twain's familiar turn-of-the-century verdict. Around the same time, moreover, the art critic Scheffler was reflecting critically upon Berlin 'with its "American-tempo growth", its "Babylonian imbroglio", as a capital of "parvenu culture"' (Frisby 2001: 173).[3] No coincidence, then, that the young Brecht chose Chicago as the environment for his early play about rising urban alienation, *In the Jungle of Cities*, written some years later in 1922. Based on a diary entry (Brecht 1979: 119), Vaßen observes that at that time Brecht saw

> the big city as a 'jungle' [...] and above all as an 'area of struggle' [...] When Brecht notes 'the hostility of the big city, its malignant stony consistency, its babylonian confusion of language: in short, [that] its poetry has not yet been created', he sees it as his task to bridge this gap and to get to grips with the new reality of the city.

(1998: 75)

Brecht set an even earlier play, *Drums in the Night*, in the Piccadilly Bar of the landmark Haus Vaterland at Potsdamer Platz (see chapter nine). Written a few days after the 1919 Spartacus riots raging in the streets outside, it records one of the most decisive moments in German twentieth century history, as Bienert explains:

> The decision by the Social Democratic leadership to suppress the communist uprising using troops loyal to the emperor, encumbered any attempts during the Weimar Republic to establish understanding or an active alliance between social democrats and communists. The bloody suppression of the Spartacus uprising is part of the prehistory of the National Socialists' victory over the political left.

(1998, 54)

More or less desecrated by the Russian army in 1945, perhaps the last piece of *action* Potsdamer Platz saw before it was properly put to sleep in 1961 was when the brutal confrontation between Soviet tanks and protestors during the East German workers uprising of 17 June 1953 spilled over from Unter den Linden and Brandenburger Tor. As an eye-witness, Heiner Müller has it down as the 'main battlefield' (1992: 133); and Brecht himself became famously embroiled in controversy relating to his response to the events, as the next chapter shows. After 1961 the area annexed by the Wall – most of the intersection, that is – was razed of any buildings. All that remained, as photographs show, were rusted relics, those few material features stubborn enough to have hung on as the scorching mid-century winds passed through: the odd street or traffic sign, the railings round the staircases leading to the Underground, a semi-circle of chains linking concrete bollards where the pioneering traffic lights had been. Tramlines, embedded in cobblestones, bisected the central circus from the west, stopping dead in the middle where they disappeared below a close-knit double row of criss-cross anti-tank obstacles. Lining either side of Leipziger Strasse, the main thoroughfare due east, were tall, thin poles presumably used to support the overhead network of electric tram wires. Vestiges of a former civilisation. In the south-east corner of the zone, immediately beyond the point at which the bright red Info Box would raise its head some 30 years later, was one of those watchtowers, surveying the deadlands.

If you're going to take the radical step of turning your back on your neighbour, it makes sense to perform that act with maximum intensity at precisely the point where its antithetical effect will be felt most keenly. In that respect *total* standstill at Potsdamer Platz – it was not used, for instance, as a border crossing-point – represented a logical move. By the same token it becomes a kind of theatre-of-reconciliation-in-waiting. In other words: if reunification occurs, *here* is where it will be played out in its most concentrated, telling form. That implies not only a reconnection with its previous state as 'bustling hub' but also that *here* is where both the future identity of the city itself and East-West German relations as a whole will be defined. It is at this point, when the lights turn to green and things begin to move again – the original traffic lights have indeed been restored to their erstwhile location – that its status makes the transition from anaesthetic non-land to ground zero, a landscape with untold potential. Whilst that sounds like – and, indeed, is – a very optimistic moment, it is perhaps most accurately described as opening a crisis.

This Babylonian Confusion

In a published interview entitled 'Architecture Where the Desire May Live', Derrida elucidates the correlation between the practices of architecture and writing via the notion of the *Riss*: a tear, ripping action or engraving. A way is opened up spatially 'which – without knowing where it will lead to – inscribes its traces [...] This writing is truly like a labyrinth since it has neither beginning nor end. One is always on the move' (Leach 1997: 321). Architecture imitates this action and '[f]rom here originates the attempt [...] to create a different kind of living which no longer fits the old circumstances, where the plan is not oriented towards domination, controlling communication, the economy and transport, etc.' (322). Architecture is then a form of writing the city, one which changes the directions one may take in it. To illustrate his point Derrida invokes the parable of the building of the tower of Babel, which I think is worth reproducing here:

> There too the sky is to be conquered in an act of name-giving, which yet remains insep-arably linked with the natural language. A tribe, the Semites, whose name means 'name', a tribe therefore called 'name' want to erect a tower supposed to reach the sky, according to the scriptures, with the aim of making a name for itself. This conquest of the sky, this taking up of a position in the sky means giving oneself a name and from this power, from the power of the name, from the height of the meta-language, to dominate the other tribes, the other languages, to colonise them. But God descends and spoils the enterprise by uttering one word: 'Babel', and this word is a name which resembles a noun meaning confusion. With this name he condemns mankind to the diversity of languages. Therefore they have to renounce their plan of domination by means of a language which would be universal.
>
> *(322)*

Benjamin occupies similar mythical territory in one of his very early essays, published in *One-Way Street*, on the nature and function of language ('On Language as Such and on the Language of Man'). In it he explicates the consequence of God's pronouncement as being one in which 'man has fallen from the paradisiac state', and that fall 'marks the birth of the *human word*' (1997: 119). For Benjamin things have no proper names except in the 'pure state of God': 'For in his creative word, God called them into being [...] In the language of men, however, they are over-named' (122). The young Benjamin constructs a densely-argued case around the mistaken perception of language as something *through* rather than *in* which humans communicate (108): 'In stepping outside the purer language of name man makes language a means [...] and therefore also in one part at any rate, a *mere* sign; and this results in the plurality of languages' (120). Abandoning 'immediacy' for 'mediateness' in the communication of the concrete represents, then, a fall into the 'abyss of prattle' (120). Seemingly pointing to a resultant failure of language (amongst mortals) – Adam's act of naming as indicative of the fall into an imperfect human knowledge, of infinite language becoming finite – Benjamin states:

> Signs must become confused where things are entangled. The enslavement of language in prattle is joined by the enslavement of things in folly almost as its inevitable consequence. In this turning away from things, which was enslavement, the plan for the tower of Babel came into being, and linguistic confusion with it.

(1997: 121)

For Derrida, though, God's intervention in architecture 'represents the failure or the limitation imposed on a universal language in order to foil the plan for political and linguistic domination of the world'. This 'says something about the impossibility of mastering the diversity of languages, about the impossibility of there being a universal translation' (Leach 1997: 322). Not only does this mean, then, that 'the construction of architecture will always remain labyrinthine' but also that the issue should therefore be 'not to give up one point of view for the sake of another, which would be the only one and absolute, but to see a diversity of possible points of view' (322).

The reconstruction of Potsdamer Platz after 1989 began briefly with the 'babble' or 'prattle' of diverse voices. Alan Balfour takes up the story:

> Within months of the removal of the Wall, all kinds of imaginations were projecting onto this place, most of them with thoughts far removed from architecture. The official maps of West Berlin had always described East Berlin exactly as it was in 1939, with all the property lines clearly demarcated. The most immediate response to the demise of Socialism was a blizzard of law suits reclaiming land lost in the division [...] And even before architects began to offer visions, the city attracted international developers who were keenly aware of the vast profits to be made from the transformation of a free Berlin into a world financial and corporate centre.

> Potsdamer Platz was viewed as the most opportune field for speculation. Corporations and developers struggled to acquire possession of the extensive areas of land [...] By the end of 1991 the battle for land acquisition was over. The northwest sector went to Sony, the south-west sector to the Asea Brown Boveri

Corporation [ABB], and the largest, the south-west, to the Debis Development corporation, a wholly owned subsidiary of Daimler Benz [now Daimler Chrysler].

(Balfour 1995: 65)

Balfour's account gives a clear sense not only of the speed with which everything
was sewn up, but also the extent to which the space allocation of Potsdamer Platz
was accounted for by less than a handful of major 'name-giving' corporate players.
Before the city had even been officially reunited, first Daimler Benz, then the Sony
Corporation had snapped up these prime tracts of land at bargain prices. The
former in particular caused controversy because of its one-time 'hand-in-glove'
relationship with the Nazis (see chapter eight and Large 2002: 553–4). The motive
of these companies was to establish a credible business *presence* for themselves in
the 'new capital of Europe', as well as to act as real estate developers, hiving off
portions of their land to other commercial entities for vast profits. So, as far as the
development of Potsdamer Platz was concerned, there appeared to be little in the
way of democratic 'babble' in the public interest, as Ladd outlines:

> So much for diversity and street life, thought some critics, envisioning the area as a
> desolate zone of self-enclosed office towers. So much for planning, thought others:
> the decisions had been made before either planners or the public contributed their
> thoughts. What ensued was a messy set of negotiations between the city, trying to
> salvage something of Potsdamer Platz's urban diversity, and the corporate landown-
> ers.

(1998: 122)

Ownership established, the next stage was the awarding of highly prestigious
architectural commissions on the basis of several competitions attracting the major
international names. The rupture brought by the Wall had produced a vacuum
whose exciting architectural challenge was to connect the 'sad remnants of the
nineteenth century' in the east with the 'intentional "misorder"' in the west
(Balfour 1995: 65). Little interest appeared to exist, though, not least on the part of
the city authorities, to take up that challenge imaginatively. An overall 'master plan'
for the entire area was chosen first, being awarded to the Munich architects Hilmer
and Sattler. Their task was to reallocate responsibility for the various sections to
other architects – with the approval of the corporate players – on the basis that their
grand design would be adhered to.

Essentially the division of the area broke down into three parts: Helmut Jahn's Sony
centre, Renzo Piano's Debis section (further subdivided) and Georgio Grassi's

ABB portion. A fourth section, the so-called Lenné Dreieck (triangle) in the north-west, owned by the department store Hertie Karstadt, lagged behind and is still under construction at the time of writing. The point about the master plan was that it was required to conform as far as possible to what were referred to as 'pre-war', but were actually 'pre-modern', dictates of city patterning. So, even where architects may have wanted to introduce an innovative hand, they were severely constrained. Ultimately, the Hilmer-Sattler plan emerged, in Balfour's words, as one 'shaped to be consciously modest, free from utopian desire, free from the promise of reformation. A plan without a future' (1995: 69).

Recourse to pre-modern blueprints for the lay-out of the city gave birth to the most hotly debated architectural issue of the immediate post-89 era in Berlin, that of critical reconstruction.[4] What the notion enshrined in essence was a conforming to certain conditions of building in the centre of the city based on historical ground plans: height limits, street patterns and building 'lines', fixed proportions of residential provision, and maintenance of the 'character' of an urban building. Whilst its retrospective pre-modernity appeared to lean towards outright nostalgia, the point according to its defenders was that it should be *critical*, implying the application of a contemporary interpretation. It was, moreover, viewed by the city authorities as an important control device in the rampant property speculation promised by the collapse of the Wall. Detractors, on the other hand, pointed to its misconception of history as the retrieval of a fixed, linear phenomenon. As Gerd Kähler argues:

> In Berlin the so-called historical blueprint of the city actually amounts to a patch-work of diverse points of departure – ranging from the old town of the middle ages through to Hobrecht's [nineteenth century] plan – the individual elements of which came about in each instance in response to new circumstances of place, time and society. As a rule the 'historical' blueprint – and not exclusively in the case of Berlin! – is made up of the sum of ruptures, each marking the new, not a supposed contin-uum. There is no *one* historical blueprint of the city because that pre-supposes a *condition* that has only ever existed as a *changing* one.

> *(Kahlfeldt 2000: 383)*

This was a position which seemed to be iterated by Daniel Libeskind who proposed (and had rejected) one of the most radical designs for Potsdamer Platz. Dismissing critical reconstruction as 'a battery of arbitrary constraints that go under the guise of "rationalism", the "rhetoric of order"', he argued in an essay entitled 'Deconstructing the Call to Order' that 'Berlin is in reality a fascinating

38.

montage of conflicting histories, scales, forms and spaces – a rich mix of substance and imagination' (Balfour 1995: 35–36). As such, he commented elsewhere,

> the identity of Berlin cannot be refounded on the ruins of history or in the illusionary 'reconstructions' of an arbitrarily selected past [...] The transformation of the shape of the future city must be accompanied by corresponding changes in the mentality associated with pre-war lot lines, anachronistic visions, dreams that money can buy.

> *(Libeskind 2001: 142)*

Libeskind's view clearly resonates with Derridean echoes of God's exhortation of the Semites to renounce their plan of domination. Importantly, as Bennington's gloss on Derrida's preoccupation with the parable points out, 'it also gives us something to think about in the direction of the proper name and the common noun. For God's shouting out a proper name which can be heard as a common noun suggests the becoming-common of the proper' (Bennington/Derrida 1993: 175–6). The linguistic shift from the proper to the common, arising as a result of one thing being uttered and another being understood, simultaneously marks the turn from the space of private to that of public ownership. Libeskind's proposal, an irregular criss-cross matrix of 'thunderbolts' (a term which recalls the lightening flash of the Jewish Museum) epitomises, moreover, the architectural *Riss,* producing a 'site-as-puzzle' (labyrinth) which 'like Humpty Dumpty's shattering act […] cannot be "put together in place again"' (Libeskind 2001: 142). As Derrida suggests, the *Riss* should not be mistaken for the *Grundriss*, the ground plan or blueprint (Leach 1997: 322). It urges a breach, which is encapsulated in the plural imperative *brecht* that accords with the writer Brecht's own name (as we have seen in chapter two). In fact, the proper/common name relation addressed by Bennington is effectively replicated by Brecht/*brecht*; the owned name that would demand it be sprung open into public 'crisis', the 'Brechtian in Brecht' or the poet passing 'through a gate upon which, in weather-worn letters, a BB can be deciphered' (Benjamin 1977: 58). As it happens, one of Brecht's 1920s city poems, 'This Babylonian Confusion',5 seems to point to Kähler's notion of the 'historical blueprint' as a 'sum of ruptures, each making the new' (Kahlfeldt 2000: 383). Grappling with the failings of history, the narrator realises the 'effort/It would cost me to tell/That story to those not yet born/But who will be born and will live/In ages quite different from ours' (Brecht 1976: 125). The events of history reflect, then, plans that have 'only ever existed as changing ones' (Kahlfeldt 2000: 383):

They said to me: […]

Tell us, why did you not have

A blueprint, if only

In books perhaps of earlier times –

A blueprint of men, either drawn

Or described, for it seems to us

Your motive was quite base

And also quite easy to change. Almost anyone

Could have seen it was wrong, inhuman, exceptional.

Was there not such an old and

Simple model you could have gone by

In your confusion?

I said: Such models existed

But, you see, they were criss-crossed

Five times over with new marks, illegible

The blueprint altered five times to accord

With our degenerate image, so that

In those reports even our forefathers

Resembled none but themselves.

(Brecht 1976: 125–6)

In Libeskind's view the Berlin taste for 'totality', 'uniformity' and 'master planning' should now be well and truly *over* in both west and east (Libeskind 2001: 142). Clearly, a montage or mosaic form is one which seeks a representational relationship to history that is based on *change* rather than 'truth', one which affords the possibility of overcoming the conflicts of the past. If there is indeed any form of reconstruction of historical moments, it should reside in the remotivation of the square's one time multifarious *movement*: 'The lost centre cannot be reconnected like an artificial limb to an old body, but must generate an overall transformation of the city [...] no style or system should be given priority over others. A heterogeneous, pluralistic reality is the goal' (143).

Kähler considers the 'babble of Berlin' over critical reconstruction and its alternatives to have petered out rather than be resolved: 'At some point there are no more arguments, interest – even amongst a specialist public – stagnates, the discussion goes to sleep. Whether it even took place is questionable; in truth it was no more than a swapping of arguments – discussion presupposes the critical incorporation and evaluation of an opponent's argumentation' (Kahlfeldt 2000: 386). Since it was the will of the city authorities, critical reconstruction has largely asserted itself, though, typically at key locations like Friedrich Strasse and Pariser Platz (adjoining Brandenburger Tor). And, Kähler adds, it is the implementation of *western* planning in the interests of capital that is being witnessed (386–7), a dismissiveness deemed by Libeskind as fatal: '[O]ne must take the existing context in the GDR seriously, not because one likes the ill-conceived buildings, but because its history and its people must be respected' (Balfour 1995: 36). It is important to see in this not a blindspot, Libeskind's own form of the nostalgia he reviles, but the recognition that '[p]lanning and architecture should not condone demolition; they should deal with construction and the incorporation of difficult conditions in a new ecologically responsible manner' (Libeskind 2001: 196).

Whilst a verdict on Potsdamer Platz's future may have been reached very quickly by the judges at the planning stage, the public jury is still out. Although the Hilmer-Sattler plan was deemed 'boringly safe' by architecture critics like Balfour, it seems to have defied certain of the strictures of critical reconstruction as they have been insisted upon elsewhere, allowing high-rise buildings, for instance. Moreover, as James-Chakraborty points out, '"good" design by internationally acclaimed architects in conjunction with strict regulations' has kept *outward* commercial spectacle under control. Street facing facades do not carry the luminous display of advertising and store names of the pre-war era (2000: 130). Visiting late in 2001 a substantial part of the actual construction had in any case yet to take place, above all the north-western section and the adjoining Leipziger Platz octagon. Walking through the parts that have been finished, I was inclined to feel that the whole complex needs to be completed before the populace will develop an idea of how to respond and circulate within it. At present it produces a sense of uneasy alienation, characterised by the vacuous gawping of the touristic order; a place to visit and observe from a distance rather than 'inhabit'. The bars and cafés seem impersonal and contrived, quoting ambience rather than 'being' it. Not somewhere to feel comfortably social. Elegant and discreet as the civic, European-model orientation of Piano's south-west mall may strive to be, it does not generate the sense of a happening intersection. Identified in any case by James-Chakraborty as 'frankly commercial rather than civic' in its function, despite the tempering of mercantile display (136), it even fails to galvanise a particular 'pleasure in shopping'.

Sonyc Sound

Certainly the most striking feature of the complex is the Sony Centre (appropriately) designed by the German-American Chicago-based architect Helmut Jahn. Through the sheer speed and strength of the corporation's response in the early days of negotiations over Potsdamer Platz, it managed incredibly to secure exemption from the Hilmer and Sattler master plan (Balfour 1995: 69). An aerial view shows the inner-world of Sony to have – again appropriately – the contours of a giant ear resting horizontally. A soaring forum within is topped, slightly off-centre, by what could be the speaker-element of a Walkman headset (in reality a tensile, circus-tent-like structure). Surrounding the inner sanctum is a triangulation of glass and steel building blocks, marked at its eastern point by a pronounced 'lobe', a rising 26-storey semi-column of tinted glass (now the headquarters of German state railways).

Sensing yourself shrink with every meandering step you take into the high-tech innards, you are confronted first by the glassed-off corner of what looks like the ostentatious set for a restoration drama. In fact it's the restored remnant of a neo-rococo 'breakfast suite' belonging to the once-exclusive Grand Hotel Esplanade, one of two buildings more or less surviving the war on the western side of Potsdamer Platz. Jahn has incorporated elements of the hotel, in the case of two of its rooms involving complex and spectacular 75 metre relocation operations. The breakfast suite was one, though it didn't move lock, stock and coffee-pot; the corner you witness here is the original north-west interior. The north facing side of the Sony complex has performed a similar *in vitro* annexation of the former Esplanade facade. Jahn's purpose, apart from the obvious, museum-like preservation of the remains, was to establish 'a compositional tension between historical and modern architecture' (*Info Box: der Katalog* 1998: 184). In the context of the vast corporate

39.

monolith that is the Sony Centre, it comes over as rampant twenty-first century appropriation, turning it into a stage-set so genuine it looks fake behind its shop window. This is not the refunctioning of historical architecture in the manner of Tacheles, where the troubled, shifting narratives can be read off the fabric and structure of the building, but its slick commodification. As I'm turning away, two women have ambled up to the grand, ornate mirror over the fireplace. Without a flicker of self-consciousness they retouch their make-up and puff up their big hair, like actors in the neo-neo-rococo powder-room of the state opera house.

The complex as a whole incorporates a range of organisations and functions alongside the Sony headquarters itself. There are several cinemas (including an IMAX screen), a film museum, offices, apartments, bars, cafés as well as Sony sound installations with which the public can interact. The innovative roof construction of steel, glass and fabric elements provides for natural-light-sensitive shifts in atmosphere during the day; when darkness falls a lavish, multi-coloured bonanza of both functional and staged effects lights up the night sky. Entering the forum is an awe-inspiring experience. The circus really has come to town for good, but its 'noise' is visual. The sheer scale of things is overwhelming. It is an enclosed,

40.

essentially circular cosmos, but irregular: here a café, there a cinema, jutting into the spectral plane. See-through elevators glide swiftly up and down its eleven floors, escalators lead off into unknown recesses, a sliver of transparent flooring in the middle offers a glimpse of a subterranean realm. People mill around the concourse, stopping to chat in hushed, reverential tones or sit by the fountain, but always *gazing:* up and around, or down if they've worked out a way to the upper levels. It is a visual feast that can leave you feeling dwarfed and incapacitated. You don't really know what to do there except admire the spectacle. The all-round translucent glass offers impenetrable facades, a gargantuan crystal cathedral that envelops you but does not let you in. Somewhere there must be something going on, but you just can't fathom what or where.

In a way I'm reminded of the situation evoked by the enigmatic smaller-than-life-size figures in Juan Muñoz's 2001 *Double Bind* installation in the turbine hall at Tate Modern in London: trapped in a purgatorial, twilight world between floors, where empty lifts tease you with their caged inaccessibility as they shuttle, empty, between the heaven and hell of basement and rafters. But at least there's a hint of something there, a louch underworld partially lifting its veil. In planet Sony you have a space of hypnotising plenitude which is devoid of life. That's the double bind. For this 'play of American desire', as Balfour terms it (1995: 185), holds me in thrall but, like a toy that 'does too much', doesn't really allow me to play. It's akin to Augé's over-determined non-places of supermodernity in which the more we are exposed to the '"spectacular display of the world" […]the less we can be sure we are still able to really look' (2000: 10–11).

For some individuals the estrangement holds true in a literal sense. Finding my way to one of the underground cinemas on one occasion, I observed a security guard approach and firmly eject what appeared to be a homeless person. An undesirable, not drunk and disorderly, just not looking the part. It's like banning someone from walking on the pavement. This may be public terrain right at the heart of the new Berlin but it's a *certain* public, acquainted and complying with the rules of private (or proper) behaviour, that is held in mind. That's the double bind for this person, dependency on public space which increasingly seeks to constrain or exclude the public. The shrinking zone of tolerance. Effectively it's a revived practice, reminiscent of the nineteenth century arcades, as Rendell's observation of Burlington suggests:

> It was at the threshold between street and arcade, where decisions were enacted by beadles concerning who could and could not enter the Arcade. Men and women could be excluded on grounds of class [...] In capitalism, where space as commodity is confined and controlled, [such] thresholds are feared.

(Coles 1999: 175)

41.

42.

Uwe Rada warns of the growing tendency in Berlin to create such areas of exclusion, a literal and figurative dichotomy of centre and periphery, haves and have-nots, observable in other global cities (not least London). In the mid-nineties a special 'operative group', OG City-West, was formed to issue on-the-spot *Platzverweise* – literally the term used in football for a sending off – to undesirables in designated areas of the city (Rada 1997: 189–99). Vidler relates this kind of practice to the indiscriminate branding of members of the public as vagabonds who 'were guilty of no crime but that of vagabondage; *potential criminals*, outside the law not for a crime committed but for what might be committed in the future as the product of a wayward life' (1992: 210). Rada identifies Potsdamer Platz as one of the new 'citadels' of urban zoning, a 'city-within-a-city' which hasn't yet introduced entry controls as such – though that is effectively what I observed in operation – but certainly functions like a hermetically-sealed fortress. In this scenario access is permitted to the urban underclass only if it has come to perform lowly but necessary services – toilets always need cleaning – in these centres of power (Rada 1997: 201–2). In a variation on Barthes' identity-giving, civilising function, then, the new centre of the twenty-first century is organised around the formation of a not-so-invisible security cordon – a new kind of Berlin Wall – which, aided naturally by surveillance, allows the business of the consumerist order to take its untrammelled course. It is a site, to use James-Chakraborty's succinct terms, for an 'emphatically bourgeois subject' conflated with the 'presumed universal subject' of global corporatist discourse (2000: 126). Ultimately, as Jameson suggests, the privilege of wealth is to be able to buy the right not to have to deal with too many 'awkward humans', simply to erase the spectre of their 'problematic presence'. His analysis here of the domestic withdrawal to 'gated' rural conditions is unexpectedly apposite in its evocation of the kind of exclusionist aspirations involved:

[M]y money buys me the freedom from hearing anyone else: sound also violates, and submission to other people's sounds is a symbolic index of powerlessness and vulnerability. All of this suggests some deeper drive to repress the social and sociability as such: my reward for acquiring a fortune is my possibility of withdrawing from everything that might remind me of the existence of other people in the first place.

(Leach 1997: 264)

In this present-day, central urban context, then, there is the same withdrawal action of the private in operation but, being a 'public space' the obverse applies in terms of the manner in which it is enforced. The 'static' produced is what does the crowding out here; the sheer corporate *presence* of the Sony centre produces a visual noise so powerful and hypnotic it turns dazzling white. It truly forces you to bow to the name-giving meta-language of Derrida's tower of Babel orthodoxy, forcing out the babble of the plague-ridden rabble: a conquest of the skies, a permanence – or definitive 'thus and not otherwise', against which Benjamin warns in his city writings (1997: 169) - which is asking almost to be knocked down. That's a sentiment expressed in a recent film entitled *Berlin Babylon* (2001), directed by Hubertus Siegert. It's a kind of aestheticised documentation of the city's rebuilding process in the latter half of the 90s, featuring the major architects, planners as well as construction workers. The centre of Berlin is being built up to such an extent that it is making itself ripe for destruction by the upcoming generations, declares one of the prominent but unnamed participants interviewed. It is over-determined space which leaves no room to move and breathe, no questions: an understandable paranoia in the context of the city's history. Angela Winkler, a renowned actor, reads from Benjamin's angel of history text in accompaniment to a slow-motion wind of progress sweeping across the city's evolving building sites. And it strikes me as she does so how it is a mad and unpredictable wind, foretelling further wreckages because it is an unseen and unseeing force.

With fitting irony the music for the film is by the legendary Berlin indy band Einstürzende Neubauten, a name which means literally 'collapsing new buildings'. A track from a recent album reflects on the 'lie of the land' at Potsdamer Platz:

Across the scarfaced terrain

slowly disappearing

only phantom pain remains.

Scarcely audible, foul laughter seeps out

from the red Info Box

making some turn quietly in their graves.

[…]

The temples are already cracked

future ruins

one day grass will grow over the city

over its final layer.

(Einstürzende Neubauten, 2000)

On the western flank of the Sony Centre, where it borders the former threshold of civilised West Berlin – the so-called cultural forum with modernist edifices such as Hans Scharoun's yellowish State Library and Philharmonic concert hall, and Mies van der Rohe's New National Gallery (amongst other institutions) – there is an innocuous street running north through Tiergarten towards Strasse des 17 Juni. On my map of the city its name is in brackets, perhaps because it's seen as provisional whilst building is in progress. It's called Entlastungs Strasse, a performative name, doing what it says: a street that acts as a *release valve*, taking the strain. I suppose it's been doing service as some kind of outlet or temporary relief road. Eventually it will become obsolete once the tunnel underneath it, forming part of the city ring-road, has been completed (*Infobox: der Katalog* 1998: 37). Juridically *Entlastung* refers to the act of being exonerated. That's how I feel now as I escape Potsdamer Platz, freed from the static of supersonyc law.

Notes

1. Apparently, its various parts were sold off and the money donated to charity. See *Info Box: der Katalog* (1998) for documentation of the projects covered by the exhibition.

2. Writing in 1970 Barthes begins by pointing to the unease caused by newer cities, such as Los Angeles, which are organised according to a continuous spread of 'quadrangle, reticulated' networks without an obvious core (Barthes 1982: 30). See also Dejan Sudjic's *The Hundred Mile City* (1992).

3. For a full theorisation of Berlin as an Americansied city 'unlike other metropolitan centres in Europe' at the beginning of the twentieth century, see Frisby (2001: 165–77).

4. In fact the term had already come into play in West Berlin at the seminal exhibition of international architectural plans for the city (IBA) in 1987.

5. The poem refers to a 'wheat speculator' who formed the basis of another Chicago-based play begun in the 1920s, the unfinished *Joe P. Fleischhacker* (Brecht 1976: 542). As the diary entry quoted earlier in the chapter in Vaßen's citation testifies, the 'babylonian confusion of language' was an expression Brecht bandied about in connection with developing ideas towards his earlier 'Chicago play' *In the Jungle of Cities*. Brecht was keen to stress the Chicago factor was not 'the result of a romantic disposition. I could just as well have picked Berlin, except then the audience, instead of saying, 'That character's acting strangely, strikingly, peculiarly', would simply have said 'It's a very exceptional Berliner who behaves like that'. Using a background which naturally suited my characters, covering them rather than showing them up, seemed the easiest way of drawing attention to the odd behaviour of widely representative contemporary human types' (Plays 1: 437). Brecht's *St. Joan of the Stockyards* (1930) and *The Resistable Rise of Arturo Ui* (1941) were, of course, also set in the Chicagoan jungle.

8. Strasse des 17 Juni: the Space of (Dis)unity

Someday you ought to take the U-Bahn all the way to the end of the line in the East. A real mind-blower, even now. Make sure to look at the faces of the old people, at the cobwebby bramble-filled heads of those who've survived it all. There aren't many left, but they're there. Think of what this century has been like for them, compared to, say, the Americans: empire, revolution, Versailles, Weimar, depression, Hitler, war, occupation, Ulbricht, Honecker, reunification, democracy. An extraordinary sequence, don't you think? And they're still here in this city.

(Cees Nooteboom, All Souls' Day)

'Dissolve the people'

Until reunification 17 June was a national holiday in West Germany. It was named the Day of German Unity and marked the East German workers' uprising of 1953. Owing to its awkward commemoration of 'an event that happened in another country and that called for mourning rather than celebration', it was never really embraced by West Germans, according to Confino (Buse and Doerr 1998: 682), other than as a day off work. Arguably the lack of identification arose because there was both general bemusement over the day's purpose and a sense of ambiguity surrounding the political nature and implications of the actual events of 17 June 1953. On the face of it, declaring a holiday – particularly on the basis of 'national unity' – looked like a provocation by the West, one seeking to drive a wedge between the East German populace and its government by pledging a supposed solidarity with the former. The people were *evidently* against the socialist system, and the state's heavy-handedness in dealing with delicate political matters, as well as its blatant dependence on if not subservience to the Soviets at moments of crisis, were there for all to behold. So, this was a revolutionary moment that required to be highlighted.

Whilst there obviously had been an immature, knee-jerk reaction on the part of the GDR leadership at the time, there was a distinct whiff of psychic sabotage about this position: a destabilising patronisation not to say *Schadenfreude* from the land

43.

of rampant economic miracles. There were, moreover, rumours suggesting the violent escalation of events had been stoked by *agents provocateurs* from the West, that it was a leaderless revolt which actually lost momentum as quickly as it had gained it.[1] A protest over raised production norms begun on 16 June by seasonal construction workers on Stalin Allee had turned into a general strike in the whole of the country by the following day, with the immediate removal of the government being called for.

Richie reports that government ministers had in fact already backed down in panic on the matter of the productivity quotas on the first day of demonstrations, but that there was far more at stake (1999: 686–7). Coupled with the fact that of the 250 or so people killed on the day, half were in the camp of the suppressing forces – some Soviet soldiers, but mainly GDR police (*Volkspolizei*) – whilst at the same time a good many of those in the latter's ranks had categorically refused to fire on the protestors, it is not difficult to see how the event did not make for the kind of clear-cut commemorative circumstance the western authorities might have liked.

It seems to have been a similar kind of desire to polarise the situation for the sake of political gain that characterised the infamous vilification of Brecht at the time as a hardline sympathiser with the Socialist Unity Party (SED). Brecht wrote a 'long letter' to the general secretary Walter Ulbricht on 17 June, the last line of which was published on its own four days later in the daily news organ of the party *Neues Deutschland*: 'At this moment I feel I must assure you of my allegiance to the Socialist Unity Party of Germany' (Brecht 1990: 516). This sentence, taken out of context for defensive propaganda purposes by a put-upon Stalinist government – though Stalin himself had died earlier that year – at a moment of high political tension, was then picked up by the 'opposition' and re-directed in its mis-represented form against its original source. It is a clichéd narrative in the world of cabalistic power-mongering. Brecht ended up in a clinch: co-opted by the SED as an unequivocal supporter of its actions, which he was not, and correspondingly attacked by (western) detractors, whose desire to dismantle the idea of an East German state *per se* he certainly did not share either.

As with so many details of Brecht's complex life, it remains unclear to this day exactly what the course of events and motives were, above all what it was Brecht actually wrote to Ulbricht. Only a slightly extended version of the 'last sentence' has appeared in print (Brecht 1990: 515–516), but Esslin refers to Brecht's desired use of 'the opportunity for putting forward his criticisms of the methods of the regime in a long and closely argued letter'; and a witness's quotation, which Esslin

Street Scenes: Brecht, Benjamin, and Berlin

deems irrefutable, talks of 'that whole long clever piece of writing' (Esslin 1965: 163–4). On the other hand, Fuegi uses exactly the same evidence, 'differently organised', to construct the case against Brecht (Fuegi 1995: 547). Be that as it may, the published extract itself already makes mention of the need for a 'great debate with the masses about the tempo of socialist construction', pointing to the supposed contents of the rest of the letter. Where commentators and politicians wanted only to apply schematised interpretations of the protest that was taking place to political ends, it seems that Brecht saw the chance for debate at a critical moment in the fledgling socialist state's development. As Willett reports, he wrote similar letters of encouragement to the GDR Prime Minister Grotewohl and the Soviet high commissioner Semyonov (Brecht 1990: 673). A visit to Brandenburger Tor is recorded, moreover, to see for himself what was going on. Here the *agent provocateur* theory gains currency; in a subsequent letter to the publisher Suhrkamp he notes the 'gross brutish figures from the Nazi era, the local product, who hadn't been seen gathered into bands for years, *but who had been here the whole time*' (1990: 517 and 673–4). A further letter, to *Neues Deutschland* on 23 June, not printed in his collected letters but sourced from the newspaper by Jesse, calls for the workers not to be allied mistakenly with the *provocateurs* (Jesse 1996: 257). And, back in Buckow, his country retreat, two months after the event, Brecht reflects in his journals on what could have been – but evidently was not – the decisive role of the leadership:

> the important thing would have been to use this first encounter to full advantage. this was the first point of contact. it came not as an embrace but as a slap in the face, but it was contact nonetheless. – the party had reason to be alarmed, but it didn't need to despair [...] here, however ill-timed, was the big chance to win over the workers. for this reason I did not find the terrible 17th june simply negative. the moment I saw the proletariat [...] exposed to the class enemy again, to the capital-ism of the fascist era in renewed strength, I saw the only force that is capable of cop-ing with it.
>
> *(1993: 454–5)*

It appears, then, that Brecht was encouraging the SED in his letters to seize the moment, and it is in the context of this emboldening advice that he declared his continuing support for the party (though he was not actually a member). Many of the poems in his last formal collection of poetry, the *Buckow Elegies* (1976: 439–445), betray Brecht's preoccupation with the events of 17 June 1953 in Berlin. Above all his disappointment both at the SED leadership's handling of the situation (Jesse 1996: 260), and the evident urge to discredit him personally. Under these circumstances he produced his famous poetic riposte to the accusation expressed formally that 'the people/Had forfeited the confidence of government', which was: 'Would it not be easier/In that case for the government/To dissolve the people/And elect another?' (1976: 440).[2] Those who were gunning for Brecht naturally saw this as a retrospective 'correction' in which he was trying to ingratiate himself with the people, as well as evidence of his shadowy opportunism, in an oft-repeated myth (Richie 1999: 686; Fuegi 1995: 549 and Large 2002: 429). More plausible, as Völker suggests, is his sheer frustration at the failure of the socialist project in the GDR (1998: 396). But where (western) antagonists were happy to draw the general conclusion from this failure, of an inevitable dysfunctionalism, and to tar the writer with the same brush, Brecht himself preferred to view it as the specific shortcomings of the existing leadership. It was not just a missed opportunity but a lasting wound to the East German people, one out of which the West was eager to make capital.

Topographies

Leaving the Sony cauldron at Potsdamer Platz, I'm walking now parallel to Entlastungs Strasse through Tiergarten, Berlin's vast central park. Within a matter of ten minutes I hit the broad east-west-coursing avenue that is Strasse des 17 Juni. Facing me are two Soviet T-34 tanks. They're guarding a war memorial. Popular myth alleges these very tanks were the first two to roll into Berlin in 1945. The memorial pays respect to the many Soviet soldiers who died in the fierce battle for the city. It's a concave colonnade symbolically constructed out of the granite and marble remnants of Hitler's New Reichs Chancellory, with an immense statue of a Red Army soldier perched on the central plinth. The sight of these liberating tanks on Strasse des 17 Juni is just one of many paradoxical montages of history in this part of Berlin. Given enough time, they'll probably morph into the later generation of tanks that lined up against the protesting masses in 1953. In a sense they already have.

Nearby, looking eastwards, is Brandenburger Tor, the single remaining gateway of the eighteen that once punctuated the medieval customs wall that encircled the city. Brandenburger Tor is probably Berlin's best-known architectural icon in global terms (Haubrich 2001: 36). Modelled on aspects of the Athenian acropolis its construction in the late eighteenth century introduced classical forms to the baroque city. Somehow, amidst the thick and thin of Berlin mythology, it carries the aura of always having been there. The most significant physical change was probably when the famous Quadriga – the goddess, chariot and horses that sits atop it – was held hostage for a while by Napoleon in Paris. A further popular Berlin myth maintains that the Quadriga has been given regular 180 degree turns, sometimes facing east, sometimes west. Ladd disputes this, however, asserting it was always intended to face inwards towards the centre, not just in East German times, though Ulbricht may well have been responsible for the spread of the myth to bolster his own importance (Ladd 1998: 76–7). The Second World War left Brandenburger Tor looking shell-shocked but structurally intact, though the

Quadriga itself had to be replaced by a replica. After 1961 the gateway found itself, like Potsdamer Platz, right in the middle of the death zone between the eastern and western parts of the city. But whereas Potsdamer Platz suffered a crisis of identity, descending in its state of razed no man's land into quasi-oblivion as we have seen, Brandenburger Tor retained its imposing physical presence. Clearly visible as it was from either side, it arguably became the single-most suggestive embodiment of a past linkage between the two halves of the city, one which suggested it still had a unified future. Certainly the most powerful media images of the Wall's fall in 1989 were those of its occupation at Brandenburger Tor, and the masses streaming along Strasse des 17 Juni, many in their flimsy two-stroke Trabant cars. According to one report, within hours of that occurring, the street signs had been temporarily 'pasted over with paper strips renaming [it] Strasse des 9 November' (Holland 1990: 35). (The Wall itself was not actually breached that night at Brandenburger Tor, though; crossings occurred at the official checkpoints of Bornholmer Strasse, first, followed by Sonnen Allee and Invaliden Strasse.) As with the Day of German Unity itself the re-naming of the avenue by the West as Strasse des 17 Juni – previously it had been known as Charlottenburger Chaussee – purported to honour the victims of the 1953 uprising. Unlike the holiday, though, the street was not a phenomenon you could easily overlook. It formed a broad, multi-lane axis, stretching four kilometres due west from Brandenburger Tor, through Tiergarten and the centre of (West) Berlin to Ernst Reuter Platz.

Halfway along it is Grosser Stern, the 'great star' roundabout where five major streets converge, with its imposing victory column (*Siegessäule*). This is where the spatio-symbolic narrative of German (dis)unity begins. The column, topped by the

44.

golden goddess of victory – the monstrous Victoria whose fading fame was enhanced in the late twentieth century by featuring as one of the vantage points for Wenders' watching angels in *Wings of Desire* (1987) – glorifies the so-called Unification Wars against Denmark (1864), Austria (1866) and France (1870–71) respectively. Originally sited in front of the nearby parliament building (or Reichstag), it marked the foundation of the first national German state. Driven by the force of Bismarck's might, it was not surprising, as Richie mischievously points out, that the column's decorations, which consisted of captured cannon barrels and mosaics of victorious battles, commemorated the unification of Germany 'but, in the true spirit of Prussian chauvinism, failed to depict the contribution of any other state' (1999: 230). Benjamin writes about *Siegessäule* (as well as Tiergarten) in 'Berlin Childhood around 1900', recalling his bemusement as a youngster as to 'whether the French had gone into battle with golden cannons, or whether we had forged the cannons from gold we had taken from them' (*GS* 4i: 241). In fact, Benjamin's verdict (from the framing perspective of 1932) on the aura of the *Siegessäule*, as well as the annual parades commemorating victory against the French at the battle of Sedan in 1870 – for which the column was the focal point – is caustic. It serves, as Gilloch elucidates, as a clear instance of the way the status of monuments is transient, subject to subsequent events in history:

> Monuments to victory are inevitably transformed in time into those of defeat [...] While the city's proud monuments most clearly articulate the glorification of history, in their 'afterlife' these same structures come to unmask the modern metropolis as the locus of mythic delusion [...] For Benjamin, the monument is not to the boastful omnipotence of Imperial Germany, but is rather an emblem of the cruelty and barbarism of war [...] The symbol of German victory over the French in 1870–1 can have only a paradoxical significance after the German defeat of 1914–18 and the ensuing collapse of the Imperial system. The *Siegessäule* and the parades of Sedan Day remain as indictments of the smug complacency of the First World War, the monument of omnipotence had become a monument to impotence.

> *(1997: 73–4)*

It is ironic in a way that the *Siegessäule* should have been shifted by the Nazis to its present position at Grosser Stern in 1939, because when allied bombing of Berlin commenced, the east-west axis of today's Strasse des 17 Juni apparently 'looked like an arrow pointing bombers straight to the heart of the government quarters' (Richie 1999: 496). In which case a flashing Victoria must have acted as the semaphore incarnate, flagging in the planes. As a counter-measure, extensive camouflage netting had eventually to be erected and the golden goddess stripped and reduced to a dull bronze (496). The reason for the column being moved was that it formed an early part of the implementation of the Hitler-Speer master-plan for the city. This involved the reinvention of Berlin as Germania, a new city which would be worthy of its projected status as a metropolis of global significance.

In an exemplary development of Benjamin's theory of transience regarding the historical symbolism of commemorative sites, the *Siegessäule* provided an intriguing twist in the debate over the removal of 'undesirable' monuments in Berlin after 1989. Seemingly directed as a matter of course at the relics of socialism, both the Green Party and the (eastern) Party of Democratic Socialism threw a spanner in the works of the decision-making process by applying to have the (western) *Siegessäule* removed. Owing to its profound association with German nationalist power-mongering – first the Prussians, then Hitler – it merited being destroyed as much as, say, the Lenin statue in Friedrichshain, so the argument ran. As Robin reports, the appeal was dismissed but 'alone the fact that it had been made, and the possibility thereby raised that monuments in the West could be considered in the same light as those in the East, clearly demonstrated that the war over memory was without question a civil war' (2002: 187).

Still standing opposite the Soviet war memorial, I realise that the provisional Entlastungs Strasse alongside which I've just been walking from Potsdamer Platz is where Speer's proposed north-south axis – seven kilometres long and 300 metres wide – would have run. It would have bisected its perpendicular counterpart, what is now Strasse des 17 Juni, more or less where I am now. That's why the memorial was situated precisely *here* in 1945, to function as a symbolic block to the crass fascist fantasies exemplified by the master-plan's grandiloquence (Enke 1999: 19). The southern end of the axis was to have had an enormous triumphal arch, whilst its northern point would have been capped by a 'great hall' capable of holding 150,000 people. The east-west development was virtually the only part of the blueprint completed, though, running even further west than the Strasse des 17 Juni does today. By the eve of the Second World War it had (appropriately) reached Adolf Hitler Platz – now Theodor Heuss Platz – some seven kilometres west of Brandenburger Tor. It was unveiled on the occasion of Hitler's birthday with a march past of some 60,000 troops, lasting four hours and including artillery and military vehicles (Kahlfeldt 2000: 205).

During the Cold War the triumphal marches continued: now it was the western allied forces who held an annual parade on Strasse des 17 Juni just to reiterate the fact of their presence. One of the stipulations imposed by four-power rule was that no one was permitted to stop in front of the Soviet memorial. It was the strangest of experiences visiting this little enclave of Iron Curtain exotica on the western side of the Wall, creeping past the fenced off Soviet guards as if they might open fire at the slightest provocation. But it was *they* who were being guarded, their British keepers vigilantly holding visitors at bay in the wake of a neo-Nazi attack upon them in 1970 (Ladd 1998: 194). Again, this was one of the many anomalies of Berlin Cold

War praxis: the forced co-operation in the city of powers that were strictly at loggerheads on the world stage.

A grenade's throw north-east of the Soviet memorial is the four-square hulk of the Reichstag building. If Brandenburger Tor has served as the permanent gatekeeper of the continual flux and flow in the status of Berlin as a city, the Reichstag has certainly evolved, since its completion as the first German parliamentary building in 1894, as an index of the fluctuations of political power on a national level. For the Russians, claiming the Reichstag in Berlin at the climax of the Second World War was the single most decisive signifier possible of both Germany's definitive defeat and the Red Army's victory in the allied race to capture the capital. How ironic, then, that the famous photograph of a Soviet soldier planting the hammer and sickle on the damaged building's roof – the iconic significance of which, in Cold War terms, arguably remained unmatched until the United States sited its star-spangled banner on the moon in 1969 – recently turned out to have been 'a little staged'. Appearing to have come about exactly on schedule, on 1 May 1945, as the spontaneous climax of a furious battle for the Reichstag – in which just short of five thousand soldiers were killed in total – it was in fact enacted in improvised circumstances the following day. As *The Times* reported, the photographer concerned revealed on his deathbed in 1997 that there had been no flags large enough available, so red tablecloths had quickly to be conjured from Moscow instead. Even the identity of the heroic actor-soldier was incorrectly attributed (Richie 1999: 1006).

A further irony of the Red Army's conquest is that the Reichstag ended up falling just inside the British sector when it came to the four-power zoning. However, the Soviet authorities still managed to hold sway over it, vetoing any proposal to use the building – restored and modernised during the Cold War years as a debating chamber with attendant offices and facilities – for West German parliamentary sittings (Ladd 1998: 91). In a sense this ensured that the Reichstag simply continued to reflect the reality of its adopted position, which corresponded to the exact opposite of its originally foreseen identity. In truth it spent most of its first hundred-year history standing as a symbol of Germany's disunity on the one hand and of the instability of its democracy on the other (James-Chakraborty 2001: 122). Michael Wise sums up a commonly-held post-reunification view thus: '[I]t was depicted as a bombastic, war-scarred fossil, the scene of Germany's darkest hours, an unwelcome symbol of democracy's failure to grow deep roots under either the monarchy or the succeeding Weimar republic' (1998: 121).

In the context of what has occurred the prominent inscription on its portal, 'For the German People' (*Dem Deutschen Volke*) has come to read more like a harbinger's message of turmoil and disaster. Taking over twenty years after the formal foundation of a unified Germany to build, the Reichstag still only performed, as

Wise says, the 'appearance of democracy [rather] than its reality' in the time of the monarch Wilhelm II. Renowned for his disparaging remarks about both the building and the institution it represented, he not only retained the sole right to appoint and persist with the chancellor of his choosing, but also held the formal openings of parliament in his palace down the street (Wise 1998: 123). Even the Weimar era that followed, after the First World War, was a republic formed 'elsewhere', as its name implies. Because of the volatility of the political situation in Berlin, legislators moved to Weimar to form the republic's new constitution, and didn't return until 1920. In the event the Reichstag managed to host a 'functioning, if never fully healthy, parliamentary democracy for only about a dozen years' (Wise 1998: 125–6). It should not be forgotten, moreover, that the *symbolic* status of the building, much talked about in the heady days after 1989, had become its actual *function*: since the decisive fire of 1933, it had not been in use for the business of politics. One of the records that had to be set straight in the argument against its resurrection as the new parliament (Bundestag) of a reunified Germany on the grounds that its past was tainted, was, as Wise observes, that it hadn't actually served as a Nazi power-base (122).[3]

The Third Coming

In the Hissens' 1996 film about Christo and Jeanne-Claude's *Wrapped Reichstag* project, there is an archive scene early on which is shot in the snow-covered environs of the building. It is the time of the Cold War, presumably during their first visit to Berlin in 1976, and the artists are being accompanied round the site of the Reichstag by Michael Cullen. The latter was an American living in Berlin, who takes the credit for first suggesting the project to the artist team in 1971. All of a sudden Cullen points to an S-Bahn commuter train trundling its way across the divide towards Friedrich Strasse station in the eastern sector. His excitement, not only at the everyday act of 'transgression' itself but also at being able to *demonstrate* to his guests this piece of Berlin exotica, is palpable. The film captures the kind of emotional response which, as testament to what was moving about an era, easily becomes erased once circumstances change. Cullen's animated state in the shadow of the sorry hulk of a *déclassé* Reichstag – about which he was to produce several historical studies[4] – celebrates the ordinary-but-extraordinary occurrence of movement (ultimately of people) within gridlocked conditions. As such it seems to epitomise the principle of Christo's project, astonishingly set in train nearly a quarter of a century before its actual realisation in 1995.[5]

Where the wrapping of the whole Reichstag building in silvery polypropylene material began as the idea for a spectacular intervention into the situation of the Cold War, it reached completion in the transitional hiatus produced by the breaking of that particular stalemate. In one respect, then, Christo's work remains fixed in its form. For much of his practice is in fact related to the unexpected wrapping of familiar objects, large and small, anywhere in the world. The Reichstag veiling *in itself* would have been broadly the same whether it had taken place in 1971 or 1995. What emerges as significant resides, first, at the interface between the formal functioning of the work; second, what it actually takes to bring it about; and, lastly, how it mobilises its viewing constituency in the contextual circumstances – historical, political, topographical – in which it ultimately occurs. Each one of these aspects is premised on generating *movement*. Bureaucratic authorities are moved to negotiate, debate and legislate in what Christo refers to as the software stage (Hissen/Hissen 1996). Spectators are moved to participate in the event physically – by being there and responding to it – and imaginatively, by speculating creatively over the broader significance of its impact. The formal act itself, finally, occurs as both a time and motion-based event. Lasting a fortnight and incorporating a three-phase process – the hardware stage – of *becoming*, then *being*, wrapped, as well as becoming *un*wrapped again, the estranged building also reproduces the remarkable sense of a breathing movement as the tied fabric envelops it and the wind gets under its skirts. The machinery of 'wrapping' corresponds formally in fact to the Brechtian sense of a 'staging of a veiling' in which a familiar object or circumstance is not just made strange but *shown* to be made so. The phenomenon in question both is and is not itself, resembling the Brechtian actor's *demonstration* of a character or situation and pointing to that character/situation's capacity to 'be otherwise'. Here a 'sick' building – one that is 'not quite itself' – is bandaged (or mummified), undergoing a two-week period of healing and convalescence in which

45.

it is 'wrapped as the Reichstag and unwrapped as the Bundestag' (Large 2002: 612). Effectively it has had 'the gift of life' breathed back into it, a repackaged present (or swaddled rebirthing) to the city from the artists. What you witness at each individual stage and as a whole is the ritualised performance of democracy in action.

In its software phase there was considerable right-wing opposition to Christo's project, which viewed it variously as unsuitably experimental and irreverent, ambiguous in a way that would polarise rather than unify the populace, and unprecedented in other comparably respectable democracies (Ladd 1998: 93–4 and Large 2002: 612). The important thing for the project, though, was that it provoked a parliamentary debate at all, one which resulted in a fairly narrow majority in favour. Without a stitch of the fabric even having been woven, the project had already produced intense discussion. This was, on the one hand, over the writing of German history and, on the other, over the future of both the Reichstag as the refunctioned site of parliament and the nation as a whole: what would this act of wrapping suggest about the state of German unity and democracy if it were permitted to take place? Also remarkable about Christo and Jeanne-Claude's 24-year struggle – as a crucial element in the functioning of the eventual piece itself – was the way its fluctuations had become indicative of the health of German-German relations. The birth of the 'big idea' just as a *possibility* in 1971 coincided with the tentative beginnings of East-West *détente*, as the more co-operative Brandt-Honecker years set in. Typically, though, the conservative parliamentary president Carstens was unwilling to run with the project in 1977 because the Reichstag was supposedly a symbol of German unity with which one should not tamper (Baal-Teschuva 1995: 31). Choosing to view Christo's proposed intervention as a trivialisation rather than facilitation of unification, then, the Reichstag is paradoxically preserved in this reactionary reading as the rigid embodiment of a past ideal of nationhood, one with which a reconnection will be made once the 'aberration' that is the GDR has run its course. Finally, at the project's culmination in the 1990s, the parliamentary decision to take the risk and allow such a radical act to occur correlated with its own sense of being on the cusp of a new but undefined era of democratic unity.

Whilst the materialisation of that unity remains a vexed question, there is no doubting that its possibility contributed to the extraordinary response to the Reichstag's wrapping in the summer of 1995. The veiling, originally scheduled – naturally – to occur on 17 June, was delayed slightly, but that did not prevent an estimated *five million* visitors from attending in the fortnight of its duration. Effectively the site, surrounded by vast, 're-opened' space, became the focal point for spontaneous gathering and festivities. The troubled colossus had been turned momentarily into a people's fun palace, its gloomy threat spirited away, presaging its recasting as the locus of democracy. Everybody could have their piece of it, a fact that was encapsulated literally by the distribution of millions of little pieces of the shiny fabric used. Now people could create their own personal installations by wrapping up their fragments of Wall chipped off six years earlier. As Willy Brandt had predicted in the early days of the project, it was something in which all German people would find themselves reflected.

Whilst Brandt doubtless meant what he said, and was warmly quoted by Jeanne-Claude in this spirit, there were certainly no idealistic sentiments on the part of the artists, no empty rhetoric claiming they were 'doing it for the people' (Hissen/Hissen 1996). On the contrary, one of the more thought-provoking responses to the launch of the event was when the artists categorically stated at the press conference that they had done it only for themselves: to see if they could, to see what it would be like. Sitting alongside a visibly twitchy Rita Süssmuth, the parliamentary president at the time, who, as one of a minority of conservatives voting in favour of the project, had heroically championed the artists' cause, it was a poignant moment. After all, this was a project that had really been premised on the exhaustive task of persuading politicians of its relevance to the broader populace. Importantly the artists added that if it attracted the interest of others, the public, then all the better, but that was not the starting point. It was a controversial declaration from an artist team that refuses any form of commercial or public sponsorship, that pays for everything itself, and therefore has arguably earned the right to make the kind of direct, independent-minded pronouncement which for a politician – or, indeed, a subsidised artist – might be professional suicide. Where politicians purport to serve the people and spend a considerable part of their time 'proving' that this is what they are doing, Christo and Jeanne-Claude simply allow their actions to speak their own significance to the public. It is an act of galvanisation. An idea is set in train; how people react to that idea is ultimately what makes the work, but that is not something that can be predicted or determined in advance. The situation determines the work's importance.

'Lighthouse of the Nation'

If Christo's ephemeral wrapping introduced a respiratory action to the Reichstag building, Norman Foster's original architectural design for its refunctioning seemed to provide the perfect sequel. (Whether Foster was responding directly to Christo's design is a moot point; the architect's proposal preceded the fulfilment of the latter's project, but Foster would surely have been aware of the plan since the artist's intentions had been known for a long time.) A horizontal, translucent canopy, propped up by twenty slender poles and covering both the building and generous pedestrian expanses on its northern and western sides, appeared to be lifting Christo's veil and giving the new ideal of unity and democracy a thoroughly cathartic airing. Emphasising *lightness* above all, the Reichstag's dour, intimidating grandeur would be given a refreshing aura of accessibility. However, mired in

46.

extensive, anxiety-laden debates weighing the building's capacity to respond 'to the Bundestag's needs while at the same time turn[ing] the Reichstag into a new and convincing emblem of parliamentary democracy', Foster 'experienced how difficult it was to work with a legislative body as his patron, which meant having several hundred deputies and ministers peering over his shoulder as he drafted' (Wise 1998: 127–8) – just Christo's point regarding subsidy. Whilst the architect's gutting and redesign for the interior seemed to meet with general acceptance – a 'new chamber housed in a vast transparent hall within the shell of the old building' (Balfour 1995: 73) – the enormous canopy evidently chilled feet after initial enthusiasm. It was a *dome* that was wanted, an echo of Wallot's original cupola which had been damaged in World War II and eventually removed altogether in 1954 (Schulz 2000: 35–6). And the strength of that desire was evident: the Reichstag emerged as the most expensive public building in post-reunification Berlin at a cost of 600 million Deutschmarks (Large 2002: 615). Where a commanding Sony Centre at Potsdamer Platz might (coincidentally) evoke the contours of an ear – albeit one deaf to anything other than its master's own voice – the glass dome that Foster eventually came up with sits like an all-seeing eye in the socket of the new German parliament building. You have in this coupling the embodiment of the new, dominant Berlin: the eyes and ears of business and politics. On the one hand there's the privatised public space of strategic, commercial enterprise; on the other is the incarnation – for the time being – of Chancellor Schröder's so-called new centre ideology, literally *in* the new centre of the city. This incorporates the Reichstag as well as an adjacent 'federal strip', the brand new 'Band des Bundes', conceived by the architects Axel Schultes and Charlotte Frank, which bisects the course of the former Wall and extends from the chancellery in the west to parliamentary offices in the east.

From the terraced roof of the Reichstag you can look *outwards* over the surface of the whole city and, as you enter Foster's dome, *downwards* into the concentric debating forum in full swing below. A central cone of angled, oblong mirrors, widening as it rises to the top, reflects natural light into the chamber, whilst a double helix of ramps, hugging the glass interior, guides visitors to the cupola's apex and back down again. The intention is clear: this represents a highly polished performance of free circulation, openness and transparency. You could view it as a striking inversion of the Foucauldian panoptic metaphor, which, not a sideways glance away, used to be actually-existingly evoked by East German watchtowers over the death strip. Here, supposedly, it's the people gazing down – or not, as the self-regulating panopticon theory would have it – at the power-brokers below, holding them to account as they set about their representative business, 'a real subjection [...] born mechanically from a fictitious relation' (Foucault 1991: 202).

I don't know how aware the debating politicians really are of the public they serve peering down at them, but there isn't in any case much of the chamber to be seen from the dome. If you care to stop being dazzled by the myriad mirrors for a moment, you might just make out what looks almost like a smaller dome within the obvious one – an inner eye. It draws your attention, if you can catch a glimpse of it, to the way the debating chamber is sealed off from the outer public shell, like a bell

jar, unaffected by the flies buzzing around outside. In this view, you could see Foster's architecture of democracy as a diversion – a Baudrillardian simulation perhaps – which makes us believe what is happening inside is visibly subject to the interests of the populace through the dazzling brilliance of its seduction. There's no doubting the building's welcome striving to maximise public access, nor the elegance as well as technical excellence of Foster's design in the circumstances. But you can't help thinking that the architect's highly compromised position, in which Wise's general observation about German politicians' tendency to pursue with exaggerated rigour 'simplistic semiotic equations – like the notion that glass facades amount to transparency' (1998: 19), has ultimately held sway. So, even if Foster would have liked to have avoided heavy-handed

47.

attributions, the building is subject to them, come what may. The problem with such a rigid, mimetic taking of 'the symbol for the reality itself' (19) is that it easily and rightly invites playfully contradictory readings for the sake of it. In other words, if you are too eager for your building to *represent* something – rather then be a building, as it were, and allow its significance to emerge through *use* – it is more than likely that it will fail to receive the

48.

response you seek. On the other hand, the potential for that kind of 'undoing' of prescriptive symbolism may prove to be precisely the blessing the building deserves.

Blurred Identities

One person who has sought to play the game of provocatively rewriting messages in Berlin is the artist Hans Haacke. He is renowned for his 1990 death-strip montage featuring a rotating Mercedes Benz star – identical to the neon one on the Europa Centre (see chapter seven) – perched atop a former GDR watchtower sited

at Stallschreiber Strasse.[6] Inscribed on one side is a Shakespearian slogan, *Bereit sein ist alles*, corresponding also (as it happens) to the honourable Boy Scout motto 'Be prepared'. At the same time it resonates darkly with associations of the gateway at Auschwitz (*Arbeit macht frei*). Clearly ambiguous, the message incorporates the controversial notion of willing collusion: being prepared to do *whatever it takes*. On the one hand this refers ironically to the position of the former guards, whose defensive gaze was supposedly directed westwards at continuity-fascism, but actually went the opposite way towards its own citizens. Haacke himself recounts how the doormat of the watchtower in question had precisely this motto emblazoned on it (Herzogenrath 1990:

49.

100). On the other hand, it relates to Daimler Benz, who used the slogan in advertising (and who own, as Daimler Chrysler, the largest section of the new Potsdamer Platz complex, as we have seen). In Haacke's words, the company

> vigorously promoted Hitler's rise to power. Its chairman and president were both members of the SS. Like other companies during the war, Daimler Benz relied mostly on forced labour [...] and has since agreed to pay compensation of 434 Deutschmarks to each of the forty-eight thousand labourers who worked during that period.

> *(Stein 1999: 180)*

Haacke drily points out the staggering lack of proportion between the crime and its supposed atonement. This is thrown into relief, moreover, by a continuing opportunism in which Daimler plays off being Germany's 'largest producer of defence material' against being its 'most conspicuous sponsor of art exhibitions' (180).

A quotation from Goethe on the other side – also used for advertising purposes – proclaims that 'Art will be art' (*Kunst bleibt Kunst*). Again, it deliberately produces an ironic ambiguity: is it the aesthetics of the watchtower as an architectural construct that is meant or Daimler's 'contaminating' involvement as big business in the art world? Haacke entitles his work 'Freedom is now simply going to be sponsored – out of petty cash'. The installation inserts itself awkwardly, then, in the deathly gap between Daimler's duplicitous strategy of massively exploiting situations of terror under the cheap 'moral' guise of promoting a civilising humanity through high art. West Berlin's prime symbol of freedom nestles comfortably now on top of its antithetical counterpart in the East. Where cosy capitalism tries to wave its soothing, colonialist wand over bankrupt socialism, here, in the former anti-fascist defence zone between east and west, the art work seems to be hitting back by juxtaposing signs which, amongst other things, controversially suggest: 'You want to sponsor art, how about this?'

The installation recalls Brecht's 'collusion' with Steyr in the 1920s, the company who supplied him with a free car in exchange for an advertising poem. Steyr also produced weapons, a fact to which Brecht drew attention in the opening lines (see chapter three, note four). In a sense Brecht was posing the same question in far less loaded circumstances since there was no evidence of moral corruption or hypocrisy as such in the company's actions. His position throws into relief the more fundamental – and very contemporary – conundrum of whether you would oppose the production of armaments and defence materials *per se*. If not, at what point does their implementation or sale become immoral (if at all)?

Haacke was commissioned to make a major piece for the northern courtyard of the Reichstag building. This time he literally re-wrote a message. Looking down on to the courtyard from the giddy heights of the terrace, large, luminous letters spell out *Der Bevölkerung*: 'For the Populace'. Echoing the style of Behrens's 1916 gothic characters, it's a clear riposte to the imperious, nationalistic inscription on the Reichstag's entrance portal. But it also subverts the kind of protracted

50.

handwringing over the promotion of 'appropriate representations of national identity' that accompanied – or dogged – Foster's contribution to the building. At a point where difficult questions are being weighed regarding not only the reunifying of two ideologically separated Germanys, but also how to deal with waves of Eastern European immigrants – to say nothing of the continuing presence of first and subsequent generation guest workers – the reformulated message challengingly asks what it is that constitutes a nation in the first place: the reality of a highly differentiated populace or an ideal of Germanness? The historical resonance of that provocation goes without saying. It is as charged as Daniel Libeskind's call for the development of the 'non-identity of Germany', for 'blurred structures': 'I would say why would you want an identity […] I have never thought that nations and national architecture is of relevance any more' (Leach 1999: 135). Evidently touching on raw nerves right at the heart of the German legislative body, Haacke's work was also made subject to parliamentary approval, narrowly squeaking through in April 2000 with only two conservative votes in favour. As with Brecht's gravestone, though in a manner far more public and critically immediate in this case (as the writer himself would have applauded), the extent to which two words can reverberate is remarkable.

In fact Haacke's installation constitutes a lot more than that. The neon letters appear to hover just above an overgrown bed of varied plant life that virtually fills out the rectangular dimensions of the courtyard. All MPs were requested by the artist to supply a quantity of earth from their local constituency, as well as the seeds of a plant typically associated with their region. This is allowed to grow untended until the MP concerned leaves parliament, when it is replaced by a new offering from whoever takes over. Seeking a correlation between the natural cycle of seasons and the cycle of parliamentary life, the seedbed installation offers precisely the reconsecration of previously 'soiled' or 'fallow' terrain for which Christo's wrapping ploughed the way.[7] It is indicative not only of the 'stake of responsibility' held by individual parliamentarians but also of the changing constellation of the nation's population and, hence, the imperative of the former to stay attuned to the demands of the latter. This is not a people that sits easily within the neatly trimmed and weeded borderlines of 'nationhood' – a culture based on the racialised roots of soil, space and folk once invoked by the likes of Herder (in Brouwer and Mulder 2002: 46) – nor one that can be conveniently dissolved and re-elected.

The Politics of Fun

Triumphalist Prussians, marching SA troops, protesting East German workers, parading western allied forces, delirious post-Wall revellers: Strasse des 17 Juni has witnessed every conceivable form of politicised mass event wherein the question of unity has been a factor. The long avenue has produced, under different names, its own unique index of modern Berlin history, stretching back to the commemoration of the victorious Unification Wars embodied by the victory column at its heart. Carrying it into the twenty-first century is the world's largest regular gathering of partying people, the annual Love Parade rave. Entering its fifteenth year of existence in 2003, it has probably already achieved legendary status. Up to one-and-a-half million participants course up and down the entire length of Berlin's east-west artery for one long, (usually) hot afternoon and evening on the second Saturday in July. When it began life, the summer before the Wall came down, the parade involved two DJs in their cars initiating a spontaneous birthday party on Kurfürstendamm, with some 150 friends straggling behind. By 1995 it had become so big that it was forced to transfer its route to the broad, protracted length of Strasse des 17 Juni. There were 250 DJs and over 50 decorated floats involved when I witnessed it in 2000.

Ever since this transplantation, its organisers, Planetcom, have fought a running battle with environmentalists seeking to have it banned or re-routed. Passing through the extensive Tiergarten as it does provides a hugely convenient outlet for the multitude of ravers, but causes havoc and desecration amongst the plant and animal life of the park. The chief complaint relates to the copious quantities of toxic urine let into the ground over a relatively short period of time. The morning after witnesses the city's water services literally hosing down trees and shrubs in an attempt to dilute the chemical mix. Alongside them is the second shift of council street cleaners, the first already having swept into action at midnight, by which time the majority of the paraders has long since dispersed into the multiplicity of clubs in the city. Entering the spirit of the occasion, the cleaners wear orange T-shirts, identifying them on the back as 'Saturday Night *Feger*' (sweepers), a witty play on the cultic disco movie of the 1970s starring John Travolta. Emblazoned on the front is another anglified pun, which even pokes self-deprecating fun at the common sibilatory mispronunciation by Germans of the definite article: 'Dose [do the] right thing – save the rave', it says. *Dose* itself means 'can' or 'tin': in their plurality they form one third of the vast mounds of rubbish collected by the sweepers.

The 300 tons of waste that accumulates – and we're talking, of course, carelessly discarded rather than helpfully placed in an appropriate receptacle – is the other main bone of contention at the Love Parade. Thus, the street cleaners' slogan constitutes an appeal: not reducing the number of ditched cans imperils the event's future. This touches, further, on the pragmatic significance of waste disposal in the whole staging of the Love Parade in the first place. Planetcom has persuaded the city council to give the event the official status of a *political demonstration*, which implies the city takes responsibility for the considerable costs of instituting rubbish clearance (as well as maintenance of Tiergarten's well-being). It has been willing so far to do this because of the revenue the event generates generally for the city, estimated at approximately DM 250 per person in 2000 (Oloew 2000: 9). Paradoxically, then, we're witnessing here the political demonstration packaged as profitable commodity. (Compare that to the 1953 uprising.) Intimations of withdrawal of this status in 1998 owing to environmentalists' pressure were met with organisers' threats simply to transfer the parade lock, stock and can to another city.[8] The council's acquiescence with Planetcom was testament both to the enormous popular momentum the Love Parade had gained in the meantime and the city fathers' desire to carve out for themselves an image of cosmopolitan largesse: tolerant and trendy on the one hand, capable of handling such a monumental event on the other.[9] Amongst the most trenchant criticisms of this attitude is that it blithely ignores the fact that rave culture is all about drug consumption. The Love Parade thereby qualifies as the largest celebration of sanctioned drug-taking in the world (Grunert 2000: 9).

The chances of the number 123 bus reaching its terminus stop at the junction of Strasse des 17 Juni are remote. The approach road has been taken over by streams of ravers making their way to the hub of the action. Parked vehicles on either side have in any case reduced the thoroughfare to but a single lane. Some folk have made themselves at home: from their white hire van a group of six or seven 'student-types' have hauled a battered settee and requisite non-matching armchairs, which they've arranged cosily on the grass by the pavement. It's shortly after two o'clock and the Love Parade has just got underway, but they're supping their first beers of the day and are in no hurry to enter the fray just yet. Giving up on making headway, the bus driver opens his doors and we all pile out. I reel as if I'd just narrowly avoided being run over by a juggernaut. It's the surge not so much of booming techno, pure and hard, as of ambience, the sheer thrill of being here amongst this massive throbbing throng. Retrospectively the energetic charge of that baptismal moment strikes me as being the all-enveloping mega-blast of consumerist culture. An irresistible whoompf – perhaps the pleasurable antithesis to the heart-stopping gust of Weigel-Steiner's screaming wind of terror (see chapter five) – which sweeps you away into a carefree perpetual present. Welcome to the carnival of forgetting where no one need fear losing face because we're all wilfully lost and faceless anyway. According to Rada, the world of techno is portrayed as providing a means of handling the permanent and excessive demands of daily existence where identity is constantly being required to adopt different roles. Techno provides a necessary release from such complications of communication, resigning itself to a strategy of survival rather than change (1997: 121).

The parade makes its way down Strasse des 17 Juni from both ends. Floats begin simultaneously at either Ernst Reuter Platz or Brandenburger Tor, congregating several hours later round the Prussian victory column at Grosser Stern. Most of the floats are hired and decorated by Berlin clubs. They're small, representative mobilisations of what is normally an after-hours, clandestine scene. Night becomes day. Blinking hard, DJs and ravers alike come crawling out from this showy subterranean world to hang out their dirty linen. Not that there's much in the way of 'fabric'; the most shocking visible aspect of this 'soul-baring' for those ignorant of clubbing style is the sheer state of undress. (In truth the Love Parade contradicts the original, raw impetus of the rave event, which was to take place secretly and spontaneously – as indeed its first occurrence in 1989 did – time and place being passed on by word of mouth.) Down below, at street level, are the densely packed mortal masses who hail each float as it crawls by. God is a DJ. Or Karl Marx is God is a DJ: a huge polystyrene effigy of Marx, complete with headphones, floats by. It's been fashioned by a club from the city of Chemnitz, the former Karl Marx Stadt in East Germany. His bust of old in the main square has become the place's principal tourist attraction. It's used as a branding symbol to market the city, which is now known as the *Stadt mit Köpfchen*. Literally that means 'the city with the head' but it simultaneously refers to the notion of being clever and quick off the mark (*Köpfchen haben*).

Many of the ravers aren't from Berlin at all. German Railways alone lays on special trains for 350,000 visitors. In fact, many Berliners – even hip ones – want to have no truck whatsoever with the Love Parade. For them it represents an invasion from the outside which the clubs exploit; kids from the provinces come to indulge in the big city experience for a weekend (Brock 2000: 25). (That's another reversal of the original spirit of rave culture where it was all about city kids escaping to clandestine rural locations.) Displaced parades have been spawned by the sense of chagrin arising as a result of this hijacking; for a while there was a Hate Parade, now there's the more provocatively-named Fuck Parade, which occurs simultaneously in the Scheunenviertel and Prenzlauer Berg areas of the city. The warm weather and E-fuelled capacity to party through the night means the visitors to the Love Parade don't really have to worry about banal details like accommodation. If they end up in bed, it's most likely to be a hospital one. All through the night the slow melancholy wail of ambulance sirens bears testament to a steady flow of unconscious, dehydrated, exhausted, or overdosed bodies. For one of my flat-mates, a doctor at the local Moabit hospital, the Love Parade is nothing but a disaster zone.

Designating the Love Parade a political demonstration isn't only a smart commercial move, at least if you believe the hype of DJ Dr Motte. One of the two originators of the event, he claims the intention always was to forge a new form of demonstration which 'isn't *against* anything but *for* what you might call *Lebensfreude*' or the joy of being alive (Michaelis 2000: 26). Given a new slogan each year, it was the unity-seeking 'One World, One Love Parade' the year that I went. Echoing the sentiments of Bob Marley's well-known reggae anthem (to which the slogan alludes) – 'Let's get together and feel alright' – Motte's vision is to establish a *global* Love Parade day: 'the morphogenetic field around the earth would become charged in such a way that peaceful dancing would produce world peace' (26). Whether Dr Motte is deluded, a sharp self-publicist or just taking a journalist for a ride here, the Love Parade would do better to proclaim no other motive or aspiration than simply to be the intense but highly temporary distraction from the humdrum that it is. It's not really worth taking the philosophy too seriously, but if you wanted to accord it the honour, it reveals a trite, reactionary politics of seamless global unity. Ultimately this seeks to reproduce cultural otherness as the same for the purposes of promoting a profitable image. For 'One World' we might just as well substitute 'First (White) World'.

As I squirmed my way through the bobbing crowds, I kept missing something. Perhaps like the sensation of a phantom limb. Even by the evening, when the parade had come to a rest at the victory column bottleneck round Grosser Stern – where doubtless someone was proclaiming Bismarck or Victoria to be a DJ – I wanted to know what I'd actually come to see. But if I was missing anything, it was the point. *Nothing* happens. It's a circular narrative whose points of reference are blurred. Through the sheer, vibrant force of its sound techno creates that kind of expectation, of something 'big and exciting going down'. What I'd come to see was all around me, and nowhere. It was just about *being there* and absorbing the presentness of the moment. Sharing that with a million or so people generates a contradictory sense of anonymous but unconditional belonging. Drugs help, of course. You 'become' the parade; at the same time it passes through you. That's why there's no point in merely spectating because then it just passes you by, like watching people shopping. And when you've ditched your empty cans on the street and pissed in Tiergarten's bushes, you can go home, perhaps relieved.

I wondered whether this was what it was like when the masses poured through the Wall in 1989; whether the Love Parade, born in the same year, is a kind of transferred but ready-made replication in commodified (or canned) form of that

51.

feeling of euphoria. So much of that was premised on the fact of being there physically, of testing and occupying the forbidden lands for real when the unthinkable happened – the *Wahnsinn* or 'madness' that everyone used to describe the indescribable. Love, as John Berger tells us, is, after all, the opposite of separation (rather than hate), which is what the city had been experiencing for some 30 years. It 'aims to close all distance' (1984: 89–90). Arguably that instant in 1989 was also a kind of distraction from the cold light of day that would follow. But, although Chancellor Kohl attempted to buy the moment by spontaneously forking out DM 100 to each eastern citizen, it still maintained a performative identity as a spontaneous intervention of consequence. Something physical was lastingly transformed.

Woodstock is frequently portrayed as the social antidote to the Vietnam War, decisively crystallising for a generation its sense of necessary liberal-pacifist rebellion. As Brock puts it: '[it] presented a type of action which sought to counter the behaviour of the mass of soldiers, of formations. *Informare* means to submit to a formation. You produce information by conforming to a social formation' (Brock 2000: 25). The information generated by the Love Parade does not produce change in anything other than the temporary desecration of Tiergarten. But nor does it strive to. That's why it cannot be seen as a political demonstration. Love, moreover, which 'celebrates the unique and unrepeatable' (Berger 1984: 90), is merely an expression it borrows. In truth, it recycles, reproducing the circular rhythm of a feel-good culture of excess. According to Pornschlegel, any claims for it to have been the 'new Republic's magic ingredient', which, by refusing discourse, came closest to truly unifying the city in the 1990s, could be seen to be hollow in the event's steady demise the further the twenty-first century progresses: 'In the end what came out of it was no more than what went in: the old Federal Republic plus the East' (2003: 13).

By lunch-time on the following day, everything – including the parade's abject side, the expulsion of the worthless consumed commodity – has disappeared from view. All is as it was until the same time next year. As Hessel observed of the city back in the 1920s already: '[f]ilth and rubbish don't remain lying around for long in Berlin. There's nothing the city likes better than clearing up' (1984: 213). At the same time it is precisely the clearing up, the paradoxical foregrounding of the features of the obscene in the playing out of the whole event, that catches the eye. As Gilloch says of Benjamin's recognition of the rag-picker's importance, he or she 'inhabits and recycles the ruins of modernity [...] an urban 'archaeologist' who unearths the old-fashioned commodities that in turn reveal the truth about new ones: namely, that they are the same old rubbish' (1997: 165).

Notes

1. The GDR novelist Stefan Heym famously developed the notion of external destabilisation causing the escalation of the uprising in his novel *Five Days in June* (1977). Although this would have chimed with the State's own version of events, the novel's general critique of GDR society meant it remained officially banned in the East until 1989 (Robin 2002: 211).

2. Brecht's response via the poem was to a poetic statement issued by the first secretary of the GDR writers' guild Kurt Barthel. In it he declares his shame at the workers' behaviour and warns of the sheer difficulty of regaining trust (Jesse 1996: 259).

3. The Bonn parliament voted in June 1991 to relocate to Berlin, at which point it had not yet been determined that the Reichstag would be its home. That was a decision which followed 'logically' – according to Schulz (2000: 30) – five months later, not without the kind of protest typified by this SPD politician: 'We are not a German Reich but a Federation and we want to underscore that federalism' (Large 2002: 611). It is noticeable that the reconstituted building has not as yet been able to assert its new official name of Bundestag. The new Berlin parliament opened in April 1999.

4. See Michael S. Cullen (1983), *Der Reichstag: Geschichte eines Monumentes,* Berlin: Fröhlich und Kaufmann; (1998), *Der Reichstag: Parlament, Denkmal, Symbol*, Berlin, be.bra verlag; and, with Uwe Kieling (1992), *Der Deutsche Reichstag: Geschichte eines Parlaments*, Berlin.

5. The period corresponds almost exactly to the time-span between the supposed birth of parliamentary democracy and the completion of the Reichstag one hundred years earlier (1871–1894).

6. For full documentation of the project see Herzogenrath *et al.* (1990: 81–104).

7. Historically speaking the Reichstag building can be said to be in the fourth phase now of 'parliamentary rotation' after a long, fallow third phase.

8. In the meantime the Love Parade has released the trademark for its brand name to be used by other cities, which included Tel Aviv, Vienna and Leeds in 2000. Discussions are underway with Mexico City, Hong Kong and Buenos Aires (Oloew 2000: 9).

9. In fact, in 2001 the federal court formally denied the Love Parade its political status. It seems an agreement has been reached between Planetcom and the council gradually to phase out the latter's

subsidy. By 2004 ravers themselves will be picking up the tab (Melle 2001: 21), a development which will surely reduce significantly the already dwindling appeal of the event.

9. Karl Liebknecht Strasse: the Space of Light

[T]he notion of *parallalax* [...] involves the apparent displacement of an object caused by the actual movement of its observer. This figure underscores both that our framings of the past depend on our position in the present and that these positions are defined through such framings.

(Hal Foster, The Return of the Real)

When depth of time replaces depths of sensible space; when the commutation of interface supplants the delimitation of surfaces; when transparence re-establishes appearances; then we begin to wonder whether that which we insist on calling *space* isn't actually *light*, a subliminary, para-optical light of which sunlight is only one phase or reflection.

(Paul Virilio, The Lost Dimension)

A Street Fit for Heroes

Once you've filtered through the Doric columns of Brandenburger Tor and on to Pariser Platz, the east-west axis through the centre of the city extends for approximately a kilometre and-a-half as Unter den Linden. You are entering the heart of the old royal Berlin. Established by the Great Elector Friedrich Wilhelm in the seventeenth century as part of the general expansion of the city, the tree-lined Unter den Linden (literally 'underneath the limes') evolved in the following century into Berlin's grandest avenue – a golden mile – and has remained so ever since. Situated on it now are a mixture of heavyweight or exclusive institutions, ranging from the vast Russian embassy and luxurious, turn-of-the-century Hotel Adlon in the west to Humboldt University and the State Opera House in the east. When it reaches the bridge over to Spree Insel at its eastern end – a narrow island formed by the Spree River separating for some

52.

two kilometres in the centre of the city – the street makes a slight curtsey to the left. That's the first deviation of what is an arrow-like urban thoroughfare, incorporating several streets and stretching for some eleven kilometres in total. And it marks the point at which Unter den Linden transforms into Karl Liebknecht Strasse. Across the bridge on the right is the expanse of Schloss Platz where the royal family of the Hohenzollerns began to build a grand palace, the Stadtschloss, in the middle of the fifteenth century. When Unter den Linden eventually materialised, as the bounded medieval town began to open out, part of the conception behind it was to permit the Great Elector easy access from the palace to his personal game park, Tiergarten (which means 'animal garden'). Subject to constant elaboration and expansion through the centuries, involving the leading architects of each respective age, the Stadtschloss was finally completed in 1850 (Haubrich 2001: 13).

As you might think Karl Liebknecht Strasse, which continues in a north-easterly direction for a couple of kilometres (past the television tower and Alexander Platz), only acquired that name in the era of the GDR. Prior to that it had had a royal designation, Kaiser Wilhelm Strasse, which indicated its late-nineteenth century origins as an oblique extension to Unter den Linden, designed to permit traffic to flow past the palace. The customary Berlin act of rewriting street names in accordance with ideological vanquishment was not merely played out at a level of substituted signs, however. In 1950, exactly five centuries after building had first commenced, SED party secretary Walter Ulbricht decreed that the war-damaged might of the Stadtschloss should be blown up and removed for all time as the reconstruction of 'Berlin, the socialist city' got under way. Not only would this be indicative of a clean break with the palace's undesirable aristocratic, not to say militaristic, past – seen as the logical pre-cursor to fascism[1] – it would also pave the way for a vast area in which the masses could gather for large-scale state pageants. The refunctioning involved a further name-change: royalist Schloss Platz became communist Marx-Engels Platz. Only one segment of the Stadtschloss remained; one of its baroque portals was preserved and later incorporated into the facade of the adjacent GDR council of state building.[2] From its balcony Karl Liebknecht, leader of the pro-Leninist Spartacus movement, had proclaimed the founding of a Free Socialist Republic of Germany on 9 November 1918. That proved to be wishful thinking and the movement was brutally crushed in January of the following year as it tried to seize Berlin by force (Richie 1999: 300–9). Liebknecht, who considered himself to be 'Berlin's Lenin' – partly because the Spartacists were receiving direct Bolshevik support – seemingly personified the ineptitude and disorganisation which eventually ensured the uprising's defeat. Supposedly released after being apprehended in the riots, he was hit over the head by a rifle on his way out from his place of arrest, driven to Tiergarten, and shot (307–8).[3]

Brecht's early play *Drums in the Night* was written the same year, 1919, and draws on the Spartacus riots as an integral element in the drama of a returning First World War soldier, Andreas Kragler. The latter's fiancée, Anna, thinking him dead, is busy celebrating her engagement to an obnoxious, petit-bourgeois war-time profiteer in the Piccadilly Bar at Potsdamer Platz. Failing to persuade Anna to hook up with him once more, the returned protagonist finds himself on the point of joining the Spartacists, more in a fatal replication of the romantic impulse characteristic of the onset of the War – a form of suicide – than any ideological conviction. Anna finds him again, however, on the riot-torn streets of the city, and pledges herself to him after all. Tired after years of fighting, Kragler accepts her back, musing: 'Is my flesh to rot in the gutter so that their idea should get to heaven?' Instead he makes the epigrammatic declaration that 'Everybody is Top Man in His Own Skin', that he is 'a swine and the swine's going home!' (*Plays* 1: 114–15). Brecht supposedly attempted to soften the anti-revolutionary, or at least ambiguous, tenor of the piece much later in life as a 'solid citizen' of the GDR (Esslin 1965: 247–8). But one of the play's achievements is surely the way it draws attention to both the lack of sound leadership and cohesion in the revolution itself and the sense of post-War enervation being experienced by a shell-shocked, defeated nation. Moreover, it raises, as Meech points out, the whole question of the dubious need for heroes in the first place (Thomson and Sacks 1994: 49–50). That would have been a poignant issue at the end of a war that had commenced with such misplaced patriotic fervour, but it also bears critical relevance to the GDR's subsequent martyrdom at Marx-Engels Platz – let alone as a general tendency elsewhere – of a dubious hero like Liebknecht.

Erichs Lampenladen

Later in the GDR's history, at the onset of the Erich Honecker era in the early 1970s, plans began to be developed towards constructing a new, socialist 'palace for the people' at the eastern edge of the square, to be called officially Palast der Republik. Opening its doors in 1976 it amounted effectively to a multi-functional centre, comprising a comprehensive mix of arts, community, political and conference events, and including several café-bars and restaurants, flexible auditoria with room for up to 5,000 people, as well as a separate plenum for the GDR state parliament (*Volkskammer*). It even had its own post office, and a bowling alley. The intention clearly was to provide a public meeting ground in the middle of the East German capital in which the formal activities of politics and the more informal ones of the citizenry were seen to be of the same order. Ladd is quick to point out, though, that the parliament 'met infrequently and had as little public visibility as it had power' (1998: 59), real politics remaining exclusively in the hands of the communist party executive (or politburo). Doubtless the most significant decision ever taken there – symbolically the last – was in August 1990 when the GDR's first freely-elected parliament voted to join the Federal Republic.

But there is a clear sense in which the building has emerged from East German popular history with some considerable credit for its amenability and vibrancy as a centre for socio-cultural interchange (Heidler 1998). Whether or not anyone ever considered it to be an attractive architectural construction is another matter. Certainly the official GDR line was that it had brought to its capital city a modern, post-Bauhaus package of aesthetics and functionalism, the clean-lined, see-through pragmatics which had since transmogrified in the western world into a widespread 'international style'. The importance of that departure lay above all in the Honecker-era's desired distancing from the power-play of preceding socialist bombast.

However, the building was vilified aesthetically and technically after the fall of the Wall by western architectural discourse as an exemplar of 'grandiose mediocrity', an oblong box of bronzed glass and dull marble applications (Haubrich 2001: 206). At the time of its construction it had been viewed by its audience in the East with comparable scepticism, arising though from a perception of 'glamour and status craving' on the part of the GDR leadership rather than formal shortcomings. As Ensikat reports, this led to its original nickname of 'Palazzo Prozzi', *protzen* being the infinitive 'to boast' or 'show off'. When the glittering lights were finally switched on – one thousand spherical glass lamps in all sizes, hanging at varying heights in the capacious, two-tier public reception area of the building – there was one nick-name above all that seemed appropriate: *Erichs Lampenladen* (lamp-shop) (Heidler 1998: 60). The gentle fun-poking evoked by that designation betrayed a popular affection for the Palast der Republik. It was an emotion which, after the fall of the Wall, saw itself hardening into a stubborn defence – part of the 'civil war' referred to by Robin (2002: 187) – of one of the few remaining bastions of GDR society.

Western calls for its immediate removal as the epitome not only of poor aesthetic taste but also of a dehumanising regime, coincided with the setting in motion of a campaign for the resurrection of the far more extensive royal palace. The socialist people's palace served as a rallying point for a former East Berlin culture which did not wish simply to be steamrollered in every respect by a 'victorious West'. Reviving the Hohenzollern's Stadtschloss, on the other hand, represented for its supporters not only a 'rightful reinstatement' in historical terms but also, for some, a punishment for Ulbricht's outrageous recklessness in 1950 (Ladd 1998: 61). Thereby perhaps the most heated, and certainly longest-running, of post-1989 debates was unleashed on the city. It amounted once again to a struggle for the right to foreground certain historical narratives over others in determining the future identity of Berlin. As Ladd, who provides a comprehensive account of both the debate and the progression of events (1998: 47–70), summarises:

> By no means all opponents of rebuilding the royal palace wanted to preserve the
> Palace of the Republic, but the empty GDR showpiece and the ghost of its baroque

predecessor were competing for the same site. We can see rival nostalgias at work in the efforts of their respective advocates. Those who longed for a return of the royal palace wished to restore not the monarchy (though one could probably find a few monarchists among them), but rather a cityscape and with it a civic wholeness that had been lacking since 1950, or 1933, or 1918. Those who wished to keep the building that was there, the Palace of the Republic, may have had certain practical considerations on their side, but their deeper wishes were no less fixed on the past. They did not want to restore the Communists to power (though in this case there probably were a few more exceptions), but they sought to hold onto certain memories and experiences of life in the Communist state.

(59–60)

The cause of the Palast der Republik was not helped when it was discovered in 1990 to be utterly contaminated with asbestos and immediately closed. Literally and figuratively the lights went out in Erich's lamp-shop, an event which seemed to replicate perfectly the jocular verdict on East Germany's fate at the time: 'that was the GDR that was – last one out switches off the lights'. A parliamentary decision in 1993 to demolish the building appeared to have sealed its fate. This was strengthened in the same year by the installing on the exact site of the original palace of a *mock*-Stadtschloss. It was a life-size, painted canvas incorporating the majority of the northern, western and southern facades of the former royal palace, stretched over a large, steel frame and pushed up at right-angles against the Palast der Republik. Gigantic mirrors placed on the latter's western facade effectively doubled the size of the perpendicularly-positioned 'fake palace', as well as conveniently effacing the GDR building. The intention really was to seduce the public by offering a plastic vision of how a resurrected Stadtschloss would look. Financed by a private backer, Wilhelm von Boddien, it was a brilliantly executed idea which functioned very effectively to garner public support. Pre-dating the wrapping of the Reichstag, it amounted to a kind of inversion of the formal action of that later event, though it had no pretensions as such to being art. Where Christo *veiled* what was a visible relic, the Stadtschloss *conjured* an invisible ghost from the past. Arguably, the motives in each case were antithetical, too. Christo's installation was unsettling, 'making strange' as a way of facilitating transition to the new. The Stadtschloss, with its warm, yellowish glow, spread a sense of comfort, the reassuring familiarity of an idealised past. One question stood out, though: was it the mock-up event the public liked, the idea of the real thing as a temporary phenomenon, or the possibility of the thing itself?

Without going into the complex detail of events here, the Palast der Republik eventually secured a stay of execution and work on the removal of asbestos began.[4] Walking round the outside of the building in late 2001, as that process neared completion, it was difficult to conceive of a future for it, however. Like the remnant of Wall at Niederkirchner Strasse it resembles a carcass stripped to the bone. Perhaps, for a building diagnosed with the 'cancer' of asbestos but still hopeful of a cure, the searing effects of chemotherapy might provide a better analogy, though. Plant life grows between fissures in its facade; its once-fancy bronze windows now bear a kind of stain-glass testament to the visits of taggers. But its dereliction misleads; the word on the street is that it will be incorporated in some way into the overall re-design of the square, which has already been restored in name – since the enforced retirement of Marx and Engels – to Schloss Platz. A reconstruction of the original Stadtschloss – the remains of whose vanilla-tiled foundations have been dug up to prove its legitimacy 'archaeologically' – is still a possibility, but it may involve encompassing the Palast der Republik as its eastern flank. Designs are also being considered for a building which covers the former dimensions of the royal palace but replicates the multi-purpose socio-cultural properties of the people's palace (Paul 2001: 17). Whether or not such a plan can escape the commercial exploits of a Potsdamer Platz and contrive a truly civic space in the centre of the city – in the former, popular spirit of Erich's *Lampenladen* – remains to be seen. In March 2002 the newly-elected Berlin city council announced 2.1 billion Euro budget cuts – affecting above all the arts, heritage and education – simply to balance the city's books, let alone begin to deal with its overall debt of 49 billion Euro (Hooper 2002: 18).[5]

53.

Loss in Space

Walking eastwards along Unter den Linden at night, I notice a faint bluish shimmer over the central area of a cobblestone square on my right. Looking for a sign I discover this is Bebel Platz, an open, pedestrianised space a short distance from the point at which Karl Liebknecht Strasse begins.[6] When I return my gaze to the strange light I fancy I've just seen, it has gone. A will-o'-the-wisp. In its place I can just make out a shadowy huddle of human hulks, gathered as if round a grave. As one or two shift position, I catch sight again of the light, chinks of it spilling through the gaps. Approaching I find a quadrilateral glass pane, perhaps a square metre in size, embedded in the ground. Peering into it I am faced with a bright, peppermint white room stacked with vacant bookshelves. 'It's called *The Empty Library*', someone is explaining to the gathering.[7] 'On 10 May 1933 Goebbels got a group of students to form a human chain at the Humboldt University library over there', she says, pointing vaguely to a building flanking the western side of the square. 'They collected about 20,000 works of world literature – you name it: Jewish, pacifist, antifascist – chucked them in a pile outside and set them alight'. She gestures to a plaque set in the cobblestones nearby. It contains a prophetic inscription by the nineteenth century poet Heinrich Heine: 'What starts off as the burning of books ends with the burning of people'.

Where de Certeau separates the book from the body by metaphor (1988: 140), Heine locates them on a continuum. Perhaps that marks the point at which the representational becomes performative, where the book is no longer *like* the body but becomes it (Phelan 1993: 150). Already in exile at the time, and naturally one of the targeted writers, Brecht later wrote an amusing satirical poem about this event entitled simply 'The Burning of the Books'. It related to the actual instance of a writer-colleague perversely aggrieved at the dishonour of having been *left out* of what he evidently considered to have been a form of quality as well as truth assessment exercise:

54.

55.

When the Regime commanded that books with harmful knowledge

Should be publicly burned and on all sides

Oxen were forced to drag cartloads of books

To the bonfires, a banished

Writer, one of the best, scanning the list of the

Burned, was shocked to find that his

Books had been passed over. He rushed to his desk

On wings of wrath, and wrote a letter to those in power

Burn me! he wrote with flying pen, burn me! Haven't my books

Always reported the truth? And here you are

Treating me like a liar! I command you:

Burn me!

(1976: 294)

I don't know for sure whether Goebbels would have classified Proust as an honourable degenerate – though the chances are good since he was both Jewish and 'experimental' – but twelve of those 20,000 burnt books are more than likely to have constituted the latter's multi-volume *magnum opus, À la Recherche du Temps Perdu*. And, if you juxtapose the empty library of Bebel Platz with the desired revival of the royal palace at Schloss Platz, that is in a sense just what is staring you in the face: spatial stagings of loss, evocations of an anxiety of lost time. In fact, Sontag refers to the Berlin writings of Benjamin, who had translated Proust's work jointly with Hessel, as 'fragments of an opus that could be called *À la recherche des espaces perdues*. Memory, the staging of the past, turns the flow of events into tableaux', a process which is trying to 'condense it into its spatial forms, its premonitory structures' (Sontag1997: 13). The sunken installation of Bebel Platz attempts to magnify a moment from the past in terms of a spatial present that has moved on from that point and continues to do so. It is an event from the past – 'a moment when the future announced itself to us', as Szondi remarks of Benjamin's relationship to the past (Smith 1988: 21) – marked in the present *as loss*.

The historicist retrieval of the Stadtschloss, on the other hand, implies a pining for the return of a wholeness that is perceived once to have existed. This is the main practical argument for the palace's resurrection, that it formed the absolute cornerstone of the surrounding cityscape, as well as setting the standard in terms of building norms for the development of Berlin's centre as a whole, at least since the early nineteenth century (von Boddien 2001: 2–3). What is meant is the perspectival, neo-classicist *mise-en-scène* of Karl Friedrich Schinkel, which he devised for the Spree Insel area from 1815 onwards. As Boyer explains:

> It was this island that Schinkel would transform into a theatrical stage set for leisure and living. Through a series of designs for churches, city squares, a civic theatre and new museum, warehouses and residential structures, Schinkel turned the centre of Berlin into a series of pleasing vistas and perspectives, varying in scale and orientation.

(1998: 99)

It was no coincidence that the architect-cum-stage-designer 'explained his idea of a totally composed architectural setting' via a proscenium arch stage set in a theatre, the intention with his 'totally balanced and organised urban scenography' (Boyer 1998: 99) being precisely to theatricalise for the pedestrian the experience of the space of the city. And it is a perspective which constructs its centre as that of the observing subject, a bourgeois *mise-en-scène* which facilitates the owning gaze of mercantile capitalism (Burgin 1996: 42). Ulbricht's destruction of the Stadtschloss in 1950 naturally introduced a destabilising factor to Schinkel's vision of a fully composed tableau. But if the latter had been developing the notion of a 'landscape created by man, offering an ordered and stable vista […] the scenographic arrangement of the modern city' (Boyer 1998: 102) from a neo-classicist perspective, the former was, for better or worse, simply trying to set a similarly specific experience for socialism.

Enlightenment Space

One of the criticisms of the historicist argument is that the mourning for a spatial organisation belonging to times past is quite willing to erase the perceived aberration of a more immediate, GDR history. Ulbricht's act of removal was brutal; by contrast doing exactly the same to the Palast der Republik half a century later supposedly amounts to an act of cleansing (Ladd 1998: 67). One (earlier) period in history is preferred to another because the perceived aesthetic equilibrium of that age – its 'rightness' – is taken to equate with social stability: the good old days before the disruptive, ugly 'dark times' of twentieth century terror and totalitarianism arrived. It is the promise of a return to 'intactness'. The bourgeois theatre of Schinkel is the 'finished theatre', reflecting a self-satisfied world in which everything has been decided and put in place.

What is ultimately paradoxical about such a turning back of the clock is that it arguably flies in the face of the original enlightenment impulse it would embrace by seeking to fix it as absolute. The space that the enlightenment 'saw' in Berlin was one of outward expansion – that is, *movement* – from the 'clustering defensive medieval city' (Balfour 1995: 9). In more 'universal' terms, this corresponded to Galileo's seminal and unlimited opening up of a bounded medieval 'space of localisation', as Foucault argues:

> [T]he real scandal caused by Galileo's work was not the discovery, or rediscovery, of the earth's movement around the sun, but the assertion of an infinite and infinitely open space, in which the space of the Middle Ages was to some extent dissolved. The location of a thing, in fact, was no longer anything more than a point in its movement, its rest nothing but its movement slowed down infinitely. In other words, from Galileo onward, ever since the seventeenth century, localization was replaced by extension.

> *(Leach 1997: 350)*

Brecht's theoretical portrayal of Galileo represents the perfect human embodiment of the epic notion of 'making strange'. For that is exactly what he did as a scientist: looked at the world 'strangely', anew, entertaining the possibility of it actually being otherwise. In the first scene of the play he expounds his vision to the young boy Andrea Sarti, later to become his disciple:

> Our cities are cramped, and so are men's minds. Superstition and the plague. But now the word is 'that's how things are, but they won't stay like that'. Because every-thing is in motion, my friend [...] What is written in the old books is no longer good enough. For where faith has been enthroned for a thousand years doubt now sits. Everyone says: right, that's what it says in the books, but let's have a look for our-selves. That most solemn truths are being familiarly nudged; what was never doubt-ed before is doubted now [...] The universe has lost its centre overnight, and woken up to find it has countless centres. So that each one can now be seen as the centre, or none at all. Suddenly there is a lot of room.

> *(Plays 5i: 6–8)*

Brecht's concern, of course, is to deal with the relationship between progressive science (or 'new discoveries') and the power of authority. In Galileo's case this produces the paradox of the enlightenment man who 'criminally' hides his light under a bushel. Though there is an argument in the play to say that Galileo recanted his findings in a shrewd move to buy time secretly to complete his work on the *Discorsi*, the character himself refuses this heroic view in Scene 14: 'I betrayed my profession' (109). The right and imperative of science to exercise doubt has bent to the rigid dominance of a prevailing (Catholic) ideology. Where pure science's motive is to find out whether or not it is right, authority's is to assert that it is. If there is a tragedy, it is one of circumstance rather than any individual: the fact that the situation would produce the call for the actions of a hero in the first place. As Galileo himself retorts when an older Andrea Sarti accuses him of failing his country (and, as Meech points out [Thomson and Sacks 1994: 49], in an echo of Kragler's anti-heroic sentiments in *Drums in the Night*): 'Unhappy the land where heroes are needed' (*Plays* 5i: 98).

Brecht suggests, moreover, of the fate of pioneers in his foreword to the play, that '[t]errible is the disappointment when men discover, or think they discover, that they have fallen victims to an illusion, that the old is stronger than the new [...] that their age – the new age – has not yet arrived' (116). It is surely the need continually to provoke uncertainty over ingrained, received knowledge for which Brecht sought to make the case. With Galileo it is, of course, a momentous proposal: the human being is after all replacing God at the centre of the universe. Even so for Brecht, Galileo's crime is still that he did not permit – or at least delayed – the unfolding precisely of the *idea* of the possibility of change that his discovery seemed to represent. So, whilst the materialist Brecht is naturally gripped by the historical shift implied by Galileo's paradigmatic transference of the 'sovereign gaze' effectively from a vertical to a horizontal axis, his main preoccupation is with the reception and application of the 'new' in a transformed world centuries later. As he states in the *Short Organum*, 'We must leave [past periods] their distinguishing marks [but] keep their impermanence always before our eyes, so that our own period can be seen to be impermanent too' (Willett 1978: 190). And nowhere is the implementation of that method more graphically illustrated than in the extensive rewriting on *Galileo* itself, more than on any other of his plays (*Plays* 5i: 162). Beginning in 1938 each fresh version corresponded, as Willett and Manheim observe, to 'crucial moments of our recent history [...]: Hitler's triumphs in 1938, the dropping of the first nuclear bomb in 1945, the death of Stalin in 1953' (*Plays* 5i: xix). In a sense, then, Brecht takes Galileo's telescope and looks through it with Benjamin's eyes, bringing into focus the distant actions of the enlightenment scientist against successive foregrounds of a changing twentieth century present. We are made aware of the way the space of modernity opened up by Galileo and his instrument has been subject to a process of constant re-visioning, each change in turn produced by advances in technology and the broken tensions of competing discourses of power.[8]

Relative Uncertainty

If there is a figure who emerges as a problematic latter-day incarnation of Galileo's conundrum over what to do with ground-breaking discoveries, it is surely Werner Heisenberg. For the physicist was not only instrumental – as one of several – in developing the revolutionary theory of quantum mechanics, for which he received the Nobel prize in 1933, but he also played a distinctly ambiguous role during the Nazi era as one of the principal scientists working on experiments to split the atom. You could say the hypothetical shape of their 'relationship' is configured as an inversion that meets at a point where the far away and minute respectively are brought into focus: the telescope and the microscope. The former's problem was that state authority did not wish to 'know' what he knew (fearing its effects would be dangerous); the latter's was – eventually – that it did want to know (hoping its effects would be dangerous).

Allied with the Einsteinian modern – what was seen in Germany as the 'Jewish physics' of quantum theory – Heisenberg was derided initially and formally discredited as a 'white Jew' by those upholders of classical 'German physics' who saw the chance to assert their superiority under a national socialist regime (Walker 2001: 19). In fact, Brecht presciently lampoons the type in the narratory prelude to one of the collection of scenes in *Fear and Misery of the Third Reich* entitled 'The Physicists': 'Enter the local Newtons/Dressed up like bearded Teutons – /Not one of them hook-nosed./Their science will end up barbarian/For they'll get an impeccably Aryan/State-certified physics imposed' (*Plays* 4iii: 45). The scene itself portrays two compromised physicists, forced by circumstance to toe the line of official science whilst secretly trying to conduct the 'real research' of modern physics. In a sense this was Heisenberg's dilemma as someone who wished to carry on working in Germany after 1933. In reality, though, he was able through influential contacts to re-establish his credibility with Nazi officialdom by arguing for the potential value of modern physics to the nation. Himmler was convinced but stressed to Heisenberg that any public reference to Einstein had to emphasise a distinction between the man and his work (Walker 2001: 19).

It is with Heisenberg's acquiescence with this deeply implicating condition – to say nothing of the other Jewish colleagues he let slip from his plane of vision – that the points for his 'ambiguous practice' are set. For inevitably he was not simply left to pursue his research but increasingly asked formally to speak for the role of modern physics in the context of the Nazi German state. This involved numerous ambassadorial lecture trips abroad in which he is recorded as making mostly slight, but nevertheless clear, statements of support for Germany's prosecution of war. The most significant of these was the 1941 visit to his close Danish colleague and friend Niels Bohr in Copenhagen. To this day there is disagreement over the meeting's purpose as well as over what exactly was uttered and/or meant on this occasion. At its heart was the question of the development of an atomic bomb.

Heisenberg, it seems, tried to justify to Bohr Germany's war aims and convince him of the inevitability of victory. Was the motive for this ultimately a pacifist-humanist one, however, to hold escalation and the terrible implications of a nuclear strike in check? In other words: 'Don't go there if that's where you're heading because it won't help your side anyway', a move which may have been premised on calling Bohr's bluff. Or was he on a spying mission to ascertain the state of play regarding allied intentions and progress in developing a nuclear capability? (Frayn 2002: 1 and 3).[9]

One of the unverified myths surrounding Heisenberg after the war is that he deliberately slowed down or withheld research on uranium fission so as to prevent its application to the development of an atomic bomb (Walker 2001: 19). In Heisenberg's memoirs, moreover, he asserts that he hinted to Bohr at their meeting in 1941 that this was essentially one of two options open to physicists at the time: 'They could [...] advise their governments that atom bombs would come too late for use in the present war, and that work on them therefore detracted from the war effort' (Frayn 2002: 3). Whilst Heisenberg makes no claims here to having followed this direction, according to Frayn, merely to have set forth the choices available, he is quoted elsewhere as stating to Bohr that he knew an atomic bomb was 'in principle possible, but it would require a terrific technical effort, which one can only hope cannot be realised in the war' (Frayn 2002: 3). What has recently emerged is that Bohr interpreted Heisenberg's position as being in favour:

> I also remember quite clearly our conversation in my room at the Institute, where in vague terms you spoke in a manner that could only give me the impression that, under your leadership, everything was being done in Germany to develop atomic weapons and that you said there was no need to talk about details since you were completely familiar with them and had spent the last two years working more or less exclusively on such preparations.

> *(Frayn 2002: 3)*

Of course, Heisenberg may have been engaged in the effort Bohr describes but could still have been hopeful of it not being realisable in time. Alternatively he could simply have been trying, again for the good of humanity, to 'scare off' Bohr. In fact, Bohr's view was expressed in a letter he redrafted several times but never sent, and which has only recently been released from his archive, paradoxically draping a further shroud of mystery around the episode: why did Bohr, on his home patch, not confront Heisenberg? Thus two of the leading exponents of quantum physics, specifically its relation to the principle of uncertainty, remain, now that both are dead, locked in an unresolved difference over what was said and what was meant – though I suspect the latter is the more significant – at their famous Copenhagen meeting in 1941. What is noteworthy in Bohr's letter, though, is his utter conviction of his own correct recollection of events, and Heisenberg's corresponding failure: 'I think that I owe it to you to tell you that I am greatly amazed to see how much your memory has deceived you [...] Personally I remember every word of our conversations' (Frayn 2002: 3). No room for doubt there, then. Bohr seems to be claiming infallible knowledge of both what was uttered and what was meant by it in terms which echo in a figurative way the certainty of measurement of Newtonian physics. Heisenberg, on the other hand, appears never to have made any claims to that kind of objectivity. As the instigator of the meeting, who would presumably have been clear about its agenda if not its outcome, it was perhaps in his interests both at the time and subsequently to maintain a deliberate 'double-agent's ambiguity' about his position, one as undecidable as the uncertainty principle he developed in his practice (Walker 2001: 19). As Peggy Phelan, ultimately seeking a correlation between physics and performance as praxes, puts it:

> Observation and measurement themselves both absorb and emit energy; thus the act of observation transforms the activity observed. The theory of the quantum marks the transition from 'objective' measurement to 'uncertainty', from deterministic rules to probability and chance. Quantum mechanics erases the possibility of classical physics' belief in a mimetic relationship between matter and measurement. Within the quantum universe it is impossible to derive a physical 'law' without accounting for the conditions of measurement and experimentation which produce that law. Merely by looking (?) at matter we alter its action.

> *(1993: 116)*

Transfiguring the principle expressed here, then, Bohr does not seem to be allowing for the fact that as the leading representatives of nuclear science on opposite sides in a world war, but, unusually, still capable of meeting as academic colleagues and friends, there were bound to be areas of considerable 'greyness', if not black holes, in the way the 'matter of their exchange' was perceived in their respective minds, both as it took place *and* in its subsequent interpretations. Moreover, the instrument of retrospective measurement, memory, seems to him relative only in Heisenberg's case, not his. Bohr appears guilty of failing to apply to his assessment of the encounter precisely *his own* theatrical analogy – which echoes Brechtian self-reflexivity – of being both spectator *and* actor, in this case in his own drama. Phelan again:

> Physicists and playwrights, then, are necessarily and unavoidably involved in both metaphysics and metatheatre. Experiments are designed to isolate how we understand our understanding, and how we perceive perception, when all that is certain is that neither can be certain.

> *(1993: 115)*

Marking Time

If there is one observation that might be made about the socialist experiment as its traces continue to reveal themselves in and around Karl Liebknecht Strasse, it is the extent to which East German officialdom's untrammeled certainty of its project was misplaced. To be clear, it was not necessarily the experiment that was so but the demonstrative certainty in its particular direction. Overstating your case inevitably invites the locating of cracks in the armour as well as ridicule. Ulbricht's desire for an expansive parade ground at Marx-Engels Platz, capable of staging mass celebrations of socialist civilisation, didn't take long to transform into a wind-blown car park of Wartburgs and Trabants (though arguably that still conforms to some extent to the vision). When Honecker came along with his plans for the Palast der Republik – Erich's Galilean cosmos of a thousand glittering lamps – it meant banishing from Spree Insel the GDR 'national monument to the spiritual fathers of Marxism', after whom the square had been named, to the other side of the people's palace (Haubrich 2001: 224). Now the two grand old fuddy-duddies, Marx and Engels, popularly known as 'the pensioners', stare fixedly at the television tower soaring 365 metres into the sky over towards Alexander Platz. Friedrich, standing, hasn't batted an eyelid at the dollop of bird shit that's dropped on his forehead and trickled onto his bushy moustache, whilst Karl, sitting, must be relieved to be able to take the weight off those elephantine legs of his. The trousers and shoes alone appear to weigh a tonne. (It's the same problem the immortalised Brecht has outside the Berliner Ensemble's theatre. Same sculptor – or clothing designer – involved, too. But at least the writer hasn't had his eponymous square pulled from under his feet just yet.) Marx and Engels, a couple of displaced tramps if I ever saw them in their coarsely-tailored outfits. From the front their pedestals look like suitcases and the joke in the time of the GDR used to be that they were waiting for their exit visas to the West. Now, uncertain as it is whether or not they're coming or going, it's more Vladimir and Estragon.

Crossing over to the television tower, the *Fernsehturm*, I am resolved to let myself be whisked to the top. It's an overcast day but looking like it might brighten. The city will still be spectacularly visible for miles around. I have experienced the tower from below when its prominent, spherical bulge two-thirds of the way up (containing the viewing areas and café-bar), and its distinctive red and white needle-point have been shrouded entirely in winter mist. It's a ghostly sight, this colossal, windowless column in the heart of Berlin, a concrete beanstalk, disappearing mysteriously into the fog. The unwitting stranger to the city witnessing this apparition must wonder what on earth it is. When the weather's good, conversely, there's a well-known trick of the light towards sunset on the south-west side of the glass sphere. It produces the distinctive, reflected outline of a cross, always proving something of an embarrassment to those who foresaw the tower as the pinnacle of socialist technological achievement. Maybe *this* is what Marx and Engels wait for so patiently, day in day out: the mark of God(ot). They'd

56.

have a pretty good view. Deeply uncertain what to make of it they await the reappearance of this powerful presence, not knowing whether it will oblige. 'Presence is impossible without doubt', suggests Phelan, and: 'doubt is the signature of presence, rather then the security of re-presentation' (1993: 115). The TV tower is the embodiment *par excellence* of socialist Man's claims not only to the space of God but also to the space of the capitalist west. In a curious way it was East Germany's most impressive contribution in terrestrial terms to the cold space war being fought out by the Soviets and Americans. Completed in 1969, the same year Apollo 11 was landing on the moon, it's a phallic representation of technological, space-race presence. In the semiotic battle of post-War Berlin it had no equal in the West; it was so obviously *there, signalling,* literally and figuratively. No wonder there were calls by westerners to have it hauled down after 1989, an act which would have amounted to envious revenge for its hubris. Perhaps the disarming blessing of the cryptic cross, an accidental inbuilt iconoclasm – which GDR architects sought desperately to explain and remove – saved its life there. Furthermore, it should not be forgotten that whilst the tower was winning the battle for visible dominance, it was invisibly losing the televisual one, effectively serving as a constant and ironic reminder of the illegal but unregulatable practice of East Berliners tuning into western broadcasting stations.

Just before ascending the tower I nip to the other side of Alexander Platz station, which skulks in its eastern shadow. Sandwiched in the gap leading to the square itself is the *Weltzeituhr*, another 'space age' innovation installed in 1969. Marking East Berlin as the centre of the universe, it's a ten metre high, twenty-four-hour 'world clock', a gyrating drum of aluminium and enamel which tells you the time of day in all the major cities of the globe. Twelve noon in Berlin is 16.00 hours in New Delhi is 21.00 hours in Sydney is 08.00 hours in Rio. Perched on top of the drum is a representation of the solar system: a galaxy of planets pursuing their orbital trajectories in a tangled ball of spiralling steel rods.

The clock represents another one of those GDR ironies, laying itself open to gentle mockery: a country hermetically locked into a rigid socialist grid making audacious

assertions of worldliness and technological advancement. But it is not only that. Shusterman notes Richard Sennett's invocation of 'the temporal emptiness of mechanical time' in relation to the organisation of cities. It is 'an 'empty volume' through which time could be made objective and visual, thus allowing diverse activities to be more easily ordered'. Sennett apparently 'sees the renaissance invention of the mechanical clock as central to the emergence of the modern metropolis' (Shusterman 2000: 242). The *Weltzeituhr's* reference to the absolute time and space of classical physics was intended to be indicative, then, of urban and social order in the GDR. A smooth functioning city that had its place in the larger scheme of things. The clock was indicative of the attempt to assert state control over every detail of life, formally to eradicate the unpredictable, erratic or incidental. That was the impulse which inevitably led to the sense of time slowing down or 'nothing happening'. The East German historian Stefan Wolle's summary of how history was viewed officially bears this out:

57.

In GDR schools and universities the history of one's own state was the most boring learning material imaginable. It wasn't only because of the ideologically-determined distortions of reality. These existed to no less an extent in other subject areas, and falsified history can be very interesting, too. The reasons for the inner dreariness emitted by these official representations of history, which were printed on poor-quality paper and always illustrated with the same old pictures, lay deeper. The history of the GDR amounted – at least in the way it was presented by school and university teachers – to a succession of party conventions, plenaries, conferences, proclamations and planning figures. Basically, the powers that be had got rid of history. Any event implied movement, and movement was considered dangerous.

(1998: 20)

It is coincidence, of course, that the abbreviation for the vast state security service, the *Stasi*, almost reproduces the term 'stasis', but ultimately that is what the organisation sought and effected with its clandestine network operations. A whole society holding itself in check around a void centre. Set up by the SED leadership to 'comprehensively control society, state and economy' in the face of a populace which it viewed as posing 'a constant security risk', the *Stasi* had over a quarter of a million people working for it in formal and informal capacities. It was, thus, the single largest employer in the GDR, but officially it did not exist.[10] It's surveillance operations covered well over a third of the entire sixteen million population of East Germany (Forschungs und Gedenkstätte Normannenstrasse 2000: 10). Not much scope for falling out of line there. Compounding the irony of 'wordly time' posed by the *Weltzeituhr* at Alexander Platz was, as the writer and film director John Burgan reports, the revelation after reunification 'that the electric current in the East fluctuated so much that public clocks were always off by different amounts; nowhere could you tell what hour it was' (Stein 1999: 166). Once again, the impulse to regulate could be seen to be subject to a subtle, unforeseen destabilisation.

The Space of Light

Berlin used, in fact, to be referred to as the 'city of light', central as it was up until the First World War to the development of the electricity industry on a global scale. That evolution took place essentially on the basis of a fierce rivalry between two innovators: Siemens, whose company adopted the same name, and Rathenau, who founded the German-Edison Company and, later, AEG. Between them these men and their famous companies invented and implemented a whole range of revolutionising electronic phenomena including the dynamo, light bulbs, street lighting, telephone systems, neon advertising, trolley buses, power stations, the telegraph and the first power cables (Richie 1999: 146–8). (And everybody presumed it was Bismarck who had been in control.) Hence, the city of light not only created new space – after dark, between distant locations – it also began to cross that space at speed.

Siemens also 'installed the first ever electric elevator, which astounded everyone with its smooth and quiet ride' (146). Whizzing up the television tower now I wonder how it would compare. Paul Virilio talks of '*speed distance* obliterat[ing] the notion of physical dimension' (1991b: 18). He's thinking chiefly of the influence of cyberspace – the screen as the new city square – but also of the way mechanisms of electronic surveillance – 'gaseous systems of control' as Deleuze has it (Leach 1997: 308) – rather than physical boundaries now govern the space of the city. On arrival, the old city gates are superceded by the electronic security procedure of the airport (Virilio 1991b: 10–11), the visible and plastic becomes undetectable. Things exist at one remove. It's a credible vision, but it feels as if we're not wholly there, here in 'old Europe', even in 'new Berlin'. For now, light as I'm made to feel as the lift soars up the TV tower in double-quick time, I still have a bodily sense of *up* and *down*, and *near* and *far*, as I emerge in the viewing area of the spheroid.

Double-quick is the speed that was adopted by the gyrating café-bar up there after the fall of the Wall. It used to take one hour to creep round in a full 360 degree circle, six degrees a minute. Now there are two revolutions every hour. Two for the price of one: it sounds like everything-must-go, free market values. But it's more like doubling profits: the 'consumer' only gets half an hour for the same all-round vista. Perhaps, now the Wall is down, the same ethereal dreams of uninhibited space once enjoyed by the GDR citizen on visits here aren't making the running anymore.

Reiterating Müller after reunification: the Wall was a temporal barrier, 'a time-wall between two speeds: acceleration in the West; deceleration in the East' (Herzogenrath 1990: 9). Burgan maintains that the image of Berlin now should still be 'two clocks, running at different speeds, never catching up with each other' (Stein 1999: 166). Time reduced or movement accelerated, it's a difference which emphasises, as Meschede points out, the contingent nature of seeing (2001: 51). He's referring to the way it seems to have intrigued the British artist Tacita Dean when she made her 16mm colour film about the tower entitled simply *Fernsehturm* (2001). For her there are evidently more than two speeds in operation.

Shot over a period of an afternoon turning to evening, the film was subsequently edited into a 44 minute sequence. For the most part the camera maintains a fixed position on the slow, revolving platform of the café-bar, allowing action to pass in and out of its viewing range, which, using an anamorphic lens, has extended the frame to double its size. So, whilst the camera rarely moves by human agency, it is constantly moving or being moved on a circular, horizontal plane, while the continuous ritual of sittings – renewed groups of guests taking their places at tables, ordering, chatting, eating and drinking, and leaving again – is played out. Meanwhile, the heavily-outlined frames of the viewing windows pass indistinct images of Berlin – North, East, South, West – before our eyes as the platform rotates, an effect which is like the gradual

58.

manual feeding of a giant-format film through a projector. But we are looking at the film itself, not its projection. As day metamorphoses into night, a slow-coming darkness in the east – which the spectacularly bright setting sun seems to be drawing magnetically over the edge of the horizon – blackens the exterior view, transforming the windows into reflectors of the interior. We're still on the move but our focus is closing inward, becoming social and intimate as natural light is replaced by the yellowish warmth of man-made electric lamps. 'Physicists', Phelan notes, 'get what they interrogate for in terms of light' (1993: 117); Dean too is recording an experience of the city by observing the play of light. Like writing with vanishing ink, it's an endlessly elusive process.

Fernsehen means literally 'seeing far'; it is also the noun for 'television' (as well as the infinitive 'to watch television'). Ironically, then, a phenomenon so bound up with technology and mediation is turned here at its epicentre to the literal function suggested by its name: the natural, human action of seeing into the distance with the naked eye. And, as darkness falls *fernsehen* has mutated here into *nahsehen*, 'seeing near'. Thus a form of unaided double-telescoping has occurred, a 'seeing-far' that has concertinaed. (As Virilio points out: 'if we look carefully at the term "telescoping", we find it is made up of two usages: [1] the noun, "telescope", examines that which is distant; and, [2] the verb, "to telescope", crushes inward, or condenses without distinction' [1991b: 66].) Like a private hour glass the steady draining of tall, slim glasses of beer, amber as the twilight (half empty or half full?), marks this shift. It is one which is not only spatial but temporal and physical: from its clear, sober beginning to its blurry, less-than-sober end a further, chemically-induced, rearrangement of time awareness has probably occurred in the realm of the guests' consciousness. Dean is concerned always to make these processes physically and visually tangible. Where time appears to be accelerating relentlessly, she forces it to slow down again by examining the performative complexity of its natural and constructed interactions. The terror of speed – what it suppresses, forgets, repeats mindlessly – is curbed into a space of contemplation.

This recalls Benjamin's view of photography as the opening up of a new space which, 'like the space informed by human consciousness' giving way to one 'informed by the unconscious', produces unforeseen moments:

> Whereas it is commonplace that, for example, we have some idea what is involved in the act of walking, if only in general terms, we have no idea at all what happens during the fraction of a second when a person *steps out*. Photography, with its devices of slow motion and enlargement, reveals the secret […] reveals in this material the physiognomic aspects of visual worlds which dwell in the smallest things, meaningful yet covert enough to find a hiding place in waking dreams.
>
> *(1997: 243)*

In 1997 Dean made a piece called *Mosquito*. It was a film too, or at least part of one, namely the soundtrack. What it amounted to was a 9.5 metre strip of 16mm magnetic tape stuck to the wall. As the artist herself explains in a pamphlet for a retrospective at Tate Britain in 2001: '24 of the small square sprockets that run along the bottom edge of the magnetic strip represents 24 frames of picture, which is one second of time'. Hence, the piece 'visually transcribes a sound in terms of its length and so physically describes the passing of time. A mosquito, with its unremitting buzz, only stops when it has settled on its frustrated prey' (Dean 2001: 1). What follows is the drawing of blood, arguably a form of intoxication – getting punch drunk – or adrenaline rush. The image enshrined conceptually in the piece can be said, then, to evoke an abrupt shift in perceptions of time. These chime with the performance artist Anthony Howells' dichotomy of sameness and anomalousness (or

59.

certainty and uncertainty): 'repetition suspends time by annulling progress, while inconsistency creates time by supplying it with a history of significant events' (1999: 171). The pattern of a particular state of being is broken by some rupture to the system; monotonous drift is surprised into a magnified intensity. What Dean captures, though, is a simultaneity of perception in the body. Like the experience of the crash victim, say, the shock of the event produces a slow motion present on the one hand and a speeded up, historical 'film of my whole life flashing before me' on the other. This is what *Fernsehturm* effects, as a film, as a location, finally as an embodiment of Berlin at the turn of the millennium. A needlepoint concentration of shifting modes of being, telescoping past and present, distance and proximity, but always moving on, leaving only fleeting images.

It has turned in the meantime into a blazingly intense mid-December dusk on this the eve of my departure from the city. Seizing the moment, the setting sun has staged a spectacular finale. I feel I've been here before. And I have – in Tacita Dean's film. I'm in the eye of the needle now, the projector's gate, the looking-glass gateway to the city. To the west the brilliant twilit sky is criss-crossed with the searing, salmon pink scratches of jet vapour trails, writing the vanishing narratives of their journeys near and far: New Delhi, Sydney, Rio, Berlin. A slight turn northwards and I can see the arrival and departure of planes over Tegel Airport, quietly drifting in from the darkening east or rising sharply to chase the western sun. Out of darkness into light, or vice versa. Tomorrow it will be me, giving up my temporary Berlin identity at the check-in, naked again in non-space, the fugitive's return. Almost on the same optical trajectory but very much in the foreground, the circular, luminous emblem of the Berliner Ensemble, rotating over the Theater am Schiffbauerdamm at Bertolt Brecht Platz. Like a slow wave to the departing travellers at Friedrichstrasse Station just across the river.

Notes

1. As Large points out, the Honecker regime reversed Ulbricht's revulsion of all things Prussian. It 'hoped to harness the residual power in the Prussian idea by transforming it – after careful sanitisation – into a worthy ancestor of the GDR state'. Amidst a general 'refocusing' of history, then, the bronze equestrian statue of Prussia's most famous king, Fredrick the Great, was returned from Potsdam, 'whence it had been banished by Ulbricht, to its former place of prominence on Unter den Linden' (2002: 499).

2. The council of state building served temporarily as the federal chancellery once government had moved to Berlin after reunification and before the new building diagonally opposite the Reichstag had been completed (in 2001).

3. As I pointed out in chapter four, his co-leader Rosa Luxemburg suffered a similar fate on the same occasion.

4. One of the reasons for the Palast der Republik's reprieve was that similar asbestos contamination was discovered in the futuristic International Congress Centre (ICC) in the west of the city in 1993. Built at a similar time and with a comparable, if more business-orientated, purpose there was no question of pulling *it* down. It was also estimated that the costs for renovating the Palast would be considerably less than complete demolition (Heidler 1998: 174–5).

5. In July 2002, having spent 50 million Euro on reconstituting the building, the German Bundestag decided to haul it down anyway and reconstruct three facades of the Stadtschloss. The form the fourth side (where the Palast der Republik was situated) as well as the interior would take remained unclear (Klein 2002: 13).

6. August Bebel was one of the most outspoken activists and theorists of the socialist labour movement between the 1860s and 1910s, founding the Social Democratic Workers' Party in 1869 and opposing Prussian-dominated unification (Buse and Doerr 1998: 84).

7. The installation was created by the Israeli artist Micha Ullman in 1995.

8. Burgin sums these up broadly as follows: 'In the early modern period it is the space of the humanist subject in its mercantile entrepreneurial incarnation. In the late modern period it is the space of industrial capitalism, the space of an exponentially increased pace of dispersal, displacement and dissemination, of people and things. In the 'postmodern' period it is the space of financial capitalism – the former space in the process of imploding, or 'infolding' (Burgin 1996: 44).

9. Michael Frayn has written a stage play about the 1941 encounter between Bohr and Heisenberg entitled *Copenhagen*.

10. Thomas Brussig's immensely successful post-reunification novel *Helden wie wir* (Heroes like Us) (1995) lampoons the idea of a vast work force not knowing by whom it is actually employed.

Bibliography

All references to the works of Brecht and Benjamin are to published English translations insofar as they have been available. Where they have not, references are to the original collected editions, respectively abbreviated to *GW (Gesammelte Werke)* in Brecht's case and *GS (Gesammelte Schriften)* in Benjamin's. Where a direct quotation has been used in the latter case, an English translation has been supplied by the author.

1. Works by Bertolt Brecht

(1967), *Gesammelte Werke*, 1–20, Frankfurt am Main: Suhrkamp Verlag.

(1970-), *Collected Plays*, 1–8, (ed. J. Willett and R. Manheim), (trans. various), London: Methuen.

(1976), *Poems 1913–1956*, (ed. J. Willett and R. Manheim), (trans. various), London: Eyre Methuen.

(1979), *Diaries 1920–1922*, (ed. H. Ramthun), (trans. J. Willett), London: Methuen.

(1990), *Letters 1913–1956*, (ed. J. Willett), (trans. R. Manheim), London: Methuen.

(1993), *Journals 1934–1955*, (ed. J. Willett), (trans. H. Rorrison), London: Methuen.

2. Works by Walter Benjamin

(1972–89), *Gesammelte Schriften*, 1–7, (eds. R. Tiedemann and H. Schweppenhäuser), Frankfurt am Main: Suhrkamp Verlag.

(1977), *Understanding Brecht*, (trans. A. Bostock), London: New Left Books.

(1978), *Reflections: Essays, Aphorisms, Autobiographical Writings*, (ed. P. Demetz), (trans. E. Jephcott), New York and London: Harcourt Brace Jovanovich.

(1983), *Charles Baudelaire: a Lyric Poet in the Era of High Capitalism,* (trans. H. Zorn), London: Verso.

(1996), *Selected Writings Volume 1 1913–1926*, (eds. M. Bullock and M. W. Jennings), (trans. R. Livingston et al.), Cambridge, MA and London: The Belknap Press of Harvard University.

(1997), *One-Way Street and Other Writings*, (trans. E. Jephcott and K. Shorter), London: Verso.

(1999a), *Illuminations*, (trans. H. Zorn), London: Pimlico.

(1999b), *Selected Writings Volume 2 1927–1934*, (eds. M. W. Jennings, H. Eiland, G. Smith), (trans. R. Livingston et al.), Cambridge, MA and London: The Belknap Press of Harvard University.

(2002), *The Arcades Project*, (ed. R. Tiedemann), (trans. H. Eiland and K.McLaughlin), Cambridge, MA and London: The Belknap Press of Harvard University.

3. Works relating to Benjamin and Brecht

Arendt, Hannah (1999), '*Introduction: Walter Benjamin 1892–1940*' in *Illuminations*, London: Pimlico, pp. 7–58.

Bienert, Michael (1998), *Mit Brecht durch Berlin*, Frankfurt am Main and Leipzig: Insel Verlag.

Buck-Morss, Susan (1989), *The Dialectics of Seeing: Walter Benjamin and the Arcades Project*, Cambridge, MA and London: MIT Press.

Caygill, Howard (1998), *Walter Benjamin: the Colour of Experience,* London and New York: Routledge.

Coles, Alex (1999) (ed.), *The Optic of Walter Benjamin* (de-, dis-, ex-, 3), London: Black Dog Publishing.

Dickson, Keith (1978), *Towards Utopia: a Study of Brecht*, Oxford: Clarendon Press.

Eagleton, Terry (1986), '*Brecht and Rhetoric*' in *Against the Grain: Essays 1975–1985*, London and New York: Verso, pp. 167–172.

Esslin, Martin (1965), *Brecht: A Choice of Evils,* London: Heinemann Educational Books.

Feinstein, Elaine (1993), *Loving Brecht*, London: Sceptre.

Fuegi, John (1995), *The Life and Lies of Bertolt Brecht*, London: Flamingo.

Gilloch, Graeme (1997), *Myth and Metropolis: Walter Benjamin and the City,* Cambridge: Polity Press.

Henrichs, Benjamin (2000), 'Die Liebe fängt erst an...', *Süddeutsche Zeitung* (Berlin Seite), 19–20 August, p. 9.

Hooper, John (2000), 'A taste of the bourgeois charms of the Brecht household', *Guardian*, 10 June.

Hörnigk, Therese (1999) (ed.), *Berliner Brecht Dialog 1998, Frankfurt am Main:* Suhrkamp Verlag.

Jacobs, Carol (1999), *In the Language of Walter Benjamin,* Baltimore and London: The Johns Hopkins University Press.

Jameson, Fredric (1998), *Brecht and Method,* London and New York: Verso.

Jesse, Horst (1996), *Brecht in Berlin*, München: Verlag Das Freie Buch.

Mahlke, Stephan (1999), 'Brecht+–Müller: German-German Brecht Images before and after 1989', *The Drama Review*, 43.iv, pp. 40–9.

Marcus, Laura and Lynda Neal (1998) (eds.), T*he Actuality of Walter Benjamin*, London: Lawrence and Wishart.

McCole, John (1993), *Walter Benjamin and the Antinomies of Tradition*, Ithaca: Cornell University Press.

Parini, Jay (1998), *Benjamin's Crossing*, London: Anchor.

Pavis, Patrick (1999), 'Brechtian Gestus and Its Avatars in Contemporary Theatre', *Brecht 100<=>2000 The Brecht Yearbook*, 24, pp. 176–190.

Reinelt, Janelle (1996), *After Brecht: British Epic Theater*, Ann Arbor: University of Michigan Press.

Rutschky, Michael and Juergen Teller (1997), *Der Verborgene Brecht: ein Berliner Stadtrundgang,* Berlin, New York and Zurich: Scalo Verlag and Berlin: Literaturforum im Brecht-Haus.

Sacks, Glendyr and Peter Thomson (1994) (eds.), *The Cambridge Companion to Brecht*, Cambridge: Cambridge University Press.

Schumacher, Ernst and Renate (1981), *Leben Brechts: in Wort und Bild,* Berlin: Henschelverlag.

Silberman, Marc (1998) (ed.), *drive b: brecht 100, Theater der Zeit/Brecht Yearbook*, 23.

Smith, Gary (1988) (ed.), O*n Walter Benjamin: Critical Essays and Recollections*, Cambridge, MA and London: MIT Press.

Sontag, Susan (1997), *'Introduction'* in *One-Way Street and Other Writings,* (trans. E. Jephcott and K. Shorter), London and New York: Verso, pp. 7–28.

Stiftung Archiv der Akademie der Künste (2000) (ed.), *Chausseestrasse 125: die Wohnung von Bertolt Brecht und Helene Weigel in Berlin Mitte,* Berlin.

Suvin, Darko (1999), 'Centennial Politics: On Jameson on Brecht on Method', *New Left Review,* I: 234 (Mar-Apr), pp. 127–140.

Vaßen, Florian (1998), 'A New Poetry for the Big City: Brecht's Behavioural Experiments in *Aus dem Lesebuch für Städtebewohne*r', (trans. K. Hall), *German Monitor, 41* (Bertolt Brecht centenary essays), (eds. Steve Giles and Rodney Livingstone), pp. 75–87.

Völker, Klaus (1979), *Brecht: a Biography,* (trans. J. Nowell), London and Boston: Marion Boyars.

Willett, John (1978) (ed. and trans.), *Brecht on Theatre: the Development of an Aesthetic,* London: Eyre Methuen.

Willett, John (1998), *Brecht in Context: Comparative Approaches,* London: Methuen.

Wright, Elizabeth (1989), *Postmodern Brecht: a Re-presentation,* London and New York: Routledge.

4. Works relating to Berlin

Averesch, Sigrid (2001), *'Gewaltbereite Skinheads',* *Berliner Zeitung,* 8/9 December, p. 6.

Baal-Teshuva, Jacob (1995), *Christo und Jeanne-Claude: Der Reichstag und Urbane Projekte,* München: Prestel Verlag.

Baehr, Ulrich (1984) (ed.), M*ythos Berlin – Wahrnehmungsgeschichte einer Industriellen Metropole,* Berlin: Verlag Ästhetik und Kommunikation.

Balfour, Alan (1995) (ed.), *World Cities: Berlin,* London: Academy Editions.

Barber, Stephen (1995), *Fragments of the European City,* London: Reaktion Books.

Barber, Stephen (2001), *Extreme Europe,* London: Reaktion Books.

Berliner Zeitung (2001), 'Polizisten wollen Entschuldigung', 5 December, p. 21.

Binet, Hélène and Raoul Buschoten (1997), *A Passage Through Silence and Light: Daniel Libeskind's Jewish Museum Extension to the Berlin Museum*, London: Black Dog Publishing.

Bloch, Ernst (1985), 'Übergrund: Berlin, Funktionen im Hohlraum' in *Erbschaft dieser Zeit*, 4 (Werkausgabe), *Frankfurt am Main:* Suhrkamp Verlag, pp. 212–228.

Bommarius, Christian (2001), 'Sabbat in Berlin', *Berliner Zeitung*, 3 December, p. 3.

Brock, Bazon et al. (2000), 'Wir bauen eine Kathedrale aus Müll', *Tagesspiegel*, 8 July, p. 25.

Cobbers, Arnt (2000), *Architektenführer: die wichtigsten Berliner Bauwerke*, Berlin: Jaron Verlag.

Connolly, Kate (2002), 'Reprieved far-right party plans election challenge', *Guardian*, 8 May, p. 4.

Cullen, Michael S. (1999) (ed.), *Das Holocaust-Mahnmal: Dokumentation einer Debatte*, Zürich: Pendo Verlag.

Dasgupta, Gautam and Bonnie Marranca (2000) (eds.), *Performing Arts Journal* (Berlin issue), 65, (May).

Emmerich, M., A. Koppietz and F. Köhn (2001), 'Innensenator entschuldigt sich bei der Jüdischen Gemeinde zu Berlin', *Berliner Zeitung*, 4 December, p. 15.

Enke, Roland et al. (1999), *Berlin: Offene Stadt – die Stadt als Ausstellung*, Berlin: Nicolai.

Flemming, Thomas and Hagen Koch (2000), *The Berlin Wall: Division of a City*, Berlin: be.bra verlag.

Forschungs und Gedenkstätte Normannenstrasse (2000) (ed.), *Wegweiser durch die Ausstellung im Haus des ehemaligen Ministeriums für Staatssicherheit der DDR*, Berlin: Astak.

Friedrich, Detlef (2001), 'Jüdisches Viertel?', *Berliner Zeitung*, 4 December, p. 9.

Garton Ash, Timothy (1989), *The Uses of Adversity*, Cambridge: Granta.

Garton Ash, Timothy (1997), *The File: a Personal History*, London: HarperCollins.

Gawthrop, John and Jack Holland (2001), *The Rough Guide to Berlin*, London: Rough Guides Ltd.

Geithe, Britta (2001), 'Mörder-Soldaten', *tip-Magazin*, 25 (6-19 Dec), pp. 72–3.

Gilman, Sander and Wolf von Eckardt (1993), *Bertolt Brecht's Berlin: a Scrapbook of the Twenties*, Lincoln and London: University of Nebraska Press.

Griffin, Matthew (2000), 'Undoing Memory', *Performing Arts Journal*, 65 (May), pp.168-170.

Grunert, Brigitte (2000), 'Im Rausch', *Tagesspiegel*, 7 July, p. 9.

Haubrig, Rainer; Hans Wolfgang Hoffmann and Philipp Mauser (2001), *Berlin: Architekturführer*, Berlin: Quadriga.

Heidler, Kirsten (1998) (ed.), *Von Erichs Lampenladen zur Asbestruine*, Berlin: Argon Verlag.

Herzogenrath, Wulf; Joachim Sartorius and Christoph Tannert (1990) (eds.), *Die Endlichkeit der Freiheit Berlin 1990: ein Ausstellungsprojekt in Ost und West*, Berlin: Edition Hentrich.

Hessel, Franz (1984), *Ein Flaneur in Berlin*, Berlin: Das Arsenal.

Holland, Jack (1990), *The Rough Guide: Berlin*, Bromley: Harrap Columbus.

Hooper, John (2001), 'German graffiti artist's number may be up', *Guardian*, 12 May.

Hooper, John (2002), 'Berlin cuts leave the arts in the cold', *Guardian*, 20 March, p. 18.

Huyssen, Andreas (1997), 'The Voids of Berlin', *Critical Inquiry,* 24.i (Autumn), pp. 57–81.

Info-Box: Der Katalogue (1998), Berlin: Nishen Verlag.

James-Chakraborty, Kathleen (2000), 'The New Berlin', in *German Architecture for a Mass Audience*, London and New York: Routledge, pp. 115–136.

Kahlfeldt, Paul; Joseph Paul Kleihues and Thorsten Scheer (2000) (eds.), *Stadt der Architektur/Architektur der Stadt: Berlin 1900–2000*, Berlin: Nicolai.

Karwelat, Jürgen (1988), 'Ein Berliner Stadtplan von 1946 – seiner Zeit voraus', in *Sackgassen: Keine Wendemöglichkeit für Berliner Straßennamen*, (ed. Berliner Geschichtswerkstatt), Berlin: Nishen Verlag, pp. 9–23.

Klein, Georg (2002), 'Nachtgewandelt in Ruinen', *Süddeutsche Zeitung*, 27 August, p. 13.

Krause, Andreas (2001), 'Die Wiederholung' *Berliner Zeitung*, 5 December, p. 13.

Kraudzun, Henning (2000), 'Das Symbol des Sozialismus kehrt zurück', *Tagesspiegel*, 8 July, p. 10.

Krüger, Thomas (1999) (ed.), *Die Bewegte Stadt: Berlin am Ende der Neunziger*, Berlin: FAB Verlag.

Ladd, Brian (1998), *The Ghosts of Berlin: Confronting German History in the Landscape*, Chicago and London: University of Chicago Press.

Large, David Clay (2002), *Berlin: a Modern History*, Harmondsworth: Penguin.

Libeskind, Daniel (2000), *Jewish Museum Berlin*, G + B Arts International.

Maier, Helmut (1987), *Berlin Anhalter Bahnhof*, Berlin: Verlag Ästhetik und Kommunikation.

Melle, Stefan (2001), 'Die Hecken werden in Sicherheit gebracht', *Berliner Zeitung*, 22 November, p. 21.

Michaelis, Nils (2000), 'Dr Motte: 'Wir füllen das morphogenetische Feld'', *Zitty,* 23.xiv, p. 26.

Museumspädagogischer Dienst Berlin (2000) (ed.), Leerzeit: *Wege durch das Jüdische Museum Berlin*, Berlin: MDB.

Nooteboom, Cees (1991), *Berliner Notizen*, Frankfurt am Main: Suhrkamp Verlag.

Oloew, Matthias (2000), 'Weniger Festnahmen, viel mehr Alkohol und Drogen', *Tagesspiegel,* 10 July, p. 9.

Paul, Ulrich (2001), 'Der Palast der Republik soll vorübergehend geöffnet werden', *Berliner Zeitung*, 20 November, p. 17.

Pornschlegel, Clemens (2003), 'Selig im Gemeinsamen', *Süddeutsche Zeitung*, 12/13 July, p. 13.

Raabe, Matthias (2001), 'Mit der Brechstange auf den Spielplatz', *Berliner Zeitung*, 3 December, p. 25.

Rada, Uwe (1997), *Hauptstadt der Verdrängung: Berliner Zukunft zwischen Kiez und Metropole*, Berlin: Verlag Schwarze Risse/Rote Strasse and Verlag Libertäre Assoziation.

Rebiger, Bill (2000), *Das Jüdische Berlin: Kultur, Religion und Alltag gestern und heute*, Berlin: Jaron Verlag.

Richie, Alexandra (1999), *Faust's Metropolis: a History of Berlin*, London: HarperCollins.

Robin, Régine (2002), *Berlin. Gedächtnis einer Stadt*, (trans. R. Voullié), Berlin: TRANSIT Verlag.

Scherer, Hans (1998), *Jetzt Berlin: Unterwegs in der Hauptstadt*, Frankfurt am Main: Eichborn.

Schlör, Joachim (2001), '"The Six is the Message:" Stadt in Bewegung' in *Berlin: Geschichte einer Stadt*, (ed. Julius H. Schoeps), Berlin: Be.Bra Verlag, pp. 212–229.

Schultz, Bernhard (2000), *The Reichstag: the Parliament Building by Norman Foster*, Munich: Prestel Verlag.

Shusterman, Richard (2000), 'The Urban Aesthetics of Absence: Pragmatist Reflections in Berlin' in *Performing Live: Aesthetic Alternatives for the Ends of Art*, Ithaca and London: Cornell University Press, pp. 96–111.

Stein, Jean (1999) (ed.), *Grand Street 69* (Berlin issue), 18.i.

Tagesspiegel am Sonntag (2001), 'Ungehinderte Randale gegen Polizeiautos', 2 December, p. 9.

Time Out (1998), Berlin Guide, Harmondsworth: Penguin.

Vallgren, Carl-Johan (2000), *Ein Barbar in Berlin: die Stadt in 8 Kapiteln*, München: Quadriga.

Van Treeck, Bernhard (1999) (ed.), *Street-Art Berlin: Kunst im öffentlichen Raum*, Berlin: Schwarzkopf und Schwarzkopf.

Von Boddien, Wilhelm (2001) (ed.), *Berlin Extrablatt*, Berlin: Förderverein Berliner Stadtschloss.

Wise, Michael (1998), *Capital Dilemma: Germany's Search for a New Architecture of Democracy*, New York: Princeton Architectural Press.

Wolle, Stefan (1998), *Die Heile Welt der Diktatur: Alltag und Herrschaft in der DDR 1971–1989*, Berlin Christoph Links Verlag.

5. Works of fiction (referred to)

Auster, Paul (1988), *The Invention of Solitude*, London: Faber and Faber.

Auster, Paul (1993), *Leviathan*, London: Faber and Faber.

Ballard, J. G. (1995), *Crash*, London: Vintage.

Berger, John (1984), *And Our Faces, my Heart, Brief as Photos*, London: Writers and Readers.

Chatwin, Bruce (1988), *The Songlines*, London: Pan Books.

Chatwin, Bruce (1989), *What am I Doing Here*, London: Pan Books.

DeLillo, Don (1992), *Mao II,* London: Vintage.

Dyer, Geoff (1992), *But Beautiful*, London: Vintage.

Dyer, Geoff (1997), *Out of Sheer Rage: in the Shadow of D.H. Lawrence*, London: Little, Brown and Company.

Kafka, Franz (1992), *The Transformation ('Metamorphosis') and other Stories,* (ed. and trans. M. Pasley), Harmondsworth: Penguin.

Müller, Heiner (1995), *Theatremachine,* (ed. and trans. M. von Henning), London: Faber and Faber.

Müller, Heiner (2001), *A Heiner Müller Reader: Plays, Poetry, Prose,* (ed. and trans. C. Weber), Baltimore and London: Johns Hopkins University Press/PAJ Books.

Musil, Robert (1954), *The Man without Qualities*, 1–4, (trans. E. Wilkins and E. Kaiser), London: Picador.

Nooteboom, Cees (2002), *All Souls' Day,* (trans. S. Massotty), London: Picador.

Ohler, Norman (2001), *Mitte*, Berlin: Rowohlt Verlag.

Wolf, Christa (1990), *Was bleibt*, Berlin and Weimar: Aufbau Verlag.

6. Films (referred to)

Fincher, David (1999), *Fight Club*, USA.

Gloor-Fadel, Samira (1999), *Berlin – Cinéma*, Switzerland/France.

Hissen, Jörg Daniel and Wolfram Hissen (1996), *Dem Deutschen Volke – Verhüllter Reichstag, 1971–1995*, Germany/France.

Palitsch, Peter and Manfred Wekwerth (1961), *Mutter Courage und ihre Kinder*, GDR.

Ruttmann, Walter (1927), *Berlin – Die Sinfonie der Großstadt*, Germany.

Siegert, Hubertus (2001), *Berlin Babylon*, Germany.

Tykwer, Tom (1998), *Lola Rennt*, Germany.

Wenders, Wim (1987), *Der Himmel über Berlin*, Germany/France.

7. Performances, installations and other art works (referred to)

Biedermann, Carl and Eva Butzmann (1996), *Der Verlassene Raum (Denkmal für die Ermordeten Berliner Juden)*, Koppen Platz, Berlin.

Boltanski, Christian (1990), *The Missing House*, Große Hamburger Straße, Berlin.

Calle, Sophie (1997), *Die Entfernung/The Detachment: a Berlin Travel Guide,* Dresden: Verlag der Kunst with Arndt and Partner Gallery and G+B International.

Christo and Jean-Claude (1995), *Verhüllter Reichstag: Projekt für Berlin*, Berlin.

Dean, Tacita (2001), *Fernsehturm*, London: Frith Street Gallery and New York/Paris: Marian Goodman Gallery.

Dean, Tacita (2002), *The Berlin Project* (Between the Ears), BBC Radio 3, 2 February.

Einstürzende Neubauten (2000), 'Die Befindlichkeit des Landes' in *Silence is Sexy*, (trans. M. Partridge), Berlin: Zomba Records/Rough Trade.

Haacke, Hans (1991), *Die Freiheit wird jetzt einfach gesponsort – aus der Portokasse,* Grenzturm Stallschreiber Strasse/Alte Jakob Strasse, Berlin.

Haacke, Hans (2000), *Der Bevölkerung*, Deutscher Bundestag/Reichstag, Berlin.

Hirsch, Nikolaus, Wolfgang Lorch and Andrea Wandel (1998), *Gleis 17*, Grunewald S-Bahnhof, Berlin.

Muñoz, Juan (2001), *Double Bind*, Tate Modern, London.

Rademacher, Norbert (1994), *Installation für das KZ-Außenlager Sonnenallee*, Berlin.

Ulmann, Micha (1995), *Die Leere Bibliothek,* Bebel Platz, Berlin.

Vrubel, Dmitry (1990), *The Mortal Kiss*, East Side Gallery, Berlin.

Wall, Jeff (1993), *A Sudden Gust of Wind*, Tate Modern, London.

Whiteread, Rachel (1993), *House*, Tower Hamlets, London.

Whiteread, Rachel (2000), *Holocaust Memorial*, Juden Platz, Vienna.

Wilson, Jane and Louise (1997), *Stasi City,* Kunstverein, Hannover.

8. General works

Adorno, Theodor *et al.* (1980), *Aesthetics and Politics*, (trans. and ed. R. Taylor), London and New York: Verso.

Augé, Marc (1995), *Non-Places: Introduction to an Anthropology of Supermodernity, trans.* J. Howe, London: Verso.

Bachelard, Gaston (1994), *The Poetics of Space*, (trans. M. Jolas), Boston: Beacon Press.

Barthes, Roland (1975), *The Pleasure of the Text*, (trans. R. Miller), New York: Hill and Wang.

Barthes, Roland (1982), *Empire of Signs*, (trans. R. Howard), London: Jonathan Cape.

Barthes, Roland (1984), *Image, Music, Text*, (trans. S. Heath), London: Flamingo.

Barthes, Roland (1989), *The Rustle of Language,* (trans. R. Howard), Berkeley and LA: University of California Press.

Barthes, Roland (1993), *Camera Lucida: Reflections on Photography*, (trans. R. Howard), London: Vintage.

Baudrillard, Jean (1983), *Simulations*, (trans. P. Foss, P. Patton and P. Beitchman), New York: Semiotext(e).

Bennington, Geoff and Jaques Derrida (1993), *Jacques Derrida*, trans. G. Bennington, Chicago and London: University of Chicago Press.

Berger, John and Katya Berger Andreadakis (2000), 'The Long Sunset', *Guardian* (Europe), 5 August, pp. 13–14.

Berger, John (2001), (untitled column), *Guardian*, 25 October, p. 7.

Berger, Peter (1977), *Facing up to Modernity: Excursions in Society, Politics and Religion*, New York: Basic Books.

Blamey, David (2002) (ed.), *Here, There, Elsewhere: Dialogues on Location and Mobility,* London: Open Editions.

Boyer, Christine M. (1998), *The City of Collective Memory: Its Historical Imagery and Architectural Entertainments*, Cambridge, MA. and London: MIT Press.

Brouwer, Joke and Arjen Mulder (2002) (eds.) *Transurbanism*, Rotterdam: V2-Publishing/NAI Publishers.

Burgin, Victor (1996), *In/Different Spaces: Place and Memory in Visual Culture*, Los Angeles and London: University of California Press.

Buse, Dieter K. and Jürgen C. Doerr (1998) (eds.), *Modern Germany: an Encyclopedia of History, People and Culture, 1871–1991, 1–2*, New York and London: Garland Publishing Inc.

Clapp, Susannah (1998), *With Chatwin: Portrait of a Writer*, London: Vintage.

Coles, Alex (2000) (ed.), *Site-specificity: the Ethnographic Turn (de-, dis-, ex-, 4)*, London: Black Dog Publishing.

de Certeau, Michel (1988), *The Practice of Everyday Life*, (trans. S. Rendall), London, Berkeley and LA: University of California Press.

de Certeau, Michel (1995), *Heterologies: Discourse on the Other*, (trans. B. Massumi), Minneapolis and London: University of Minnesota Press.

de Greef, Hugo and Tom Stromberg (1995) (eds.), *Theaterschrift (City/Art/Identity)*, 10.

Derrida, Jacques (1988), *Limited Inc*, Evanston, IL: Northwestern University Press.

Diamond, Elin (1997), *Unmaking Mimesis: Essays on Feminism and Theatre*, London and New York: Routledge.

Doherty, Claire and Jeremy Millar (2000), *Jane and Louise Wilson*, London: Ellipsis.

Etchells, Tim (1999), *Certain Fragments*, London and New York: Routledge.

Foster, Hal (1985) (ed.), *Postmodern Culture*, London: Pluto Press.

Foster, Hal (1996), *The Return of the Real: the Avant-Garde at the End of the Century*, Cambridge, MA and London: MIT Press.

Foucault, Michel (1991), *Discipline and Punish: the Birth of the Prison*, (trans. A. Sheridan), Harmondsworth: Penguin.

Frayn, Michael (2002), 'Friends and Mortal Enemies', *Guardian* (Saturday Review), 23 March, pp. 1–3.

Freud, Sigmund (1990), 'The "Uncanny"' in *Art and Literature* (14), (ed. A. Richards), London: Penguin, pp. 335–376.

Freud, Sigmund (1991), 'Beyond the Pleasure Principle' in *On Metapsychology: the Theory of Psychoanalysis* (11), (ed. A. Richards), London: Penguin, pp. 269–338.

Frisby, David (2001), *Cityscapes of Modernity: Critical Explorations*, Cambridge: Polity Press.

Frisch, Max (1950), *Tagebücher 1946–1949*, Frankfurt am Main: Suhrkamp Verlag.

Fyfe, Nicholas R. (1998) (ed.), *Images of the Street: Planning, Identity and Control in Public Space*, London and New York: Routledge.

Graves, Peter (1994), 'The Treachery of St. Joan: Christa Wolf and the Stasi', *German Monitor*, 30 (Christ Wolf in Perspective), (ed. I. Wallace), pp. 1–12.

Heathfield, Adrian (1997), 'Facing the Other: the Performance Encounter and Death' in *Shattered Anatomies: Traces of the Body in Performance*, (ed. A. Heathfield et al.), Bristol: Arnolfini Live.

Highmore, Ben (2002), *Everyday Life and Cultural Theory: an Introduction*, London and New York: Routledge.

Holmberg, Arthur (1988), 'A Conversation with Robert Wilson and Heiner Müller', *Modern Drama,* 31.iii, pp. 454–458.

Howells, Anthony (1999), *The Analysis of Performance Art: a Guide to its Theory and Practice*, Amsterdam: Harwood Academic Publishers.

Jameson, Fredric (1991), *Postmodernism or the Logic of Late Capitalism*, London: Verso.

Kaye, Nick (2000), *Site-specific Art: Performance, Place and Documentation*, London and New York: Routledge.

Klein, Naomi (2002), 'Buying a gladiatorial myth', *Guardian*, 2 January, p. 12.

Kluge, Alexander and Heiner Müller (1995), *Ich Schulde der Welt einen Toten*, Hamburg: Rotbuch Verlag.

Lacan, Jaques (1997), *Écrits: a Selection*, (trans. A. Sheridan), London: Routledge.

Lane, Jill and Peggy Phelan (1998) (eds.), *The Ends of Performance*, New York and London: New York University Press.

Leach, Neil (1997) (ed.), *Rethinking Architecture: a Reader in Cultural Theory*, London and New York: Routledge.

Leach, Neil (1999) (ed.), *Architecture and Revolution: Contemporary Perspectives on Central and Eastern Europe*, London and New York: Routledge.

Lefebvre, Henri (1998), *The Production of Space,* (trans. D. Nicholson-Smith), Oxford: Blackwell Publishers.

Libeskind, Daniel (1997) (ed.), *Radix-Matrix: Architecture and Writings*, Munich and New York: Prestel.

Libeskind, Daniel (2001), *The Space of Encounter,* London: Thames and Hudson.

Liggett, Helen (2003), *Urban Encounters*, Minneapolis and London: University of Minnesota Press.

Lingwood, James (1995) (ed.), *Rachel Whiteread: House*, London: Phaidon Press.

Lyotard, Jean-François (1991), *The Inhuman: Reflections on Time*, (trans. G. Bennington and R. Bowlby), Cambridge: Polity Press.

McEvoy, J. P. and Oscar Zarate (1996), *Quantum Theory for Beginners,* Cambridge: Icon Books.

Meschede, Friedrich (2001), 'Fernsehturm' in *Tacita Dean*, London: Tate Gallery Publishing Ltd, pp. 50–61.

Müller, Heiner (1992), *Krieg ohne Schlacht: Leben in Zwei Diktaturen*, Köln: Kiepenheuer und Witsch.

Parker, Andrew and Eve Kosovsky Sedgwick (1995) (eds.), *Performance and Performativity*, London and New York: Routledge.

Phelan, Peggy (1993), *Unmarked: the Politics of Performance*, London and New York: Routledge.

Pile, Steve (1996), *The Body and the City: Psychoanalysis, Space and Subjectivity*, London and New York: Routledge.

Read, Alan (1995), *Theatre and Everyday Life: an Ethics of Performance*, London and New York: Routledge.

Read, Alan (2000) (ed.), *Architecturally Speaking: Practices of Art, Architecture and the Everyday*, London and New York: Routledge.

Sadler, Simon (1998), *The Situationist City*, Cambridge, MA and London: MIT Press.

Sallis, Judith (1996), 'The Search for Permanence in a Disintegrating World', *German Monitor*, 38, (eds. P. Monteath and R. Alter), pp. 109–23.

Sayer, Henry M. (1992), *The Object of Performance: the American Avant-Garde since 1970*, Chicago and London: University of Chicago Press.

Searle, Adrian (2000), 'Making Memories', *Guardian* (G2), 17 October, p. 12.

Sinclair, Iain (1997), *Lights Out for the Territory*, London: Granta Books.

Sontag, Susan (1983), 'Writing Itself: On Roland Barthes' in *A Susan Sontag Reader*, London: Penguin, pp. 423–446.

States, Bert O. (1987), *Great Reckonings in Small Rooms: on the Phenomenology of Theatre*, Berkeley and Los Angeles, CA and London: University of California Press.

Sudjic, Deyan (1992), *The Hundred Mile City*, London: Flamingo.

Tester, Keith (1994) (ed.), *The Flâneur*, London and New York: Routledge.

Vidler, Anthony (1992), *The Architectural Uncanny*, Cambridge, MA and London: MIT Press.

Vidler, Anthony (2000), *Warped Space*, Cambridge, MA and London: MIT Press.

Virilio, Paul (1991a), *The Aesthetics of Disappearance*, (trans. P. Beitchman), New York: Semiotext(e).

Virilio, Paul (1991b), *Lost Dimension*, (trans. D. Moschenberg), New York: Semiotext(e).

Walker, Mark (2001), 'Die Wahrheit liegt irgendwo dazwischen', *Berliner Zeitung*, 5 December, p. 19.

Young, James E. (1994) (ed.), *The Art of Memory: Holocaust Memorials in History*, New York and Munich: Prestel Verlag.

Index of Names